WORLD BANK TECHNICAL PAPER NO. 331
Africa Technical Department Series

African Water Resources

Challenges and Opportunities for Sustainable Development

Narendra P. Sharma
Torbjorn Damhaug
Edeltraut Gilgan-Hunt
David Grey
Valentina Okaru
Daniel Rothberg

The World Bank
Washington, D.C.

First printing August 1996

Technical Papers are published to communicate the results of the Bank's work to the development community with the least possible delay. The typescript of this paper therefore has not been prepared in accordance with the procedures appropriate to formal printed texts, and the World Bank accepts no responsibility for errors. Some sources cited in this paper may be informal documents that are not readily available.

The findings, interpretations, and conclusions expressed in this paper are entirely those of the author(s) and should not be attributed in any manner to the World Bank, to its affiliated organizations, or to members of its Board of Executive Directors or the countries they represent. The World Bank does not guarantee the accuracy of the data included in this publication and accepts no responsibility whatsoever for any consequence of their use. The boundaries, colors, denominations, and other information shown on any map in this volume do not imply on the part of the World Bank Group any judgment on the legal status of any territory or the endorsement or acceptance of such boundaries.

The complete backlist of publications from the World Bank is shown in the annual Index of Publications, which contains an alphabetical title list (with full ordering information) and indexes of subjects, authors, and countries and regions. The latest edition is available free of charge from the Distribution Unit, Office of the Publisher, The World Bank, 1818 H Street, N.W., Washington, D.C. 20433, U.S.A., or from Publications, The World Bank, 66, avenue d'Iéna, 75116 Paris, France.

ISBN 0-8213-3711-4
ISSN: 0253-7494

Cover photos: World Bank/Curt Carnemark

All authors are with the World Bank's Environmentally Sustainable Development Division of the Africa Technical Department: Narendra P. Sharma is agricultural adviser, Torbjorn Damhaug is water resources and management specialist, Edeltraut Gilgan-Hunt is environmental project assistant, David Grey is senior water resources and management specialist, Valentina Okaru is regulation specialist, and Daniel Rothberg is a consultant.

Library of Congress Cataloging-in-Publication Data

African water resources : challenges and opportunities for sustainable development / Narendra P. Sharma . . . [et al.].
p. cm. — (World Bank technical paper, ISSN 0253-7494 ; no. 331)
Includes bibliographical references.
ISBN 0-8213-3711-4
1. Water resources development—Africa, Sub-Saharan.
2. Sustainable development—Africa, Sub-Saharan. I. Sharma, Narendra P. II. World Bank III. Series.
HD1699.A1A355 1996
333.91'0096—dc20

96-26382
CIP

AFRICA TECHNICAL DEPARTMENT PAPERS

Technical Paper Series

No. 132 Murphy, Casley, and Curry, *Farmers' Estimations as a Source of Production Data: Methodological Guidelines for Cereals in Africa*

No. 135 Walshe, Grindle, Nell, and Bachmann, *Dairy Development in Sub-Saharan Africa: A Study of Issues and Options*

No. 141 Riverson, Gaviria, and Thriscutt, *Rural Roads in Sub-Saharan Africa: Lessons from World Bank Experience*

No. 142 Kiss and Meerman, *Integrated Pest Management and African Agriculture*

No. 143 Grut, Gray, and Egli, *Forest Pricing and Concession Policies: Managing the High Forests of West and Central Africa*

No. 157 Critchley, Reij, and Seznec, *Water Harvesting for Plant Production, vol. II: Case Studies and Conclusions for Sub-Saharan Africa*

No. 161 Riverson and Carapetis, *Intermediate Means of Transport in Sub-Saharan Africa: Its Potential for Improving Rural Travel and Transport*

No. 165 Kellaghan and Greaney, *Using Examinations to Improve Education: A Study in Fourteen African Countries*

No. 179 Speirs and Olsen, *Indigenous Integrated Farming Systems in the Sahel*

No. 181 Mining Unit, *Industry and Energy Division, Strategy for African Mining*

No. 188 Silverman, *Public Sector Decentralization: Economic Policy and Sector Investment Programs*

No. 194 Saint, *Universities in Africa: Stabilization and Revitalization*

No. 196 Mabogunje, *Perspective on Urban Land and Urban Management Policies in Sub-Saharan Africa*

No. 197 Zymelman, editor, *Assessing Engineering Education in Sub-Saharan Africa*

No. 199 Hussi, Murphy, Lindberg, and Brenneman, *The Development of Cooperatives and Other Rural Organizations: The Role of the World Bank*

No. 203 Cleaver, *A Strategy to Develop Agriculture in Sub-Saharan Africa and a Focus for the World Bank*

No. 208 Bindlish and Evenson, *Evaluation of the Performance of T&V Extension in Kenya*

No. 209 Keith, *Property Tax: A Practical Manual for Anglophone Africa*

No. 214 Bonfiglioli, *Agro-pastoralism in Chad as a Strategy for Survival: An Essay on the Relationship between Anthropology and Statistics*

No. 218 Mohan, editor, *Bibliography of Publications: Technical Department, Africa RegionÅJuly 1987 to December 1992*

No. 225 Dia, *A Governance Approach to Reforming Civil Service in Sub-Saharan Africa*

No. 226 Bindlish, Evenson, and Gbeitbouo, *Evaluation of T&V Based-Extension in Burkina Faso*

No. 227 Cook, editor, *Involuntary Resettlement in Africa: Selected Papers from a Conference on Environment and Settlement Issues in Africa*

No. 232 Creightney, *Transport and Economic Performance: A Survey of Developing Countries*

No. 238 Heath, *Land Rights in Côte d'Ivoire: Survey and Prospects for Project Intervention*

No. 250 Rangeley, Thiam, Andersen, and Lyle, *International River Basin Organizations in Sub-Saharan Africa*

No. 251 Sharma, Rietbergen, Claude R. Heimo, and Jyoti Patel, *A Strategy for the Forest Sector in Sub-Saharan Africa*

No. 255 Mohan, editor, *Bibliography of Publications: Technical Department, Africa Region, July 1987 to April 1994*

No. 276 Johnson, *Quality Review Schemes for Auditors: Their Potential for Sub-Saharan Africa*

No. 277 Convery, *Applying Environmental Economics in Africa*

No. 298 Odaga and Heneveld, *Girls and Schools in Sub-Saharan Africa: From Analysis to Action*

No. 301 Mohan, editor, *Bibliography of Publications: Technical Department, Africa Region, July 1987 to April 1995*

No. 303 Heneveld and Craig, *Schools Count: World Bank Project Designs and the Quality of Primary Education in Sub-Saharan Africa*

No. 305 Johnson, *Educating and Training Accountants in Sub-Saharan Anglophone Africa*

Discussion Paper Series

No. 82 Psacharopoulos, *Why Educational Policies Can Fail: An Overview of Selected African Experiences*

No. 83 Craig, *Comparative African Experiences in Implementing Educational Policies*

No. 84 Kiros, *Implementing Educational Policies in Ethiopia*

No. 85 Eshiwani, *Implementing Educational Policies in Kenya*

No. 86 Galabawa, *Implementing Educational Policies in Tanzania*

No. 87 Thelejani, *Implementing Educational Policies in Lesotho*

No. 88 Magalula, *Implementing Educational Policies in Swaziland*

No. 89 Odaet, *Implementing Educational Policies in Uganda*

No. 90 Achola, *Implementing Educational Policies in Zambia*

No. 91 Maravanyika, *Implementing Educational Policies in Zimbabwe*

No. 101 Russell, Jacobsen, and Stanley, *International Migration and Development in Sub-Saharan Africa, vol. I: Overview*

No. 102 Russell, Jacobsen, and Stanley, *International Migration and Development in Sub-Saharan Africa, vol. II: Country Analyses*

No. 132 Fuller and Habte, editors, *Adjusting Educational Policies: Conserving Resources while Raising School Quality*

No. 147 Jaeger, *The Effects of Economic Policies on African Agriculture: From Past Harm to Future Hope*

No. 175 Shanmugaratnam, Vedeld, Massige, and Bovin, *Resource Management and Pastoral Institution Building in the West African Sahel*

No. 181 Lamboray and Elmendorf, *Combatting AIDS and Other Sexually Transmitted Diseases in Africa: A Review of the World Bank's Agenda for Action*

No. 184 Spurling, Pee, Mkamanga, and Nkwanyana, *Agricultural Research in Southern Africa: A Framework for Action*

No. 211 Weijenberg, Dioné, Fuchs-Carshé, Kéré, and Lefort, *Revitalizing Agricultural Research in the Sahel: A Proposed Framework for Action*

No. 219 Thillairajah, *Development of Rural Financial Markets in Sub-Saharan Africa*

No. 230 Saito, *Raising the Productivity of Women Farmers in Sub-Saharan Africa*

No. 231 Bagchee, *Agricultural Extension in Africa*

No. 234 Keck, Sharma, and Feder, *Population Growth, Shifting Cultivation, and Unsustainable Agricultural Development: A Case Study in Madagascar*

No. 242 Biggs, Moody, van Leeuwen, and White, *Africa Can Compete! Export Opportunities and Challenges for Garmetns and Home Products in the U.S. Market*

No. 251 Aryeetey, Baah-Nuakoh, Duggleby, Hettige, and Steel, *Supply and Demand for Finance of Small Enterprise in Ghana*

No. 252 Pinto and Mrope, *Projectizing the Governance Approach to Civil Service Reform: An Environment Assessment for Preparing a Sectoral Adjustment Loan in the Gambia*

No. 258 Duncan and Muvandi, *The Rate of Fertility Decline in Botswana and Zimbabwe*

No. 259 Scribner, *Policies Affecting Fertility and Contraceptive Use: An Assessment of Twelve Sub-Saharan Countries*

No. 260 Popiel, *Financial Systems in Sub-Saharan Africa: A Comparative Study*

No. 265 Gopal and Marc, *World Bank-Financed Projects with Community Participation: Procurement and Disbursement Issues*

No. 266 Venkatesan, *Seed Systems in Sub-Saharan Africa: Issues and Options*

No. 271 Parker, Riopelle, and Steel, *Small Enterprises Adjusting to Liberalization in Five African Countries*

No. 274 Marc, Graham, Schacter, and Schmidt, *Social Action Programs and Social Funds: A Review of Design and Implementation in Sub-Saharan Africa*

No. 280 Cleaver and Donovan, *Agriculture, Poverty, and Policy Reform in Sub-Saharan Africa*

No. 302 Harrold and Associates, *The Broad Sector Approach to Investment Lending: Sector Investment Programs*

No. 311 Harrold, *The Impact of the Uruguay Round on Africa*

Table of Contents

Foreword

Africa's experiences and challenges in the management and utilization of water resources provide enormous opportunities for the socially sustainable development of this vitally important resource. Water gives life to Africa's people and is essential to the region's social, economic, and environmental security. In the face of increasing demands, rising costs, and diminishing supplies, it has become a commodity of strategic importance in many of the region's countries.

Currently, about two thirds of the rural population and one quarter of the urban population are without safe drinking water, and even higher proportions lack proper sanitation. By the year 2000, approximately 300 million Africans will risk living in a water-scarce environment, and within 30 years, 20 countries in the region may be water-scarce. Recurrent and localized drought decreases food security, water-borne and water-related diseases cause millions of deaths each year, environmental degradation is increasing, and to complicate matters, all of the countries in the region share one or more transboundary river basins. The greatest and most immediate impact of this situation is felt by the poor, who often have the most limited access to water resources.

This strategy paper is one element of the World Bank's ongoing process to work with its African partners in addressing these challenges. It follows the World Bank water policy issued in 1993, supporting ways to facilitate the adoption, promotion, and implementation of the policy in the context of the needs, priorities, and constraints of African countries. This paper recommends that African countries adopt a systemic approach to water resource management, using an integrated, multisectoral framework that considers issues of social equity, ecological protection, and economic growth.

The message of the strategy found in this document is one of optimism, for the groundwork already exists for the sustainable management of Africa's water resources. Individual countries, such as Mozambique, Senegal, and Zimbabwe have already made significant innovations to meet their water resource demands. The World Bank, the donor community, African countries, and individuals should work together toward the more efficient and equitable use of Africa's water resources.

We trust that this strategy paper will stimulate dialogue and encourage a working partnership between the African people and the international community in this regard.

Kevin Cleaver
Director
Technical Department
Africa Region

Abstract

Water resources in Sub-Saharan Africa (SSA) have become a strategic commodity, with supply limited in terms of quantity and quality, and demand increasing due to population growth and economic development. The strategy developed in this document is based on the principle that water is a scarce good with dimensions of economic efficiency, social equity, and environmental sustainability. The strategy recommends an integrated, cross-sectoral, catchment area approach to water resources management in African countries. The approach builds upon African commitment and strengths, and recommends key strategic interventions for African consideration.

Based on an analysis of the current status and emerging trends in SSA's water resources, five development imperatives are identified: household water security, catchment area and wetland protection, food security, water quality and human health, and intra-national and international conflict resolution. An assessment is made of the rich collection of strengths, achievements, and opportunities in the region.

Acknowledgments

This paper was prepared by a team led by Narendra Sharma, Task Manager, and comprising David Grey, Torbjorn Damhaug, Edeltraut Gilgan-Hunt, Daniel Rothberg, and Valentina Okaru of the Technical Department of the Africa Region. The background papers (see Bibliography) have provided significant inputs to the strategy paper. It has also benefited greatly from numerous comments from individuals and diverse agencies dealing with African water resources inside and outside the Bank. From the outset, Kevin Cleaver, Jean Doyen, and Bocar M. Thiam have provided guidance and useful support to complete this paper. They have participated in various discussions with individuals within the Bank, as well as representatives of external agencies, to address key issues and to develop consensus on the solutions needed.

The paper is based on more than 20 background papers developed by Bank Staff, Africans, and external agencies (titles and authors are listed in the Bibliography). The African Advisory Group -- consisting of Ahmed Adams, Ni Boi Ayibotele, Peter Heyns, Mark Mujwahuzi, Margaret Mwangola, Ndey-Isatou Njie, General Olusegaun Obasanjo, Mamadou Sylla, and Imeru Tamrat -- met in late 1994 and 1995 to give valuable input and insight into the exercise.

The Core Team within the World Bank -- consisting of Paula Stone, Ariel Dinar, Rafik Hirji, Alfred Duda, Donald Parsons, Paula Donnelly-Roark, Mike Garn, Cyprian Fisiy, Francois-Marie Patorni, Akhtar Elahi, Geoffrey Mathews, Shimwaayi Muntemba, John M. Kalbermatten, Julia Clones, and Awa Busia -- gave input through background papers, consultation, and dialogue. Important assistance, comments, and support were also contributed by Moctar Toure, Francois Falloux, Snorri Hallgrimsson, Jean-Roger Mercier, Venkatachalam Venkatesan, Jacob Kampen, Simon Rietbergen, Leonard Berry, Letitia Obeng, Harvey Olem, Bo Applegren, Hans Wolter, Robert Rangeley, Elizabeth McLanahan, and Marc Rouleau. Guidance was also given by John Briscoe, Gershon Feder, and Ashok K. Subramanian.

The Water Thematic Team within the World Bank -- consisting of Bocar M. Thiam, Akhtar Elahi, Robert Tillman, Randolph A. Andersen, Salah Darghouth, Letitia Obeng, Assefa Telahun, Loso Boya, Walter Ochs, Francois-Marie Patorni, Max Wilton, Ebenezer Aikins-Affuls, Geoffrey Matthews, Colin Lyle, John Elder, Guy Le Moigne, Gershon Feder, Paula Stone, Alfred Duda, Paula Donnelly-Roark, Ariel Dinar, Joseph Gadek, Cynthia C. Cook, Townsend Swayze, and Lewis Campbell -- contributed comments and an interdisciplinary perspective.

Lawrence Mastri and P.C. Mohan provided editorial support, and Paula Carter, Marie-Laure Cossa, and Liisa Hietala provided secretarial assistance.

Special thanks are due to the Government of Norway, which provided major financial support for this exercise. In addition, thanks are extended to FAO, UNEP, UNESCO, AfDB, ODA/UK, ICRAF, and Duke University for their support to this exercise through selected background papers.

This report also benefited greatly from two workshops held in Nairobi, Kenya and Dakar, Senegal in February 1996. Thanks are due to UNEP and the Government of Senegal for hosting the workshops, and to ODA for the additional support it gave for production of the workshop deliberations and proceedings. Finally, thanks are extended to the 235 African participants -- from 41 countries -- at the workshop, including Ministers and representatives of government agencies, who submitted presentations, technical papers, and comments, thus contributing to consensus building and the definition of approaches for better management of water resources.

Executive Summary

Overview

In Sub-Saharan Africa (SSA), as in the rest of the world, human welfare and economic development depend on the wise use of water. Presently, many people in urban and rural areas throughout the Region have no access to safe drinking water and sanitation services. Many of the poor in rural areas have limited or unreliable access to water for even subsistence farming. The poor, who often pay the most for water services, suffer the most in terms of health and economic opportunity. Their lack of overall access is at the heart of the poverty trap and it is they who are most affected by increasing water degradation and scarcity. Combined with these factors, rising population and increasing pollution of freshwater are intensifying the pressure on already scarce water resources.

In this context, water has become a commodity of strategic importance in most African countries, because of increasing demands and rising costs, coupled with diminishing supplies of water. Developing sound water resource management programs will be crucial to the Region's poverty reduction, economic growth, food security, and maintenance of natural systems. Thus, it becomes even more urgent to secure efficient, equitable, and sustainable use of water resources for present and future generations.

This document— *African Water Resources: Challenges and Opportunities for Sustainable Management* — proposes a long-term strategy emphasizing the socially sustainable development imperatives of SSA. Based on the principle that water is a scarce good with dimensions of economic efficiency, social equity, and environmental sustainability, this document recommends an integrated, cross-sectoral, catchment area approach to water resources management in African countries. As a scarce good, water has both public and private characteristics; therefore, there is an important role for public and private participation in efficient management and development of water resources. Further, the strategy recognizes and utilizes the large reservoir of African capacity, and builds upon the numerous achievements already made in Africa. From these building blocks, the strategy recommends key strategic interventions for African consideration, and then discusses the operational implications for the World Bank.

Based on evaluations made by Africans of their own water resources, the current situation in the Region calls for partnership and country-led water resources management built on local experiences and good practices. Partnerships must be between government agencies, sectors, rural areas and urban areas, communities, stakeholder groups, co-riparian states, and international donors. Leadership and coordination for water resources management should be the responsibility of the individual countries themselves, as they will reap the greatest rewards from their efforts. Of course, partnership and country-level coordination will require commitment: to economic and social efficiency, to long-term development efforts, and to a possibly difficult transition to equitable and efficient water resource use.

This document concludes that the state of water resources in SSA requires urgent attention by African countries, with support from the international community. However, this does not mean that the industrial countries and donors should prescribe their own, non-African solutions. Africa is rich with strengths, achievements, and opportunities to manage its water resource endowment. The African countries must develop their own solutions based on a participatory approach, good governance, and environmental stewardship. The key strategic interventions proposed here — for African countries and for the World Bank — are designed to build upon these strengths and achievements, based on local ownership and commitment.

African Water Resources: Problems and Trends

SSA is a vast continent in varying stages of development with diverse physical and social characteristics. The region sees too little water or too much, in the wrong place or at the wrong time, and often of poor quality. There are too many demands placed on limited water resources and too many people, agencies, or institutions attempting to manage the resources. There are often disincentives for water resources conservation, and not enough knowledge or capacity to manage it effectively. SSA suffers because while water and hydrological systems are integrated resources, the human response—in Africa and in its development efforts— is not integrated. Also, diverse concerns and interests at the local, national, regional, and international levels require reconciliation, cooperation, and management.

Water Stress and Access. The evidence of water stress and access problems is apparent throughout the Region. Africa has a population which is expected to exceed 1 billion people by 2025. While some African countries (in West and Central Africa) have more than enough water on a per capita basis, population growth and economic development create excess demand over supply for most countries. In fact, by 2000, about 300 million Africans will risk living in a water-scarce environment. Moreover, the imbalance of demand and supply will place as many as eighteen countries in a situation of water stress (based on national averages), forcing them to make hard choices in water resource allocation and development. And with increasing population growth, the percentage of population without access to clean water or adequate sanitation is increasing, particularly in the rural and peri-urban areas. Currently, about 65 percent of the rural population and 25 percent of the urban population are without adequate water. Similarly, about 73 percent of the rural and 43 percent of the urban populations are without proper sanitation.

Poverty, Health, and Food Security. Water availability for household consumption and for productive use is closely associated with poverty reduction and food security. Making households water secure and providing water efficiently to rainfed and irrigated areas for food production will be key strategic elements in reducing poverty in SSA. This is crucial since by the turn of the century, poverty will affect an estimated 600 million people in SSA. The poor, the majority of whom live in rural areas, have limited access to clean water and sanitation for domestic use and crop production.

Water of insufficient quantity or quality leads to water-related disease, and water-borne and water-related diseases are common in the region: the diarrhea death rate of 17/1000 is the highest in the world. In urban areas, water contamination is widespread due to industrial pollution, poor sanitation practices, and discharge of untreated wastewater into surface and ground waters. With rapid urbanization, industrialization, and expansion of agriculture, point- and non-point source pollution risks will grow rapidly.

Food production in the Region has grown at about 2 percent a year over the past twenty-five years, compared with an average annual population growth of 3 percent during the same period. If farmers are to keep pace with population growth, they will have to intensify agriculture, increase crop yields, and significantly increase food production. This will require increased production on rainfed land—through better water harvesting, water and soil conservation, and improved technology, and farming practices—and on irrigated land — through increased productivity, expanded irrigated areas, increased cropping intensity, and efficient use of water.

Water Variability and Demands. Two features of African water resources are critical to effective management. First, precipitation across much of the region is exceptionally variable — both in time and in space— and unpredictable. Second, runoff is extraordinarily low. The consequence of these two features is endemic drought. Also, some areas of the region, especially the Sahelian countries, have limited supplies of freshwater and more variable rainfall, while other areas, particularly the humid tropical zone in Central and West Africa, have abundant water. Even within countries, the availability of water varies considerably because of physical features and rainfall patterns. Water management becomes more difficult as every continental SSA country shares one or more rivers with its neighbors and many countries see most of their surface waters flowing from or to other countries.

The demand for water throughout SSA is varied, although agriculture accounts for more than 80 percent of water consumption compared to other sectors (industry, energy, and municipalities). Population is growing at a rate of 3 percent annually, and the urban population will rise from 138 million in 1990 to over 500 million in 2020. Agriculture and irrigation will require more water if countries are to achieve food security. Hydropower production —which is far below potential —will increase with development. River and lake navigation will be more important in the future, and water will need to be conserved to maintain vital ecosystem functions. Finally, infrastructure services which often do not even meet current demand will be more expensive to provide in the future.

Environment and Aquatic Systems. Catchment protection through soil and water conservation, tree planting, and improved land use practices is critical. An estimated 320 million hectares of vegetated lands have been degraded over the past several decades in SSA leading to flooding, reduced ground water recharge, and reduced stream baseflow. Poor cultivation, deforestation, and overgrazing have had similar effects, negatively impacting aquatic ecosystems in the region, including water quantity and quality. The Region is also home to twenty-seven wetlands sites of designated international importance. These sites, comprising over 3 million hectares, are crucial for the maintenance of biological diversity and the functioning of aquatic systems.

Infrastructure and Costs. As easily accessible surface and ground water resources have already been exploited throughout SSA, the cost of exploiting new water supplies is rising sharply. (For example, the cost of supplying a cubic meter of water for water supply and sanitation projects is projected to double or even triple from current levels.) Also, the investment needed for new infrastructure (irrigation systems, water supply systems for domestic use, and hydropower) will be enormous. For instance, the capital requirement to provide clean water and sanitation services to all households in SSA countries over the next ten years will amount to about US$47 billion. In addition, if the African countries add another 6 million hectares to irrigation over the next ten to fifteen years, the capital cost will amount to nearly US$30 billion.

Dependency and Subsidy. Presently, African countries are highly dependent on external financing. A recent study of Bank-supported water supply and sanitation projects for FYs 87-90 shows that a much higher proportion of financing came from external sources in SSA than any other region. In SSA, external financing amounted to about 80 percent, compared to 65 percent in Asia, nearly 60 percent in Latin America, and about 55 percent in the Middle East and North Africa. In the case of rural water supply and sanitation services projects, the share of donor financing from the FYs 75-79 to FYs 90-94 period increased from 66 percent to 84 percent, while government financing decreased from 33 percent to 13 percent during this same period. This pattern of dependency and financing is also prevalent in the irrigation sector. Moreover, throughout SSA, water use is highly subsidized as water tariffs are set below the supply costs and often below the operation and maintenance costs. Consequently, cost recovery remains low, increasing the financial burden on the central government to provide capital for maintaining existing systems and developing new infrastructure.

Underlying Causes

As in many other parts of the world, water in SSA is generally regarded as a public good, and there are incentives to misuse and waste it. Also as is true elsewhere, economic, social, and political forces all influence these incentives, through market failure and incorrect policies, excessive public sector control, low capacity for effective management, and special interest groups. Moreover, water misuse and waste is a function of the widespread belief that water is in abundant supply and should be a free good. There is insufficient awareness that common water resources link rural and urban communities, sectors, or countries. In combination with difficult socioeconomic and hydrological conditions, these underlying causes can have serious effects on water supply and use in the Region.

Awareness, Capacity, and Management. Throughout SSA, the state of water resources in terms of supply and demand, quantity, scarcity, and ecological values is often unknown. People often are unaware that water is a finite resource with supply constraints, that it has a scarcity value, and that there is a cost to using it. There is also a lack of understanding of the consequences of deforestation and land degradation on the quantity and quality of water. In many countries, water management is highly centralized and the public sector plays a dominant role in management. However, management of water resources is highly fragmented among sectors and institutions, and there is excessive reliance on the public sector for services. Generally, institutional and implementation capacities are weak, and there is some scope to extend the level of stakeholder participation (private sector, local communities, NGOs) in water management. Also, past donor efforts have not resulted in significant or sustainable capacity building, nor have these efforts utilized indigenous knowledge bases or addressed gender issues in the development and management of water resources.

Policies, Regulations, and the Enabling Environment. Few countries have adequate national water policy statements, strategies, national water plans, legislative and regulatory frameworks, or mechanisms for intersectoral co-ordination and conflict resolution. Even if countries have been involved in water policy reforms, the long-term sustainability of these reforms has often been undermined by financial constraints, lack of public service capacity, and political instabilities. The regulatory framework in many of the region's countries is inadequate and often weakly enforced due to overlapping institutional responsibilities, governance problems, insufficient funds, lack of technical capacity and political interference.

Water, both for domestic consumption and irrigation, is underpriced because of inadequate pricing policies. Pricing decisions are generally influenced by political considerations, preferred priority users, and equity reasons. This not only leads to misallocation of water resources and inefficient use, but also benefits the better off consumers and commercial farmers. In addition, pricing, macroeconomic, and other sectoral policies constrain private sector investment and prevent the mobilization of domestic resources.

Data and Information. Data and information systems (physical, technical, socioeconomic) relating to water resources in terms of quantity, quality, accessibility, dissemination, and use are generally inadequate throughout the region. Surface and ground water quantity and quality networks are underdeveloped due to budgetary constraints, lack of equipment, limited sharing of information among stakeholders and riparian nations, and the lack of a link between the information base and decision-making process. Also, the development of African data and information systems has been supply driven, with no provisions for cost recovery from large users (e.g., hydroelectric plants, water supply agencies).

Framework for Addressing Transboundary Water Resources. All of the countries in continental SSA share one or more international river basins. There are at least fifty-four rivers or water bodies that cross or form international boundaries in the region. Few of the transboundary river basins in the region are effectively jointly managed, and there are many downstream countries that depend on water flow via upstream rivers. This dependency can create insecurity, misuse of water, or conflicts. If water is not allocated equitably among the riparian states (both upstream and downstream countries), it can undermine economic development, the effective management of international rivers and lakes and the protection of catchment areas.

Claims to Scarce Water and Conflicts. Competition among various activities – domestic consumption, agriculture, industry, power supply, livestock, wildlife resources, and recreation — for the use of water has now become more intense, contributing to conflicts at the local, national, and regional levels, requiring mechanisms for conflict prevention and resolution. Further, as the region is served by several major drainage systems, competition for limited water resources will increase among riparian countries. Increasing demand and growing water scarcity could cause conflicts between these riparian countries. For example, the Nile, Zambezi, Niger, and Volta River basins have potential for both serious conflicts, as well as cooperation among the riparian countries. As this competition becomes more intense, Africa will need institutionalized dispute resolution mechanisms, and economic and social data for assuring the equitable allocation of scarce resources.

Moving Forward: Building on African Achievements and Opportunities

Clearly, African people need more and better access to clean water and sanitation—and more must be done to reduce water degradation and pollution, improve local capacity, and enhance the efficient use of water for agriculture, industry, and commerce. Yet, along with these demands, there have been achievements at the local level, and there are opportunities for sustainable use of water resources. Many governments have undertaken National Environmental Action Plans, highlighting the importance of water in environmental management. Water resource assessments and the reform of water policies and institutions have been carried out or are under way in many countries. National programs for water supply and sanitation are being developed and implemented across the region incorporating new ideas that focus on participation and private sector involvement. SSA countries must now use these achievements as a base to build strategies, develop investment programs, and involve the diverse stakeholders in the better management of water resources, with a long-term perspective.

Achievements. In providing services to the poor, Africa has seen success in the community management of rural water supply and sanitation projects. The community determines its priorities and assumes responsibility, authority, and control over improvements to and operation of water services. Successful results show that effective demand must be the guiding principle, particularly for sanitation services. In urban areas, countries like Botswana have successful public utilities designed along private sector principles. Basin approaches have shown that cross-subsidization from urban to peri-urban and rural areas is justified on grounds of equity, efficiency, and effectiveness. Dramatic improvements in health have been achieved: guinea worm has been virtually eradicated, and river blindness control programs have had increasing success in West Africa. Lastly, a number of countries (such as Senegal, Mozambique, Malawi, and Zimbabwe) are moving toward a more comprehensive approach to water resource management.

Irrigation improvements have been achieved with small- and medium-scale schemes in many areas that involve water user associations, low-cost technologies, improved agricultural services, and clearly defined water rights. In the infrastructure sector, the Cameroon Electricity Company has begun using real-time management, and Sudan has developed techniques to reduce the siltation (thus extending the life) of reservoirs. Experiences with resettlement have shown the need for community consultation and partnership. Numerous countries have started to write or enact legislation that promotes water management along economic or basin principles, and with the increased confidence that this allows, governments -- such as those of Angola, Mozambique, Rwanda, Tanzania, Zambia, and Zaire --are promoting the participation of the private sector. A Drought Monitoring Project now spans twenty-one countries, and in the realm of transboundary waters, the hydrological information FRIEND project has sought to "level the playing field" between co-riparians. Finally, improved basin organizations are taking shape on the Nile and in Southern Africa (within the SADC framework).

Opportunities. Traditional African coping strategies toward environmental stress existed before population growth and relatively new international borders. These strategies, many of which are reflected in customary law, still hold promise today. There is also a tradition of participation in water management and development. Programs that have targeted community involvement and empowerment in water and sanitation services have also been successful. On the supply side of water management, the great lakes of the East African rift system, large rivers, and aquifers will become more important with more efficient technologies. Nonetheless, the use of these and other water resources will need to build upon advances in environmental economics. Moreover, the use of international waters in a coordinated and cooperative manner will create "win-win" solutions for co-riparians. Finally, SSA has the opportunity to build on the lessons of other regions. African nations can start early in the transition towards sustainable water resources management.

Strategic Response for African Countries

Vision and Challenge. The message and goal for African countries is the need for integrated water resources management (or a systemic approach) to achieve social, economic, and environmental goals to benefit present and future generations. Providing safe water and water for food production will benefit the poor significantly. Behind this message lies a vision requiring advocacy and long-term commitment. It is a vision of nations and groups of nations, cooperating regionally, sharing and using water resources rationally, ensuring clean water and sanitation services for all the region's inhabitants and providing water to key sectors such as agriculture, industry, and energy for economic development. The vision includes achieving economic growth and food security through the judicious allocation of water resources, and achieving environmental stability through the effective conservation and protection of these same scarce resources. The wise use of water resources will have enormous impact on poverty reduction, human health, and women.

However, SSA countries will face important choices and trade-offs in the use and management of water, balancing immediate economic benefits with long-term conservation and sustainable use gains. Many concerns and interest are competing at the local, national, and regional levels as various stakeholders demand water for different uses. Reconciling and managing these diverse interests will be a critical challenge for SSA. Africans will need to recognize that water is a scarce good with economic value. Furthermore, African countries will need to do more in defining the roles of the private sector, government, and local communities in water management, reflecting economic, ecological, and equity goals.

There will be roles for both the state as well as the market in water management. Countries in SSA need to make a concerted effort to accelerate a transition from an administrative command and control approach to a more participatory approach that treats water as a scarce good. Whenever feasible and appropriate, SSA countries should develop market-like solutions and adopt policies which favor the use of economic instruments in water allocation and pricing and investment decisions. The main economic instruments which could be considered are (a) market-related and demand-oriented laws, policies, regulations and incentive structures; (b) water markets with tradable water rights; (c) more extensive utilization of the private sector; and (d) economic pricing of water for specific users. It is important to recognize that the application of these market instruments will be difficult to implement in SSA countries. Even in the more advanced industrial countries, these instruments have not yet been fully adopted for diverse reasons. But as these instruments develop in African countries they will promote more rational behavior from users, both among suppliers and those who demand water resources.

National governments will have predominant roles in creating an enabling environment. The role of the government will remain important in creating laws, rules, and regulations which provide incentives to use water more efficiently and flexibly in response to changing demands and costs of water for different uses. The government can also reinforce the incentives for the improved coordination of demand and supply and protection of the public interest in the process. In addition, the governments can play a vital role in facilitating water delivery services to the poor, ensuring the protection of watersheds and aquatic systems, development of improved technologies, and cooperation among riparian countries sharing waters from international rivers, ground water aquifers, and lakes.

In this broader context, African countries should place greater emphasis on domestic resource mobilization and cost recovery. This will reduce the presently high dependency on external resources, and will generate capital for the maintenance of existing and development of new infrastructure. To this end, African countries can use appropriate pricing of water supply -- in consideration of its use (e.g., cash-crop production versus rural drinking water) -- for increased cost recovery.

Strategic Imperatives. A long-term vision will be needed to manage water resources in a way that meets the development imperatives of household water security, food security, resolution of water contamination, catchment protection, and transboundary conflict resolution and prevention. In many African countries, sustainable development would include efficient public sector interventions, market-oriented solutions, and popular participation. The strategic underpinning begins with the fact that countries in the region will need to focus on both the supply and demand sides. Water can no longer be supply driven or managed through technical and engineering solutions to capture, store, and deliver water. Policymakers need to focus more on demand management and changing people's behavior through incentives, regulations, and education. They must also turn their attention to reallocating existing supplies to higher-value uses, reducing waste, promoting conservation

Key Strategic Interventions

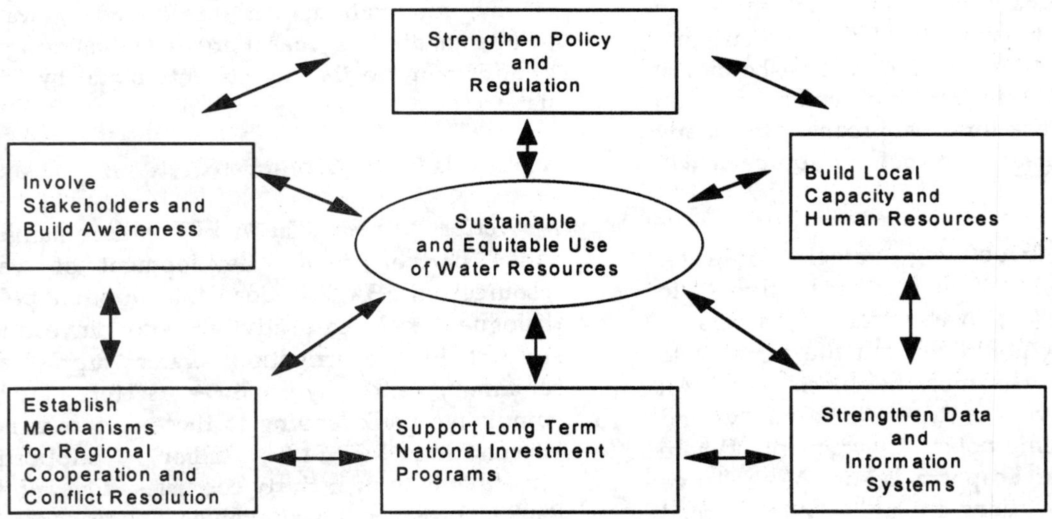

and water-saving technologies, and facilitating more equitable access. On the supply side, African countries need to modernize infrastructure, improve management practices, reduce costs, and make delivery of water from existing supplies more efficient.

Systemic Approach. African countries need to adopt a systemic approach to water resource management that reflects socioeconomic, ecological, and equity considerations. A call for a more systemic approach should not be interpreted as a call for a more extensive and rigorous central planning role and the establishment of administrative arrangements which increase the government's control of water resources. Also, this approach should not imply the development of complex projects. It requires users of water resources to think holistically and to make local and sectoral actions consistent with long-term sustainable development goals. Moreover, a systemic approach requires a broad-based partnership including all stakeholders—public and private sectors, farmers, local communities, and NGOs — to participate in water resources management. Such a comprehensive and coordinated approach will allow each sovereign country to assess its water needs in a multisectoral framework and take into account transboundary considerations. While there is a need for such an integrated, multisectoral approach, in many countries the transition to such an approach will take time.

Priority Focus. In defining strategies for water resources management in SSA, both threats to water resources (e.g., water scarcity, access to water, and water pollution) and the capacity to manage those threats must be considered. An overarching priority is to build capacity and establish an enabling policy environment. Where threats are great and capacity is low, the challenge is greatest, since actions are unlikely to succeed without prior efforts to build capacity. Building capacity and utilizing existing institutions, in an enabling policy environment implies good governance and the involvement of diverse stakeholders and use of indigenous institutions. Further, it includes human resource development, improvement of data systems and sharing information, and mechanisms for regional cooperation and conflict resolution. It also requires a sound legal and regulatory framework as well as a policy and enforcement framework to assess operational efficiency and external consequences. The figure above illustrates the key strategic interventions needed by African countries to promote the sustainable and equitable use of water resources. These strategic interventions integrate the important roles of the public sector, the private sector, and the people at large.

Activities arising out of the key strategic interventions include, within improved data and information systems for example, the granting of financial autonomy to data generating agencies, thereby allowing them to sell their product (i.e., information) on the free market. Capacity utilization efforts can target children as agents of change, especially impacting water quality and health within the home. Awareness building efforts should look to the success-stories in Namibia and Botswana, where water conservation has become a national ethic. Policies and regulations which offer structure and stability to the economy will encourage domestic resource mobilization, and lessen the need for foreign aid. Finally, cooperation over transboundary waters will be enhanced by basin organizations designed to add value to the investments made by basin states.

An Agenda for the World Bank

An Active Partner. The World Bank remains an active partner in the development of water resources in SSA. It does this through policy dialogue, technical advice, and investment support in the irrigation, water supply and sanitation, and hydropower sectors. The cumulative Bank lending to these sectors is now approaching US$4.6 billion, supporting investments in over thirty countries. Overall, the Bank's assistance has evolved in response to growing demands for increasingly scarce water resources by competing sectors, as well as the need for capacity building and utilization, and new infrastructure, reflecting the changing socioeconomic and environmental realities of African countries.

Key Lessons Learned. World Bank-supported operations have helped African countries achieve several sectoral objectives, such as providing safe water and sanitation services to many households in urban and rural areas, expanding irrigated areas to augment food production, and increasing energy supply through hydropower development. Some progress is also being made in several other ways, including beneficiary participation, private sector development, and environmental assessment. Nevertheless, efforts still need to be intensified in these areas. There has been less progress in (a) sustainable management of the water sector based on an integrated, multisectoral approach which rationalizes water use among various competing sectors; (b) capacity building, development of legal and regulatory frameworks; (c) integration of health concerns in project design and components; (d) cost recovery through sensible pricing of water services; (e) technology development to improve use efficiency and reduce cost of water supply; (f) data and information systems; and (g) gender balances in water management.

Ongoing projects will need to place more emphasis on these areas. Further, implementation must build on best practices—in policy adoption, regulatory framework, use of indigenous practices, community participation, capacity building and utilization, and successful investment programs—and on actions which have generated good results on the ground.

Implications for Future Operations. Future operations will link more closely to **poverty reduction**. During the next ten years, the Bank will assist African countries to focus on both the supply and demand sides of water management, with increased emphasis on demand management. This means that the Bank will help African countries achieve a combination of efficient public sector interventions, market-oriented solutions, and popular participation as a critical element of its poverty reduction objective.

The Bank will also assist committed countries to move towards an integrated approach to water resources management involving major stakeholders, to promote private sector development, and to a pricing system which reflects the scarcity value of water resources. Furthermore, the Bank will give more attention to the needs of peri-urban and rural areas, where most of the poor live. It must also help foster regional cooperation in managing international rivers. Capacity building, utilization, and retention —including policy changes, institution building including a regulatory framework, human resource development, resource mobilization, and the development of information and new knowledge — will be the cornerstone of Bank water sector operations in SSA.

In the context of **its principal objective of poverty reduction**, the Bank will direct its efforts to five priority areas:

- Household water security: ensuring that a large number of rural and urban poor have access to clean water and sanitation services efficiently and equitably within the next decade;
- Food security and water: supporting measures that lead to increased productivity and food production in both rainfed and irrigated areas;
- Water quality and human health: supporting actions that reduce water pollution and degradation;
- Environmental stewardship: promoting programs that protect wetlands and catchment areas;
- Regional cooperation: promoting mechanisms for conflict resolution and prevention among countries sharing water resources, and multi-national investment programs for the development of water resources.

In support of these priority areas, the Bank will ensure the integration of **environmental and social assessments and gender considerations** in its operations. The Bank will also consider making long-term, multisectoral investments in the drought-prone countries of the Sahel and Eastern and Southern Africa. Further, the Bank will need to consider financing the Hydrological Cycle Observing System (HYCOS), data collection and processing, and early warning systems. This will require Bank support for capacity building (and stakeholder participation within countries).

Need for Selectivity: Country Priority Focus. The Bank will be highly selective and concentrate on its areas of comparative advantage: policy changes, capacity building, human resources development, support of investment operations that promote the sustainable and equitable use of water resources, and improvements in donor partnership and collaboration. To this end, the Bank will focus on countries which have political stability, an enabling environment, sufficient information and data bases, and strong commitment and ownership, and where development impact can be maximized by supporting long-term national programs.

Country performance indicators (in terms of capacity, regulatory framework, policy environment, results on the ground, etc.) and the critical threats (e.g., scarce water resources, deteriorating water quality, droughts, deforestation and land degradation, and regional conflicts) facing African countries can be used to designate countries in different groups as a basis for directing Bank support and interventions. With regard to countries such as Somalia, Sudan, Angola, Zaire, and Liberia, which are characterized by political instability and low capacity, the Bank could promote their inclusion within regional initiatives, and support water and hydrological assessment efforts, the training of nationals at regional capacity building centers, and efforts of smaller group and NGOs that promote good governance at local level.

In the second group of countries (e.g., Congo, Chad, Guinea, Burundi, Rwanda, The Gambia, Mozambique, Eritrea, the Central African Republic) which are emerging from periods of instability and undergoing political transformation toward a market economy, Bank assistance could be directed mainly to capacity building, policy reforms, beneficiary participation, and targeted investments.

The third group of countries (e.g., Tanzania; Ethiopia, Lesotho, Zimbabwe, Uganda, Madagascar, Ghana, Kenya, and Senegal), where some progress has already been made toward capacity building and stakeholder participation, could be assisted by the Bank through the support of national investment programs (SIPs) for increased access to safe drinking water and sanitation, irrigation expansion, and hydropower development. The Bank could also support actions in these countries that broaden and deepen policy reforms, legal and regulatory frameworks, capacity building, resource pricing, private sector development, and stakeholder participation.

Multiple Country Focus. The prevalence of international rivers in SSA presents the Bank with an important challenge in promoting a multi-country focus and regional cooperation in the management of international waterways. International river basin management will require the Bank to move beyond its traditional support for single-country operations to supporting multi-national initiatives. Specifically, the Bank will offer, if requested by the riparian states and in collaboration with other donors, its support to potential crisis areas like the Nile Basin and the Zambezi and Inkomati Basins in Southern Africa. In this connection, the Bank may need to consider using its own intermediation to foster basin cooperation and to mediate in facilitating joint actions by the riparian states supporting specific investments, capacity building and utilization, and training. The Bank can also expand the role of the Global Environment Facility (GEF) in institution building, development of information systems, and protection of catchment areas in the management of international rivers and lakes.

Change Agenda: A New Dimension. Since the Bank's mission is to get results on the ground in poverty reduction in Africa, it needs to increase results from on-going operations in irrigation, water supply and sanitation, urban development, and hydropower. Operations need to be restructured to move toward integrated sector programs, and more attention needs to be given to the development of sector performance indicators, client consultation, and beneficiary assessment involving major stakeholders. The Bank will change its emphasis from a supervision role to one of implementation review and dialogue, and will take a broader sector approach that internalizes African country priorities and builds on existing capacity. Bank operational and sector work will be interdisciplinary and multisectoral, incorporating the "nexus" analytical concept by assessing the linkages among population, environment, poverty, economic activities, and technological variables. The sector work will lead to the preparation of brief country strategy papers produced in collaboration with the Africans and key donor agencies.

In Country Assistance Strategies, more attention will be given to addressing water related issues (policy choices, investment options, financial sustainability, private sector participation, and cost recovery), particularly as they relate to poverty, human health, and environmental degradation. Special attention will be given to cross-sectoral and transboundary considerations as well. The Bank will also make long-term commitments, understanding that processes such as the implementation of a national water policy or the development of basin-wide agreements can take place on a time-scale much longer than the standard lending cycle.

External Agencies: Need for New Partnership. Better coordination among donors and other international organizations involved in the water sector is crucial and can greatly help to accelerate the achievement of water management objectives. Without coordination, donors will continue in fragmented ways, supporting narrow goals, undermining the efforts of African national governments, duplicating each other's initiatives, or implementing inefficient projects due to limited institutional capacity in the region. As the Bank's strategy advocates a systemic approach to water management, it calls for integrated sector operations that focus on stakeholders and the private sector, require long time-horizons, or emphasize community-based systems and market-oriented approaches. Such programs are susceptible to failure when donor activity is uncoordinated. To this end, African governments will need to be proactive in coordinating donor support and in building consensus. Also, the Bank will need to work with the African Development Bank, UN Agencies, and bilateral agencies, cooperate more effectively on regional initiatives, and continue preliminary collaboration on the Global Water Partnership. Collaboration may focus on information exchange and dissemination, identification of critical water resource threats, support of national research, and mobilization of capital resources for capacity building, utilization, and sustainability.

Building Consensus: Stakeholder Workshops and Partnerships

To develop consensus and a broad coalition among all stakeholders, this strategy paper was discussed at two technical workshops in Nairobi, Kenya and Dakar, Senegal in February, 1996. In total, the workshops were attended by over 230 people, with participants including Ministers, Permanent Secretaries, and agency directors from forty-one SSA countries, and representatives from bilateral and multilateral agencies, NGOs, and the private sector. The high attendance plus the evident commitment of all participants to partnership and a broad coalition for promoting more efficient and equitable use of water resources in the region shows a consensus for a three-part **Emerging Imperative**: the need to accelerate the transition to the sustainable use of water; country-driven development that makes optimum use of African capabilities, resources, and experiences; and cooperation among sectors, among riparian countries, and among donors.

Workshop participants emphasized the positive view, counseling that African countries and donor agencies should build on the numerous achievements, experiences, and resources in the Region. To this end, the **Road Ahead** will demand the following: (a) political will and commitment; (b) stakeholder participation at all levels; (c) demand management and water conservation; (d) equitable sharing of international resources; (e) effective policy and regulatory frameworks; (f) capacity building, utilization and retention; and (g) new forms of country/donor partnership. In following this road, the participants affirmed some common principles to which Africans and donors should adhere. These principles make up a **New Agenda** for water resources management, entailing an integrated, multisectoral approach to management; co-riparian cooperation on shared rivers; partnership, integration and pluralism; water as both a social and an economic good; health and environmental sustainability; and the importance of public awareness, indigenous knowledge, and gender sensitivity.

In light of this New Agenda, the participants supported the five **Development Priorities** also identified in this strategy paper; namely, enhanced service coverage with priority for the poor, food security through irrigation and water harvesting, water quality and human health, protection of watersheds and wetlands, and intercountry river-basin cooperation. These development priorities call for **Strategic Actions** on the part of African nations and external support agencies. These actions work towards the common goal of sustainable and equitable use of water resources, and entail seven strategy elements: (a) utilization and building of local capacity and human resources; (b) development of knowledge and approaches through applied research; (c) strengthening of data and information systems; (d) involvement of all stakeholders and building of awareness; (e) establishment of mechanisms for regional cooperation and conflict resolution; (f) support of long-term national investment programs; and (g) implementation of country-driven donor coordination.

Further, the participants intensively discussed actions under five thematic topics and presented a number of challenging recommendations for priority action (the full list is contained in Annex B). For example, under the theme dealing with strategies and investment options, they emphasized community-level management and the mobilization of domestic financial resources. While discussing capacity utilization, building and retention, there was a particular call for the increased use of indigenous resources and decentralization of public sector agencies, both of which can make better use of already existing human resources. In the meeting on regional cooperation, the participants noted that riparian states and donors must work on creating "win-win" solutions reflecting equity for upstream and downstream states. With regard to information and knowledge bases, the participants supported the setting of economic objectives for information systems created on a demand-driven basis. Lastly, under the topic of donor collaboration, donor and African representatives agreed that donors should truly listen to their African clients, and rally behind country-driven national programs.

Next Steps. At the close of the Nairobi and Dakar meetings, the participants agreed to spread the messages of the workshops to a wider audience, fostering the stakeholder participation that is crucial in country and regional strategy development. There was also consensus to create an informal **Pan-African Partnership** for fostering inter-country dialogue, sharing knowledge, experience and best practices, developing consensus on key issues and actions, and reviewing progress on agreed development efforts. To this end, the **African Advisory Group** (formed during the writing of this Strategy Document and made up of nine distinguished persons from the region) will forge this Partnership and lead it during its early stages. The goal is to build upon the momentum created by the two workshops and this strategy.

For its part, the World Bank will begin to make this strategy operational. Key tenets of the strategy are already being implemented in a number of countries, including Ghana, Malawi, Mozambique, Senegal, Tanzania, and Zimbabwe, and the Africa Region of the Bank will learn from and build upon these experiences. The various country initiatives will focus on developing appropriate methods to adopt the integrated, multisectoral approach advocated here, and special attention will be given to the development of long-term national programs for the more efficient management of water resources. This will require close and better coordination and collaboration between the various sector operations staff dealing with the water sector through Country Teams and a Water Sector Association allowing staff dealing with water matters to participate in discussions to exchange ideas, information, and good practices, and to focus on cross-cutting issues that relate to the key sectors dealing with water. It will also the require development of approaches within Country Assistance Strategies that focus on integrated water resources management.

Moreover, implementation of the strategy will require, as indicated by the workshop participants, better collaboration among donors, particularly at the country level. This means that donors will need to do business differently, working in harmony to support country-driven national programs. Donors can build on important existing frameworks such as the Pan African Partnership, referred to previously, the Utility Partnership (the Capacity Building Program for Water and Sanitation), the UNDP-

World Bank Water Supply and Sanitation Program, and the GEF-sponsored Lake Victoria Environmental Management Program. Donors also need to build on the momentum around critical new initiatives like the Global Water Partnership and the United Nations Secretary-General's Special Initiative on Africa (SIA), which includes water as one of its five key elements. In relation to the SIA, a UN Agency Informal Working Group on Water has been formed under the co-chairmanship of UNEP and the World Bank, with current members including, but not limited to FAO, UNDP, UNDDSMS, UNICEF, WHO, WMO, and the Water and Sanitation Program. This Informal Working Group is already taking an important step toward developing a coordinated plan of action for the implementation of the water component of the SIA by creating a matrix of current and future agency activities at a country level.

Finally, doing business differently also means that the international community, including the World Bank, needs new approaches based on African experiences and opportunities to promote stakeholder cooperation in river basin management. This may include, among other things, multi-country lending programs and high-level diplomatic efforts on the part of the Bank. It will also require a conscious effort by the external agencies to support projects within countries which create an even playing field for all beneficiaries and co-riparian states.

1. Background

Sub-Saharan Africa's water is becoming a critical strategic commodity as demand increases and supplies diminish in areas of high population concentration. Water plays a crucial role in the region's economic development as well as in the maintenance of natural systems. Demands for water resources will increase over the next several decades as populations increase, urbanization intensifies, and economic development continues, resulting in more land degradation, deforestation, and pollution. Throughout SSA, the need to use water resources efficiently and sustainably is urgent—for the benefit of both present and future generations. African countries must treat freshwater as a scarce good and recognize that the region's social, economic, and environmental security depends on reliable access to and wise use of water resources.

A. INTRODUCTION

African countries recognize that water resources must be used wisely to improve human welfare, achieve economic growth, and enhance regional cooperation. This recognition, however, comes in the context of growing water supply constraints—particularly in the drylands which account for about 60 percent of the region's total land area— escalating supply costs, and deteriorating water quality. In many localized areas, Africans have already reached a crisis level where human health, food security, animal survival, and the environment have been adversely affected. The frequency of droughts in the Sahel and in the Eastern and Southern African countries during the past three decades has resulted in significant social, economic, and environmental costs, affecting mainly the lives of the poor.

Figure 1.1

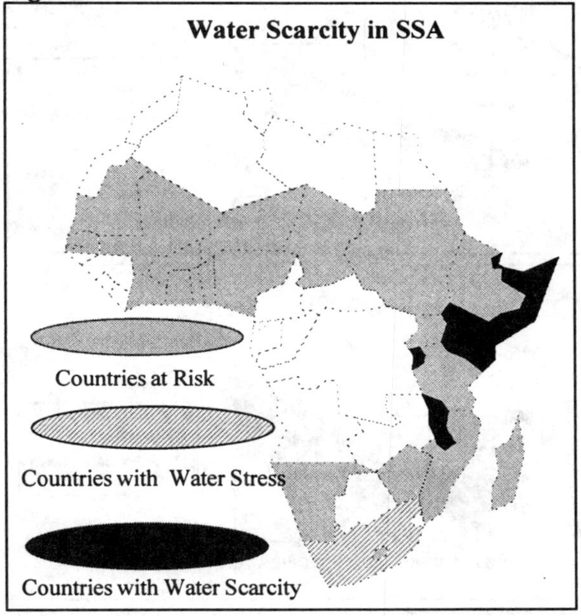

The availability of water in SSA is highly variable (within a season, a twelve-month period, and over several years) because of pronounced differences in average annual rainfall, evapotranspiration, and hydrogeology. Some areas of the region, such as the Sahelian countries, have a limited supply of freshwater and more variable rainfall, while other areas, particularly the humid tropical zone in Central and West Africa, have abundant water. Even within countries, the availability of water varies considerably, influenced by physical characteristics and seasonal patterns of precipitation. In 1990, eight countries were suffering from water stress or scarcity, and this situation is likely to get worse due to rapid population growth, expanding urbanization, and increased economic development. By 2000, about 300 million Africans risk living in a water scarce environment. Moreover, by 2025, the number of countries experiencing water stress will rise to eighteen, affecting some 600 million people (World Bank 1995e) (Figure 1.1).

Human health concerns are widespread because of a lack of safe drinking water and inadequate sanitation/sewage collection systems, and pollution of many rivers, lakes, and ground water. The proportion of the population without access to adequate water is greater in Africa than anywhere else. About 65 percent of the rural population and 25 percent of the urban population lack adequate water; 73 percent of the rural and 43 percent of the urban population lack proper sanitation (World Bank 1995d) (Figure 1.2).

Figure 1.2

Water and Sanitation - The Widening Gap*

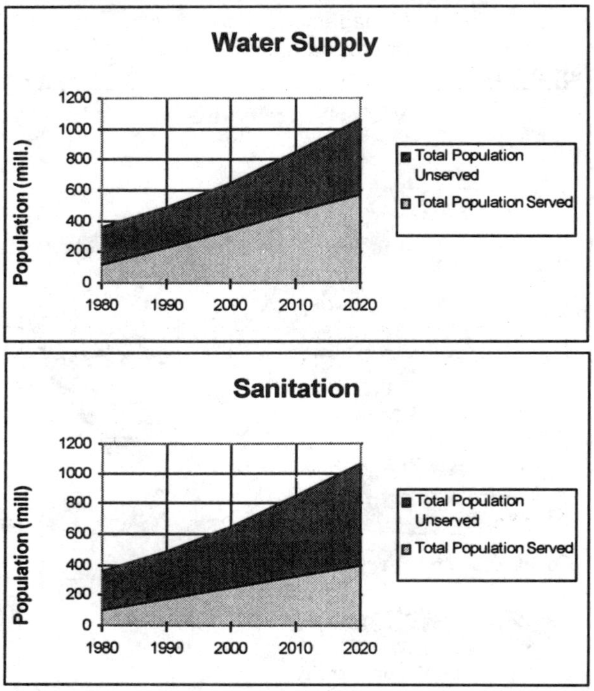

* If business as usual:
Maintaining 1980 - 1990 rate of service expansion

In SSA, the cost of exploiting new water supplies is also rising sharply, particularly costs associated with recovering ground water and transferring water from rivers and lakes to distant places. Highly subsidized pricing and inadequate cost recovery measures contribute to the over-exploitation of water resources, excessive consumption for low value uses, and the financial weaknesses of water utilities and public agencies dealing with water resources.

Competition among various activities—domestic consumption, agriculture, industry, power supply, livestock, wildlife resources, and recreation—for the use of water has become more intense, contributing to conflicts at the local, national, and regional levels, requiring better allocation procedures and mechanisms for resolving and preventing conflicts. As the region is served by several major drainage areas, competition for limited water resources will increase among riparian countries. Approximately fifty-four of Africa's rivers are shared by at least two countries, and the region has about one-third of the world's major international river basins (basins > 100,000 km^2). Although increasing demand and growing water scarcity might cause conflicts between riparian states, these very same factors are imperatives for regional cooperation. For instance, the Nile, Zambezi, Niger, and Volta river basins have the potential for both serious conflicts and cooperation among the riparian countries. Cooperation and the effective joint management of transboundary waters must be promoted, and regional economic initiatives which provide mutual benefits to all the riparian states must be developed.

In SSA, the effective management and development of water resources, particularly under conditions of scarcity, requires treatment of water not only as a social and environmental good, but also as an economic good that reflects the scarcity value of this finite resource. More important, it requires strong institutions, an intersectoral capacity to regulate both water quantity and quality, and wide societal participation in resource conservation and protection. It needs effective demand management strategies and measures through improved technology, infrastructure, and efficiency to improve supply.

As in many parts of the world, different sector agencies in the region, such as agriculture, urban and power ministries, often have some responsibility for water management and have single purpose objectives, paying little attention to intersectoral and environmental considerations. The situation is exacerbated by the widespread and entrenched weakness in formal public and private institutions—with very limited civil service capacity and an undeveloped formal private sector. In contrast, traditional and informal institutions possess untapped strengths which are relevant to sound water resources management. African countries must build capacity for effective water resources management and development in the public and private sectors and local communities. They must also build on existing institutional strengths, human resources, and approaches which generate results on the ground.

The current situation in SSA calls for renewed commitment, new approaches and partnerships, implementable actions, and regional cooperation to accelerate this transition to more efficient water resources management. Given the region's heterogeneity—and depending upon prevailing conditions, needs, and priorities—individual countries will adopt combinations of the following development imperatives:

- *Make households water secure* by providing safe drinking water and sanitation efficiently and equitably to more people in rural and urban areas.

- Protect weltands and catchment areas by involving all stakeholders.

- Increase *food security* through the efficient use of water resources and technology in rainfed and irrigated areas.

- Implement measures to address serious water quality problems (degradation and pollution) that threaten *human health.*

- Develop implementable mechanisms for *conflict resolution and prevention* both among countries sharing water resources and at the country level between people and economic sectors competing for scarce water resources.

B. Scope of the Strategy Paper

Objectives. The World Bank's WATER POLICY PAPER (World Bank 1993a) provides the guiding principles for the development of this strategy paper. The overall goal is to identify, through a participatory process of wide consultation, a regional strategy which will promote the improved management of water resources at both the regional and national level, taking full and pragmatic account of the needs, priorities, and constraints of African countries. Specific objectives of the paper are given in Box 1.1.

Box 1.1: Objectives of the Strategy Paper

•To identify and analyze water resources issues, challenges, and opportunities specific to the countries and sub-regions in SSA, giving examples from the region.
•To facilitate the implementation of the Bank's Water Resources Management Policy and promote its adoption, as appropriate, in the region.
•To pay particular attention to international water resource issues and opportunities, and thereby facilitate dialogue among the countries of the region, promoting regional initiatives where appropriate.
•To focus on the results of practical experiences, and particularly best practices, of Bank operational staff and water sector staff in the countries themselves and of those in other agencies.
•To identify a role for the Bank, through sector work and policy dialogue, technical assistance, lending operations, and less conventional instruments, to aid both regional and national water resources management actions.
•To build consensus among the key stakeholders — including Africans, bilateral and multilateral agencies, NGOs, centers of excellence, and academia — on critical issues and approaches relating to water resources management.

This paper does not seek to provide specific action plans to individual countries or groups of countries. However, it advocates that, in many cases, developing a national (or basin-wide) water resources management strategy is an effective starting point for the long-term development of water resources. The paper recognizes the link between the market and public sector in water management and that the sustainable use of water will result from a participatory approach involving all stakeholders. Further, the paper recognizes that the better management of water resources will be complex and gradual, resulting from incremental adjustments. The strategy paper does not seek to analyze and develop strategies for individual sectors in any detail—instead it takes a cross-sectoral perspective, identifying common issues and strategies that will promote an integrated approach to water resources management.

Audience. This paper will target a diverse audience, including policy makers, water sector managers, and professionals in African governments and regional organizations as well as others in the private sector and non-governmental organizations (NGOs) in Africa and donor agencies. In addition, it will target Bank operational staff, in order to share lessons from experiences and promote consensus on key regional issues and possible actions. The paper aims to improve cross-sectoral policy dialogue with African countries, promote results on the ground, and increase client consultation. Among Bank managers, the paper will signal the need for improved water resources management in Africa and increased attention to the subject in country assistance strategies and lending programs.

Partnership. This report has sought out the views and participation of a wide range of stakeholders in order to ensure its relevance to Africa as well as extensive ownership of the ideas presented. An African Advisory Group of senior policymakers and academics from seven countries in the region has provided overall guidance to the exercise, meeting in December 1994 to review and finalize the Concept Paper, and in November 1995 to review a first draft of the strategy paper. Within the Bank, a Steering Committee, including senior staff of each of the three main sectors—Agriculture, Infrastructure, and Environment— provides overall guidance, and the Africa Region's Water Thematic Team ensures wide regional, intersectoral, and operational participation.

The strategy paper is based on a wide and comprehensive range of background papers prepared by experts from many organizations, including FAO, UNEP, UNESCO, ODA/UK, AfDB, ICRAF, Duke University, independent experts, and the World Bank. A full list of background papers is given in the Bibliography.

Document Framework. This chapter provides the context for examining this topic in a broader framework focusing on important issues and solutions for the sustainable management of water resources. The next chapter describes the issues and challenges facing the region, with an understanding that these issues have created the development imperatives described here, and with an understanding that the management of water resources cuts across sectors. Chapter 3 shows that there are positive results on the ground. It says that before exogenous solutions from industrial countries are used to meet these challenges, we should look to the considerable achievements and opportunities already present in Africa. In Chapter 4, strategic options are examined to develop actions in a number of important areas, including capacity building, the enabling environment, and stakeholder participation. The final chapter (Chapter 5) develops an agenda for World Bank assistance in the water sector in African countries, building on past experiences, lessons learned, and opportunities for further collaboration with African countries and donor agencies.

2. *Current Status And Emerging Trends: Issues And Challenges*

SSA countries face important choices and trade-offs in the use and management of water, balancing between immediate economic benefits and long-term conservation and sustainable use gains. There are many concerns and interests competing at the local, national, and regional levels, with many stakeholders demanding water for different uses. Reconciling and managing these diverse interests – to promote the better use of water resources – will be a critical challenge for SSA, requiring local, national, and regional solutions. The African people will need to see water as a scarce resource rather than a free good, and African countries will have to define the roles of the market, public sector, and local people in water management, reflecting economic, ecological, and equity goals.

A. The Political Economy of Water Resources Utilization: Diverse Interests

Political Choice. Once access is at risk, water issues can bring out irrational behavior. It is rarely traded between nation states because, while threats to security or food shortages can be buffered, water shortages cannot. In every country, water resources management is fraught with political implications, tensions, and interference. Limited governance – in terms of accountability, rule of law, transparency – which is characteristic of some countries in the region and intensifies the challenges in water management. Across much of the region, water is often at the top of the list of needs of poor communities generally deprived of infrastructure and other services. Despite the important principle advocated in this strategy paper, few industrial nations treat water as an economic good, even those with leanings towards a free market economy. The effectiveness of these concepts in the region will depend on support at the highest levels in a politically stable climate, as well as a sound institutional and legal framework, a good base of information and knowledge, and the involvement of people. It will also require balancing economic, social, and ecological aims in water utilization. Ultimately, it is important to consider water not only as an economic good but also as a social and environmental good.

Correcting market and government failures (i.e., distortions in the market, goods and services that are not accounted for in the market, and policies and government interventions that lead to the misuse of water resources) will substantially improve the use and management of water resources. Management and policy reforms will be difficult, requiring strong public support and political will and commitment. Further, policies in other sectors affect water utilization. For example, agricultural, industrial, energy, and urban sector policies impact both water quantity and quality. Policy changes (both macro-economic and sectoral) could alter existing patterns of land use and water allocation and use among competing activities. Elimination of water subsidies in agriculture could shift greater use of water to industries and urban centers or even within the agricultural sector reflecting higher-valued uses.

Box 2.1: Economic efficiency and social objectives: conflict or convergence?

An important challenge facing African countries is greater economic efficiency in the pricing and allocation of water and meeting the social objectives of getting water services to the country's poor. There can be convergence between economic efficiency and social objectives by relying on market-oriented solutions, efficient public sector intervention, and public participation. Under existing conditions, formal water services — whether domestic, industrial or agricultural supplies — are commonly heavily subsidized. Thus, the higher consumption by an individual user, the higher the subsidy. In the meantime, those not reached by formal services often pay close to or above the economic cost, and consume very low volumes. In addition, the higher the level of subsidy, the fewer the resources available to extend services to the unserved. The situation is often therefore one of the better-off — living in low-density areas of cities or on large farms — benefiting greatly from the underpricing of water, while the poorer with formal services get much lower unit subsidies and the unserved pay very much higher costs, often paying more than ten times the unit cost for vended water than those with piped water.

In rural and peri-urban areas, the very poorest people often live where water is scarcest and most costly. Also, there are few incentives for utilities to extend services to the poor. In most cities, very high and very low levels of service co-exist alongside each other, creating massive inequities. Conventional targeting of the poor often does not work. For example, rising block tariffs to ensure that everyone gets some water at low cost often lead to benefits for the rich and penalties for the poor. As water lies at the heart of the poverty trap, it is necessary to reduce subsidies and extend services to the poor and marginalized areas, thus achieving greater economic and social efficiency. Subsidies for the poor, if needed, need to be highly targeted - through vouchers, income transfer, or sensible pricing.

Source: Garn 1995.

Allocations of water resources to meet basic human needs, food security, energy, and economic development; while maintaining the integrity of aquatic ecosystems; cannot be based strictly on efficiency criteria to reconcile private and societal interests. There will also be a subjective assessment by society, influenced by ecological and ethical considerations. Furthermore, individuals, special interest groups, NGOs, private sector, and government agencies may have their own agenda and respond differently to water use imperatives. These stakeholders will increasingly influence choices between competing objectives.

The complementarity between the market and public sector will also determine how efficiently and sustainably water resources are used. An important challenge for countries in SSA is to create an environment in which there is a role for the market, for the public sector, and for popular participation to achieve economic, equity, and environmental goals (Box 2.1). In this connection, it is important for African countries to make greater use of the main economic instruments (market and pricing mechanisms) since these countries have relied generally on the public sector for managing and providing water resources at highly subsidized prices.

In most cases, countries have approached water management and allocation issues as problems of control and coordination among public sector entities rather than as problems of efficient allocation and investments in water. Consequently, supply requirements derived from independent sectoral or project plans—or from more integrated and ambitious national water plans—have dominated decision-making about water allocation, development, and use. This approach has led to extensive government intervention in virtually all aspects of water management, from allocation of water to the direct government operation of supply facilities. The market will allow some choices (water allocation, entitlements, and tradable property rights) to be made, but in some cases public sector interventions will be required to address market failures and special interests to safeguard society's long-term objectives.

Inter-Sectoral Considerations. The key sectors competing for scarce water resources throughout SSA are agriculture, industry, and municipalities. Agriculture remains a high-volume user of low-cost water while municipal and industrial consumers are low-volume users of low-cost water. As noted earlier, with increased urbanization, economic expansion, and population growth, competition for limited water availability will most likely intensify and conflicts will increase among water users. Agriculture, the largest user of water (over 80 percent) is highly subsidized, even though agriculture represents low-value use. Agriculture will come under increasing pressure to share water with higher-valued uses in industries and municipalities, pay for the water utilized at higher prices, and use water more efficiently, since almost 60 percent of water used in irrigation is wasted. This could result in conflicts, given the large farming population and the need to increase food production. Interest groups, representing these sectors plus others, such as energy, tourism, and wildlife, have—and will continue to have—great influence on water resources policy decisions and management.

For instance, as in the industrial countries, when pricing water for irrigation, the irrigators can pay only a small percentage of the real cost of providing water, and water is mostly supplied at no cost, since dams and main distribution works are provided by the governments as a public capital expenditure. There is also political resistance to the re-allocation of water from irrigation to higher economic value purposes, with governments subsidizing water for domestic agriculture production, rather than using economic charges as an incentive to improving the efficiency of agricultural water use. SSA countries face an important challenge in allocating water among competing sectors in an equitable and ecologically sound manner (Box 2.2).

Box 2.2: Need for Integrated Approach: Tanzania's Pangani River Basin

Within watersheds and/or river basins, special consideration needs to be given to the ecological links between land use and development, agricultural practices, soil conservation, wetlands, flora and fauna, and human population growth. Tanzania has learned this lesson within the Pangani River Basin which flows east from the foothills of Mt. Kilimanjaro and the Usambara Mountains to the Indian Ocean. Although it is small relative to Africa's major basins, the river represents an important source of livelihood to people (in rural areas and in the capital city, Dar es Salaam) and is a vital component of the natural system. Its tributaries cut through the Masai Steppe and important protected areas, supporting abundant wildlife, including large mammals. With rapid population growth, upstream farmers have increased irrigation demands on Pangani tributaries, thereby decreasing available water downstream. Some of these formerly perennial tributaries are now dry from September to November.

The Nyumba ya Mungu is the main dam on the Pangani River, and it stores water for power generation primarily in Dar es Salaam. In recent years, power generation has been below capacity, due in part to low reservoir levels. Urban and industrial users of electricity were upset and accused upstream farmers of diverting too much water for irrigation. A second problem relates to decreasing water quality. Usambara forests have been cut for fuelwood and expanding agriculture, leading to soil erosion and landslides. These sediments flow downstream, making treatment for Dar es Salaam's drinking water more difficult. In 1993, there was a cholera outbreak in the city as well. Decreased power, health, and agricultural output and a deteriorating natural environment all contribute to undermine Tanzania's economy and increase poverty.

Source: Hirji 1995

Geopolitics of Water Management. The geopolitics of water are increasingly becoming an important issue at the country level since there are transboundary considerations. This is especially true in SSA since all the countries in the region share one or more international rivers. Water has become a strategic resource, similar to oil, and with the increasing scarcity and growing value of water resources, and concerns about access and water rights and options for future use, the potential for conflicts among riparian countries has increased in recent years and will intensify in the future. National and customary laws exist to deal with conflicts at the local and national levels but existing international laws are not adequate to fully address conflicts between countries and among riparian states. In the case of international bodies of water involving multiple countries, water utilization issues are generally addressed through treaties, agreements, and cooperation. African countries will need to develop or strengthen their institutional and legal framework to promote the equitable sharing of water resources among riparian states as well as develop viable conflict resolution and prevention mechanisms to deal with international water matters. Policy considerations among riparian states and investment decisions will need to take into account the international dimension of water resources. Externality costs associated with water use may have local, national, and regional impacts. Sovereign countries can address domestic externalities through regulations and pricing and taxation policies. However, resolution of regional externalities, resulting from pollution and degradation of catchment areas, can only be addressed through cooperation, joint investments, knowledge transfer, and sharing of costs in protecting catchment areas under existing conditions.

Since more than one country in SSA shares water from international water bodies (rivers, lakes, ground water), a number of important questions arise: How can water allocation be established equitably among the concerned states? Who should pay for the cost of protecting watersheds if benefits accrue to both upstream and downstream countries—or how should this cost be shared? Who should pay for the pollution of rivers, lakes, and ground water shared by several countries? How should the rights of downstream countries be protected to ensure a fair share of water resources? How can a basin-wide approach to management of shared water resources be developed? How should costs supporting regional river basin organizations be shared by the riparian countries? To avoid potential conflicts, these questions must be addressed.

B. Poverty, Health, and Food Security: Development Imperatives

Poverty and Water

As shown in Figure 2.1, poverty has risen steadily in SSA. It is estimated that it will affect more than 600 million people by the turn of the century. The poor have limited access to clean water and sanitation for domestic use, as well as for use in crop production.

Figure 2.1

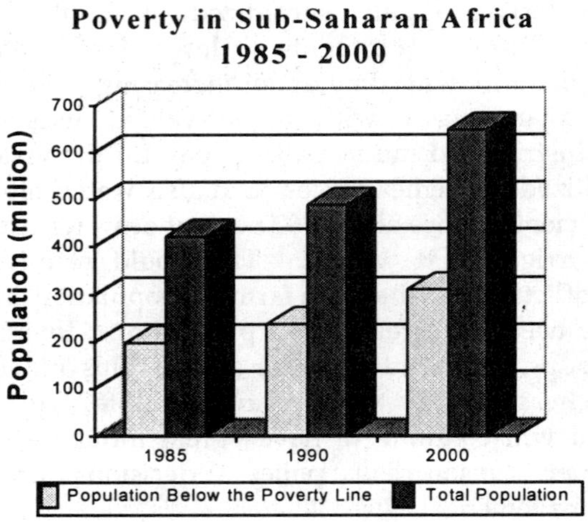

Most of Africa's poor live in rural areas. Making rural households secure regarding food, water, and energy is a key strategic element in reducing poverty. In agriculture, low-income producers can increase food production significantly by having reliable access to water and through improved water harvesting techniques and water and soil conservation practices. Also, providing the urban and peri-urban poor access to clean water and sanitation at affordable prices will contribute significantly to the health and economic well-being of many people living in towns and cities.

Health

Human Health. The primary causes of disease and poor health in SSA are water-related. The lack of safe water for drinking, the shortage or lack of accessible water for hygiene, and the scarcity of sanitation services all contribute to human health problems.

Water contamination is widespread due to industrial pollution (Box 2.3), as well as poor sanitation practices and the increasing discharges of untreated sewage into surface and ground waters. Loaded with bacteria and viruses, these waters can be a major threat to human health in the downstream localities, and water treatment is commonly inadequate or unreliable.

Box 2.3: Pollution in the Niger Delta

The multiple impacts from pollution on a major coastal system can be illustrated in the Niger Delta. The Niger Delta is the most important wetland system in West Africa. It has over 500,000 hectares of mangrove swamps. The Delta is densely populated with an estimated 4-6 million people, whose numbers are increasing at a rate of 3.5 percent per year. The Delta is also the center of Nigeria's petroleum and natural gas industries.

Petroleum Industries. Three of the four Nigerian refineries are located in the Niger Delta at Warri and Port Harcourt. The refineries generate large quantities of toxic sludge but do not contribute substantially to the wastewater except for oil and nitrogen compound discharges. Oil spills, however, have a significant impact on water quality.

Fertilizers. The National Fertilizer Company of Nigeria (NAFCON) is located near Port Harcourt. Effluent treatment systems are reported to function only intermittently. NAFCON generates approximately 50 percent of total nitrogen and virtually all total phosphorous industrial effluent in Port Harcourt. Major spills from the plant in 1992 and 1993 were reported to have resulted in massive fish kills.

Urban Wastewater. There are no operating municipal sewage treatment plants in the Niger Delta. Consequently, domestic, commercial, and industrial wastewater is discharged directly into open drains, many of which are unlined, blocked with solids, or broken. Untreated sewage contains organic matter including nutrients. High organic and nutrient inputs over large areas can result in eutrophication increasing algae blooms and dissolved oxygen depletion. In Port Harcourt, dissolved oxygen levels in some rivers are very low and are no longer sufficient for supporting herbivorous fish.

Source: Grey 1995.

Pollution: Future Threats and Responses. With rapid urbanization and industrialization (and consequent massive and localized pollutant loads) and drives for food security (and the likely increased levels of agrochemical application), the risks to water sources are growing rapidly. Soil erosion—from poor land management practices, deforestation, overgrazing, and sediment transport—is a rapidly increasing problem, affecting water quality, aquatic ecology, reservoir volumes, and estuaries (including ports). In northern Angola, for example, runoff from uncontrolled diamond mining threatens future agricultural viability of this land (Angola Country Paper 1996). In addition, erosion from poor agricultural practices causes environmental degradation from sedimentation as well as fills important hydroelectric impoundments like those on the Tana River in Kenya.

Polluted water is simply unsuitable for use in many cities and is a health hazard for drinking, bathing, and food preparation. For example, in Tanzania, 90 percent of water supplies are unsafe for drinking, while Abidjan's Ebrie Lagoon is eutrophic from waste discharges. Throughout SSA, water-borne diseases (e.g., typhoid, cholera, dysentery gastroenteritis, and hepatitis) and water-based diseases (such as scistosomiasis and guinea-worm) are common. It is difficult to overstate the impact of these diseases in the region. Diarrheal death in Africa, at a rate of 17/1000, is the highest in the world; schistosomiasis affects 28 percent of the population; malaria causes 800,000 of deaths each year; and, onchocerciasis has caused blindness in up to 25 percent of the population in some villages (Listorti 1996). The prevalence of the main water-related diseases is shown in Table 2.1.

Table 2.1. Burden of Disease in SSA by Remedial Measures in Thousands

Disease/ Condition	Yrs. Lived with Disability	Annual Deaths	DAILY (Disability adjusted life-year)
Water/Sanitation-Related	1,468	888	31,208
- intestinal worms	806	1.4	852
- diarrhea	662	887	30,356
Vector-related	7,466	855	35,819
- malaria	4,708	805	31,504
- schistosomiasis	2,887	21	3,490
- filariasis	184	NA	184
- Guinea worm	103	NA	103
- onchocerciasis	182	29.7	641

It is important to identify, monitor, and manage these risks in order to avoid the massive investments in remediation common in the industrial world. However, surface water and ground water quality networks are not well developed in the region due to budgetary constraints, lack of analytical equipment, logistical limitations, as well as a lack of appreciation of the importance of water monitoring. Laboratory services are also unreliable due to a lack of chemicals, spares, and trained staff. Water quality monitoring and assessment costs money—and in a region already pressed for financial resources, the monitoring and assessment of freshwater resources are often not seen as a priority. Many SSA countries lack enforceable legislation, water quality standards, or water pollution control programs for effectively achieving abatement of point and non-point sources of pollution. The inability of most of the countries in SSA to collect relevant water quality data is a critical issue in future water resources management and investment planning.

Food Security and Water

Future water demand for farming, including livestock production, will be influenced by strategies for food security. Increasing food supply in SSA countries is closely linked to water utilization and access to water. In many parts of SSA, a lack of water is seriously constraining increased food production. Water shortages are also becoming a serious impediment to intensifying agriculture and bringing new lands into production. Presently, about one-third of the people in the region live in drought-prone areas. In these areas, drought proofing measures; such as soil and water conservation, improved water harvesting techniques, minimum tillage, improved crop selection and varieties, and small-scale irrigation; will be important elements in the region's food security strategies. Food security means not only availability but also stability and access to food. With a focus on rainfed production, it will be necessary to address the well-known problems in SSA of low productivity, high variability from inadequate water control, and scarcity of off-farm employment and uncertain incomes. While irrigation stands out as a measure for improving agricultural productivity, it can also provide a base for growth, income, and employment in disfavored rural areas, thereby mitigating one cause of urban migration.

Water will be an important factor in increasing food production in both irrigated and rainfed areas. During the past three decades, agricultural production in the region has increased at a rate of less than 2 percent per annum, while population has risen at an average annual growth rate of about 3 percent. Under existing demand and supply trends, cereal imports are expected to rise from the current 10 million metric tons to 30 million metric tons in 25 years. As food demand is expected to increase by about 3.3 percent annually, African countries must increase food production through intensive agriculture and sustainable production systems in which water will be used efficiently. This increase must come from production from (a) rainfed agriculture (about 207 million hectares) through better water harvesting techniques, improved farming practices, better technologies and infrastructures, and efficient water conservation, and (b) irrigated agriculture through increased productivity, efficient use of water, and expanded production areas.

If the area in SSA were increased by 3 percent per year (a high investment scenario) as compared to the present expansion rate of less than 1 percent, the total irrigated area would increase from 6.5 to 9.5 million hectares by the year 2010. Assuming that the irrigated land is properly cultivated, using standard agricultural practices, it could produce about 20 percent of the value of all agricultural produce. In some countries of the Sahel, the contribution of irrigated agriculture could reach 50 percent or more. This would not only amount to a substantial contribution to food security, but would also stabilize food production in drought years, improve the nutritional balance of farming families, and provide employment in rural areas, especially during the off-season. Further expansion of irrigation is limited in some countries because of resource constraints (e.g., Sudan, Somalia, South Africa, Madagascar). However, most of the SSA countries have substantial underutilized potential for irrigation expansion, with a total physical irrigation potential of approximately 39.5 million hectares, not taking into account large scale river diversion schemes. For example, Ethiopia reports that of its potentially irrigable area of 3.5 million hectares, only 4 percent is actually irrigated (Ethiopia Country Paper 1996).

Apart from improper policies or support for large and inefficient projects, a specific issue facing irrigation in Africa is the lack of research and development (R&D) in relation to total investment. Investment for research into appropriate methods, training of local users, and development of programs and products has been small compared to the size of the infrastructure investment, and there are no studies that document returns to research investment in this area. R&D is essential for increasing productivity and the ecological sustainability of irrigation, and as will be outlined in Chapter 3 on opportunities, it should be focused on four priority areas: increasing productivity, sustainability, management transfer, and the expansion of irrigated areas (Barker 1996). Countries like Namibia recognize this fact in their own self-assessments and are making a push for applied research in the sector (Namibia Country Paper 1996).

African countries will need to use water more efficiently in agriculture as an input that has scarce value. More efficient use of water — from traditional water harvesting and moisture control practices to modern irrigation systems (mostly small scale irrigation schemes), combined with the use of improved technology, inputs, and agricultural services—will contribute significantly to food security in SSA. (Figure 2.2).

Figure 2.2

Water Yield Productivity Rainfed and Irrigated Crops

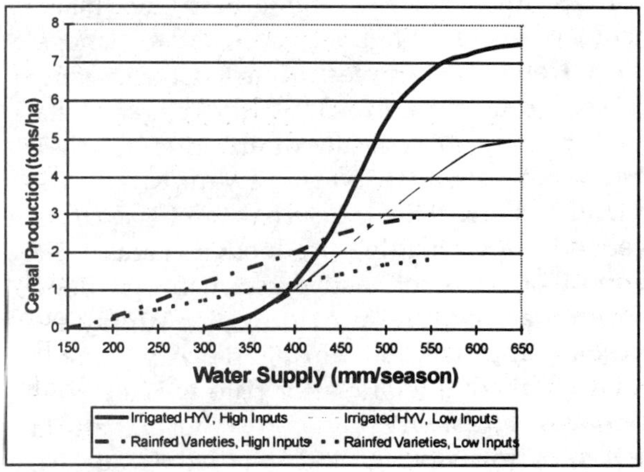

Source: FAO 1995

C. Water Resources and Water Demand: Claims for Scarce Resources

The Water Endowment

SSA spans areas which include both desert and tropical weather conditions. Precipitation over the continent varies from near zero over the Horn of Africa and the Namibian Desert to over 1600 mm/yr. in the western equatorial region. A large portion of the continent consists of semi-arid zones with 200-800 mm/yr. generally concentrated in a single rainy season. Average rainfall in this semi-arid zone exhibits a large variability as measured by the average departures of about 20-30 percent from the long-term annual mean. The mean annual renewable water resources in SSA total about 3,800 billion m^3 per year (or 3,800 km^3/year), of which 15 percent is ground water (Grove 1989) (Box 2.4).

Box 2.4: The Water Endowment

Complicating Factors:

- low total runoff relative to rainfall;
- limited highland areas of concentrated runoff;
- extreme spatial and temporal variability of rainfall and hence river flows;
- widespread occurrence of crystalline rocks with limited ground water;
- numerous international river basins;
- rapidly growing water scarcity (resources per capita).

Positive Factors:

- great lakes and large rivers: an invaluable resource;
- wetlands: fragile but valuable;
- ground water: limited but widespread.

Two features of African water resources increase the challenge of effective management. First, precipitation across much of the region is exceptionally variable — both in time and in space — and unpredictable. Second, runoff which equates to the useable and renewable water resources in Africa is extraordinarily low — only half that of Australia, North America, Europe, and Asia (despite having about the same average precipitation) and a quarter of that of Latin America. The obvious expression of this variability is endemic drought. Some parts of SSA are prone to severe droughts, especially the Sahel and Southern and Eastern Africa. The Sahel region has seen a decline in rainfall for about twenty-five years. Further, twenty-eight countries in the region experienced more than two consecutive years of drought during the 1974-1985 period (Keck and Dinar 1995). During the same period, several countries; including Cape Verde, Mauritania, Senegal, The Gambia, Guinea-Bissau, Sudan, and Ethiopia; have experienced two drought periods – with each period lasting two or more years. Another consequence of extended rainfall deficit in the Sahel has been runoff and the dramatic reduction in the size of Lake Chad.

A related expression of rainfall variability is the variation in the seasonal and annual flows in the river systems. On an annual basis, the ratio between the highest and lowest flows of the major perennial rivers (including the Senegal, Volta, Oueme, Blue Nile, Niger, Kagera, Zambezi, Okauango, and Orange) is around 3:1 and can reach 10:1. These flow variations have a dramatic influence on local production systems of millions of farmers, pastoralists, and fishermen inhabiting the river basins. Engineering solutions to variations in flow include the construction of large storage reservoirs for regulating seasonal and annual discharges. However, this can introduce other social and environmental challenges.

Limited Areas of Concentrated Runoff. A significant hydrologic feature in many parts of SSA is the concentration of runoff in limited upland areas (generating long rivers that run through dry downstream terrain.) Such uplands include the mountainous regions of the Fouta Djalon in Guinea, the Jos Plateau in Nigeria, the Cameroon Mountains in West Africa, the Ethiopian Mountains, the Aberdares and the slopes of Mount Kenya and Kilimanjaro in East Africa, and the Lesotho and Swaziland Highlands in Southern Africa. These areas, influenced by the inter-tropical convergence zone, are subject to marked seasonal and annual variation. Concentration of runoff in the upstream areas (for example, in the Ethiopian Highlands which form the headwaters of the Blue Nile) means that, in most cases, the downstream riparians (such as Egypt and Sudan in this case), often with a dry climate, are very dependent upon the actions that upstream states take to develop their water resources.

Major Rivers, Lakes, and Wetlands. The region has seventeen rivers with catchment areas greater than 100,000 km^2 and another eleven rivers with catchments exceeding 30,000 km^2. Flowing out of the highland regions of Western , Eastern, and Southern Africa, these and the hundreds of other important rivers represent a vital environmental and economic resource. Almost all important African rivers cross or form international boundaries. The region also has more than 160 lakes that are larger than 27 km^2 (Rangeley and others 1994). Most major lakes are located around the equatorial region and sub-humid East African Highlands within the Rift Valley, including the Great Lakes of Africa—Victoria, Tanganyika, and Malawi. Lake Chad is the only large tropical lake north of the equator located in the Sahel. Lakes play a vital role in the African economy as water sources for urban and rural areas, industry, livestock, wildlife, agriculture, and biological resources. They are also used for navigation, recreation, and as receptors of wastewater discharges. In addition, fishing for local and export market provides an important livelihood for riparian communities.

Africa has many important wetlands. Examples of major swamps include the Sudd swamp in the Sudan, the Okavango Delta in Botswana, Lake Chad, the Bangweulu swamps in Zambia, and the Malagarasi and Utengule swamps in Tanzania. Important floodplains include the Inner Niger Delta and the Senegal River Delta. Examples of extensive swamp forests are in the Zaire Basin and Niger Delta. Smaller, but no less important due to their abundance, are headwater 'swamps' on the upland plains—the *dambos* and *fadamas*. Wetlands are highly productive areas and support a host of activities such as flood recession agriculture, provide water supply for livestock and wildlife during the dry season, and are valuable habitats for fish, wildlife, and migratory birds. Wetlands also form natural reservoirs for storing and regulating surface flows and recharging ground water reservoirs.

Ground Water. Ground water is of extraordinary and often underestimated importance in the region, as aquifers buffer rainfall variability and continue to provide reliable sources of potable supplies in dry years when most surface sources have disappeared. Probably more than three quarters of the region's population use ground water as their main source of supply. However, the region's ground water resources, although widespread, are very limited (accounting for 15 percent of the total renewable water resources). There are few large sedimentary basins in the region with substantial renewable ground water reserves, although there are numerous smaller sedimentary aquifers along the major rivers and in coastal deltas and plains. There is little doubt that the ground water resources of the region need to be better understood and managed since their development could be key to managing rainfall variability and drought in some parts of the region, particularly the rural areas.

Unitary Resource. Water is a unitary resource, with all water in the hydrological cycle forming a part of that resource. Any interventions at or on one part of that cycle will have an impact on another part of the cycle. For example, ground water abstraction may reduce baseflows to rivers, and surface water diversion may reduce ground water recharge; wastewater discharge will affect water quality, and water quality will determine ecology. Water resources play a dominant role in several sectors— urban and rural water supply and sanitation, agriculture, power; and the environmental sectors (i.e., in maintaining environmental assets, such as the landscape)— and a lesser but nevertheless important role in others—e.g., health, forestry, industry, and transport. The inter-relationships between the hydrological cycle and the different sectors are illustrated in Figure 2.3, which seeks to show the inextricable linkages.

Figure 2.3

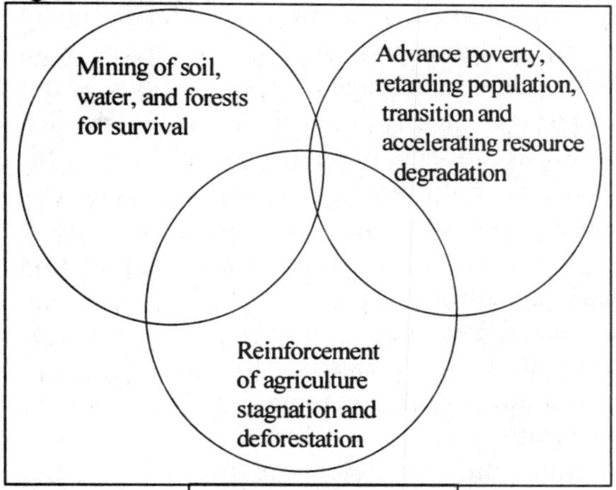

Nexus Dynamics

Land, Water, and Forests. As components of natural systems; land, water, and forests are inter-related and influence each other as well as the ecosystems. Human interventions through any of these components influence the dynamics and integrity of these ecosystems. For instance, as human interventions intensify, combined with population pressure, poverty, and poor land use practices, an ecosystem such as a river basin is altered. This alteration is in the form of increased deforestation, soil erosion and runoff, and modification of the micro-climates in the long run. Loss of vegetation contributes to the loss of soil and water quality and impedes river flows with increased sedimentation. In this context, it is important to view water resources management in a broader framework of land use and economic activities.

Intersectoral Management. As in many — if not most — parts of the world, most African countries assign responsibility for each category of water use to a different ministry or agency which can make water resources development decisions without coordinating its actions with others. The hydrological cycle— both water quantity and quality — is then affected, which inextricably impacts other users and uses. This sectoral and fragmented approach is at the core of the problem of water resources management. That does not mean that individual sectors should not continue to be free-standing users of water resources; they should and they will. It means that use needs to be planned, coordinated, and managed through an appropriate mix of institutional, policy, economic, and regulatory instruments. The sectoral demand for water highlights the need for an intersectoral approach since individual sectoral objectives are often in conflict with those of another sector. For example, calculations of hydropower potential and irrigation potential often both assume exclusive use of available water resources. Box 2.5 describes how conflict can occur between the linked activities of road construction and water conservation. Intersectoral management implies rational allocation of available resources to the highest value uses, where value is ascribed in terms of meeting a range of objectives - economic, social, environmental, or political.

Box 2.5: The Intersectoral Link Between Road Construction and Water Conservation

Among the intersectoral aspects of water resources management, road construction stands out as an area where water managers need to communicate with colleagues in the transport sector. Typically, road designers view water as an impediment or danger to the road. Therefore, they design works to remove the water quickly and far away, if possible. However, in the Sahel and dry regions of Eastern and Southern Africa, this water could be used for human and animal needs, not to mention for road maintenance itself. A World Bank-sponsored study of road works in the Sahel found that in Burkina Faso, water retention works are integrated into road design, reflecting the road agencies' awareness of the benefits of water conservation measures. In Mali and Niger, however, road agencies cited the high construction costs of water retention works as the reason for their absence. As a preliminary step in these and similar countries, water management agencies need to work with road agencies to evaluate potential socioeconomic benefits in relation to the costs of conservation.

Source: World Bank 1995d

Water Variability, Scarcity, and Drought

The region's limited water resources will come under further pressure as demand increases with rapidly growing populations. A survey of the twenty-nine Sub-Saharan African countries least endowed with water shows that in 1990 eight of them were suffering from water stress (less than 1667 m^3 of renewable water resources per capita/year) or water scarcity (less than 1000 m^3/capita/year). Using the UN medium population projection, the number of countries suffering from stress or scarcity will rise to 20 of 29 by 2025 (Husain 1993) (Figure 2.4). There are many reasons to question the usefulness of this scarcity/stress measure — it takes no account of the distribution of water availability in time and/or space, even if the actual numbers themselves are accepted as meaningful. For example, Kenya reports that it uses only 30 percent of total available water within its national boundaries, but uneven distribution of the water creates shortfalls (Kenya Country Paper 1996). Nevertheless, these numbers contribute to the gross picture of a region with a serious water problem.

Figure 2.4: UN Scarcity Predictions

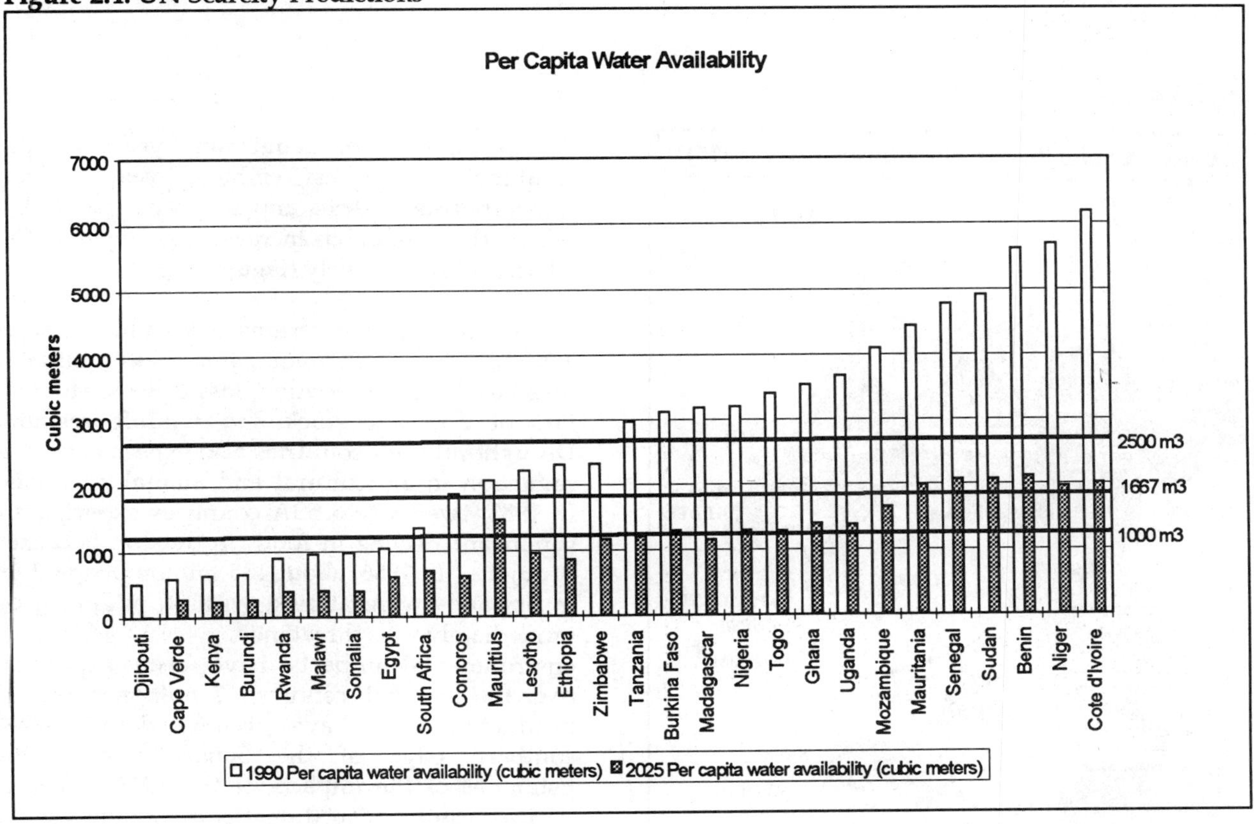

Usually water scarcity statistics are related to countries. However, Figures 2.5a and 2.5b take into account the challenges associated with international water resources by providing a river basin dimension to the water scarcity discussion. The figure to the right shows that eight river basins already face water stress and four face scarcity. These numbers will increase rapidly with population growth. Figure 2.5b illustrates water availability in the year 2025.

Figure 2.5 a

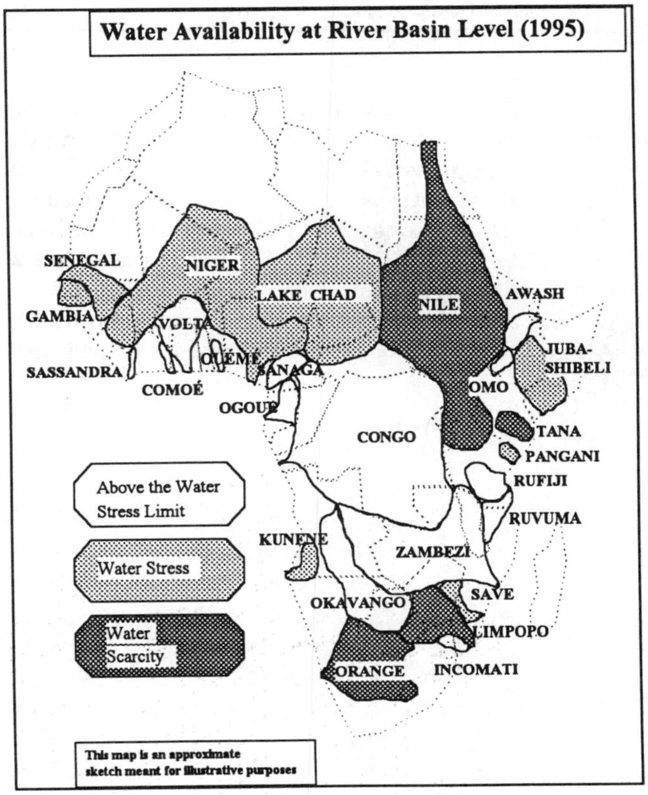

Figure 2.5 b

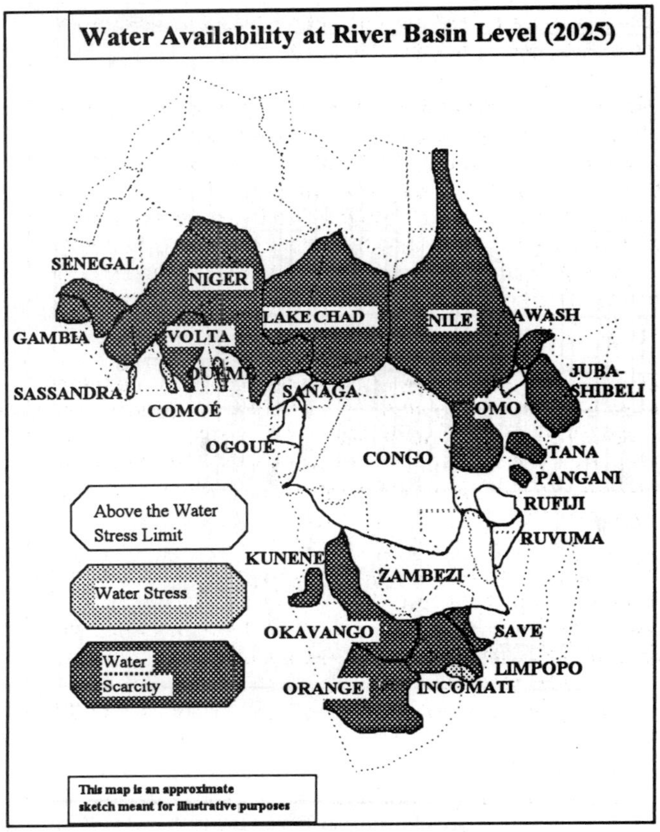

Climate variability in the region raises the specter of endemic drought. Recent trends indicate progressively drier rainfall regimes and temporal variations in rainfall in especially drought-prone zones like the Sahel and Southern and Eastern Africa. The Sahel has experienced a statistically significant decline in rainfall by 30 percent over the last thirty years, and in Southern Africa there have been marked phases of wet and dry years, each of about nine years duration, resulting in a quasi eighteen year cycle. In Equatorial East Africa and southern coastal West Africa, the rainfall has increased by 15 percent and 10 percent respectively (Figure 2.6).

Drought has serious economic, social, and environmental consequences, such as famine and diseases, land degradation, loss of vegetation, and loss of domestic stock and wildlife resources. Drought-affected countries also experience serious reduction in agricultural and animal production. In 1983, twenty-two SSA countries experienced a significant decline in food production because of droughts. In 1986, about 185 million people living in drylands were at risk, with 30 million people immediately threatened. Significant environmental impacts have been experienced over the past half-century; 65 million hectares of productive land have become desert on the southern edge of the Sahara region alone. Estimates of the impacts of the 1973 drought in Africa include 100,000 deaths in Ethiopia, a drop of 2 to 15 meters in ground water table levels, and decreased flow rates in all rivers in the Sahel. The economic impacts of drought are not easy to determine; some examples are given in Box 2.6. The costs of drought-relief programs are also high. For example, the cost of these programs in southern African countries in 1991-92 amounted to more than US$2 billion. With the dominance of rainfed farming in SSA, a major challenge is to develop systems for water management and supplementary irrigation that reduce crop losses from seasonal drought and unreliable rainfall patterns (Keck and Dinar Building Block 1995).

Box 2.6. Drought and Gross Domestic Product

There are significant difficulties in estimating the costs and economic impact of a particular drought on a country or region within a country. However, even rough estimates of these costs can help national governments, local governments, and international donors rationalize preemptive programs to reduce the risks of severe economic impact when drought occurs. Three estimates of drought's economic costs are described here.

- Wisner (1976) applied four different methods to the estimation of production losses in Kenya during the national drought in the early 1970s. Production losses to the economy focus on cattle loss (death or weight) and crop loss. Three of the four methods produce nearly identical estimates that lost agricultural production (market and subsistence) and livestock production were approximately Kenyan Pounds (KL) 25 million as a result of a national-level drought. An alternative estimate of the sum of drought relief, lost grain trade, increased social service, and public and private abatement actions suggests that the direct costs of drought in 1970-71 were KL12.8 million. The combined figure of KL37.8 million represents approximately 7.5 percent of Kenya's GNP of KL500 million in 1971. Wisner's calculations are rough estimates and should be considered in terms of order of magnitude.

- LeNay and Mathis (1989) performed a critical appraisal of four methods of livestock accounting (two methods used by the UN System of National Accounts and methods used by the governments of Mali and Niger). All four approaches were used to assess the impact of the 1984 drought on Niger's GDP. The results show that, depending upon the livestock accounting methodology, Niger's 1984 GDP declined from somewhere between 14.1 percent and 31.1 percent. The authors endorse the SNA production assessment method which shows a 16.6 percent decline in GDP in 1984 and 1.8 percent growth in 1985.

- Benson and Clay (1994) describe a model (based on the Keynsian income-expenditure approach) developed by the Reserve Bank of South Africa to assess the economic impact of the 1992 drought in South Africa. Model simulation results indicate that reduced water availability led to a fall of 1.8 percent in disposable real income (inflation-adjusted income), 0.5 percent in consumption expenditure, 5.0 percent in gross domestic savings, and 0.5 percent in gross domestic investment. The model also shows an expected net negative effect of Krugerrand 1,200 million on the current account of the balance of payments as well as a loss of 49,000 agricultural jobs and 20,000 formal sector jobs.

Source: Keck and Dinar Building Block 1995.

Figure 2.6. Index of rainfall in the Sahel 1941-1990 (departure from standard deviation).

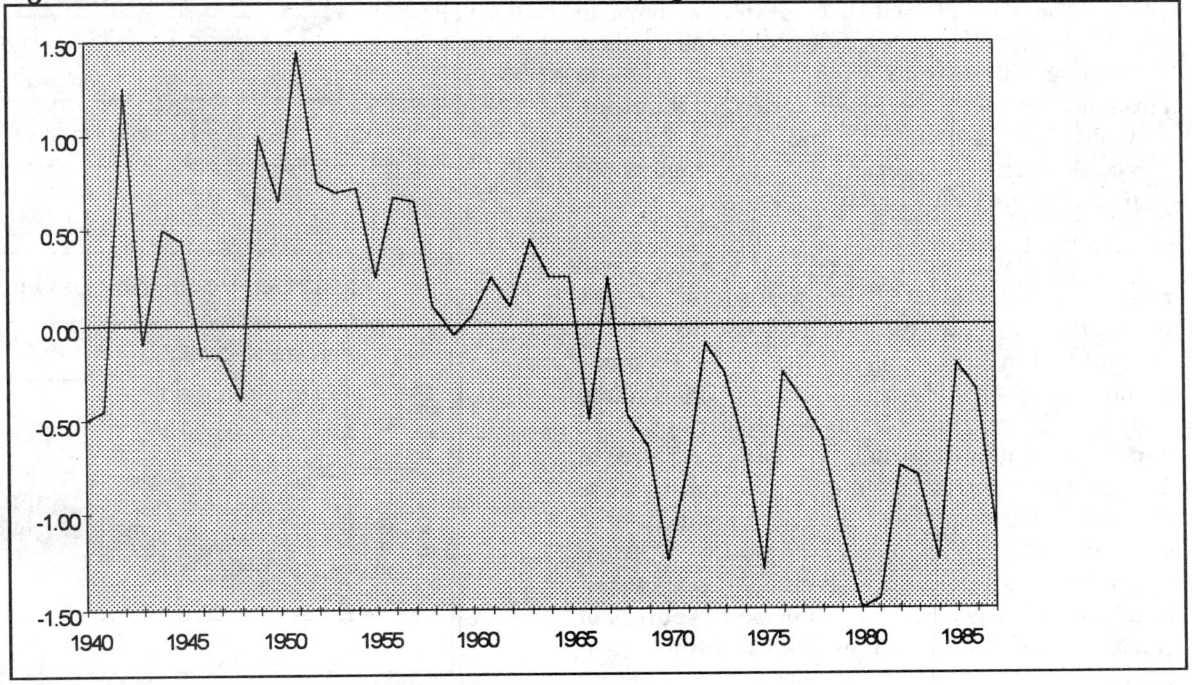

Source: Climate Prediction Center 1991.

Demands for Water

The demand for water throughout SSA is varied, supporting human and animal consumption and key economic sectors, such as agriculture, industry, and energy. Figure 2.7 shows that agriculture accounts for more than 80 percent of water consumption. These trends will continue until 2025, with agriculture accounting for the bulk of water consumption (Figure 2.8).

Population and Urbanization: Impact on Water Use. The two most important factors influencing water demand in SSA are rising population and expanding urbanization. Population growth in the region is 3 percent, the world's highest, and by 2020, the population is expected to more than double from under 500 million to about 1.1 billion people. While urban growth is a phenomenon of all developing countries, Africa, the world's least urbanized region, is now experiencing the world's most rapid rate of urbanization, at 5 percent. From an urban population of 138 million in 1990, over 500 million will live in African cities in 2020, an increase of over 370 percent. Rural populations will grow more slowly, from about 350 million in 1990 to about 560 million in 2020 (an increase of over 150 percent) (Damhaug 1995). These trends will take dramatic shape at the country level. For example, Botswana predicts an increase in overall water demand (due to population growth, increased agricultural output, and industrialization) from the current levels of 156 cubic meters per year to 336 cubic meters per year (Botswana Country Paper 1996).

Figure 2.9 shows predicted urban growth rates and illustrates the proportions of the population in medium cities (100,000 to 500,000 people) and in large ('mega') cities (more than one million people). By 2020, almost 200 million people— 20 percent of the region's population and 40 percent of the urban population will live in 'mega-cities,' in contrast to only 30 million people in 1980. This trend has implications since large cities are major points of demand which can strain water resources even in well-endowed countries. In addition, these cities are major point sources of waste water and solid waste, creating great environmental risks. Both these factors imply rapidly rising marginal costs of supply as more

Figure 2.7

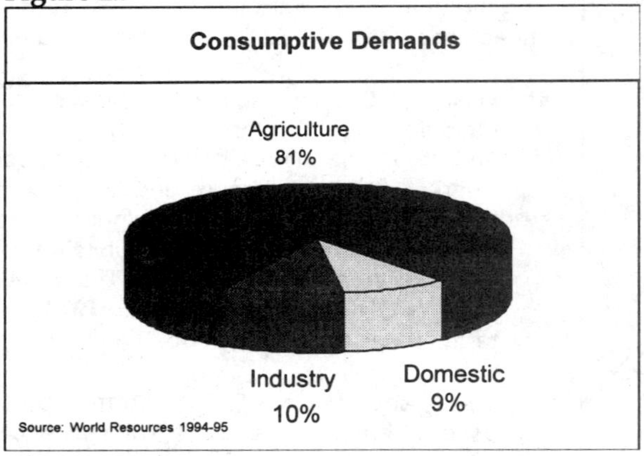

Figure 2.8

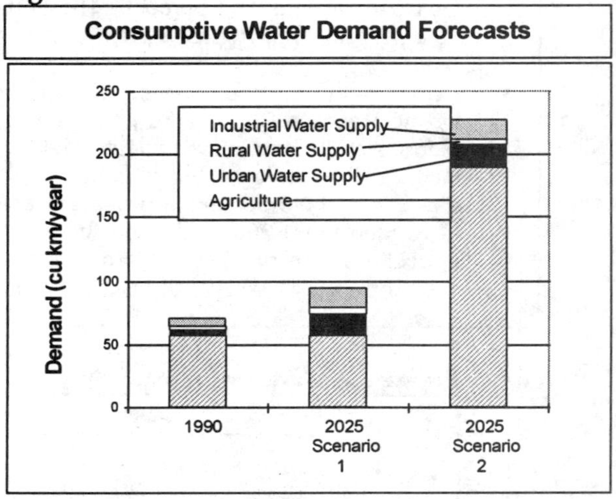

Figure 2.9

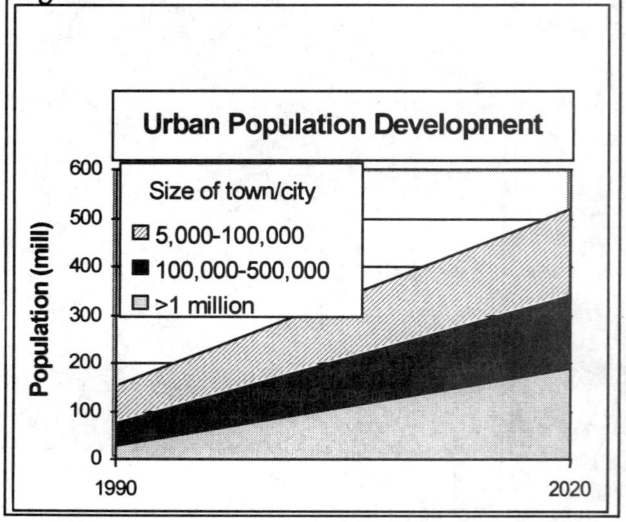

distant water sources are exploited due to the depletion and pollution of nearby sources. Compounding this demand is the likely rapid expansion of industrial demand in large cities as economic growth takes hold and market and investment opportunities grow. Water shortage, caused by scarcity as in Bulawayo, Zimbabwe or by poor reliability as in Lagos, Nigeria, can throttle industrial competitiveness.

Water Supply and Sanitation Services—a Growing Gap. Figures 2.10 and 2.11 show coverage with water supply and sanitation across the region. Coverage figures for 1980 and 1990 are actual ones; figures for later years are predicted on the assumption that rates of service expansion are the same in later decades as they were in the 1980s (the International Drinking Water Supply and Sanitation Decade). This 'business as usual' or past practices shows one very obvious trend—while coverage is expanding relatively rapidly, it is not keeping pace with population growth, and, in this scenario, the numbers of those unserved with either water supply or sanitation can be expected to increase rapidly— to over 200 million people.

Figure 2.10

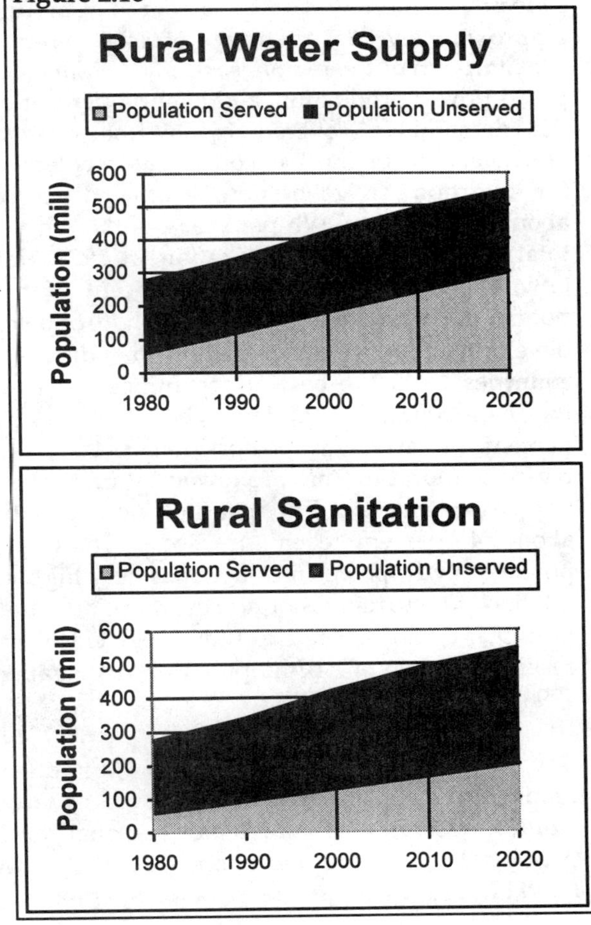

Figure 2.11

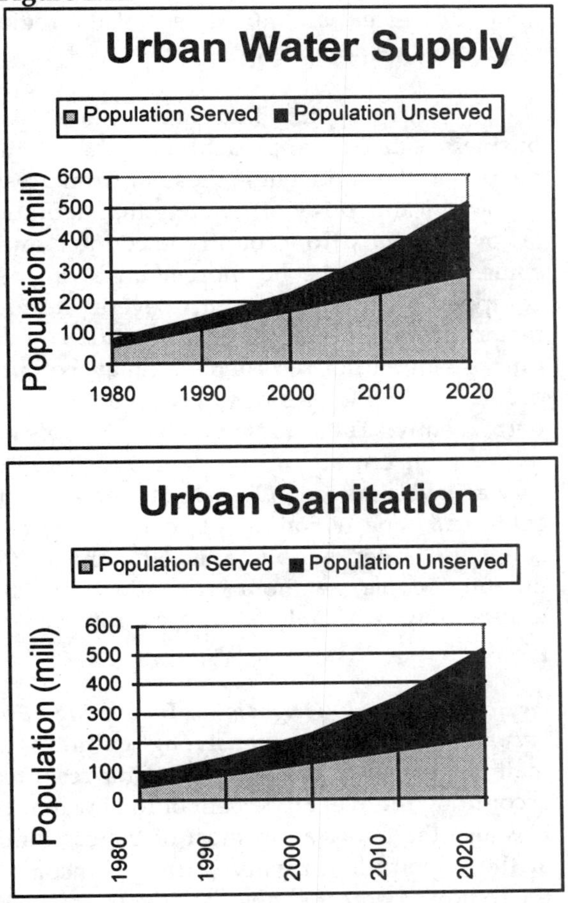

It needs to be emphasized that these gross figures hide regional and national differences and that coverage figures are themselves unreliable. Nevertheless, it is clear that a business-as-usual approach has significant negative consequences for the health and economic development of the region's cities—the engines of its economy. The implications are particularly harsh for the poor, as the unserved will be in the high-density, often informal settlements on the city margins.

The region's population remains predominantly rural, even with current rates of urbanization. Although rural population growth rates can be expected to level off over the next two decades, the rural 'story' is similar to the urban one. The figures show predicted water supply and sanitation coverage, which suggests that with a 'business as usual' approach (as above for urban services), almost 300 million people will be without adequate water supply and 400 million without sanitation in 2020—about 30 percent and 40 percent of the region's population respectively.

Once again, the implications of a business-as-usual approach for the poorest people on the continent— those in rural areas—are significant. It is worth noting that definitions of coverage vary from country to country, and in some cases may be no more than a dug well equipped with a handpump several hundred meters from the home. The condition of this pump is often not recorded— it may be out of order for long periods of time or even permanently. Thus, quoted coverage levels may be very inaccurate or may record very low service levels indeed. Overall, 50 percent of the continent's one billion people could be without adequate water supply and 60 percent (600 million people) without sanitation in 2020, unless new workable strategies replace past practices.

Agriculture and Irrigation: Increasing Food Security. As noted previously, agriculture is the main consumer of the region's water resources, accounting for over 80 percent of total water use. It is also the mainstay of most of the economies of the region, the primary source of income of the region's poorest people, and key to reducing poverty. At the same time, it is a potential threat, with an increasing number of people needing to make an income out of shrinking land and water resources, leading to a downward spiral of increasing poverty and resource degradation. The region is characterized by extensive rainfed agriculture. The estimates are that in 1988/89, about 212 million hectares were under cultivation, of which about 207 million hectares were rainfed and up to about 5.0 million hectares were irrigated. The area of potentially irrigable land in the region has been estimated at 16.5 million hectares (FAO 1986), a relatively low figure in relation to the size of the region and compared to other regions such as Asia and Latin America.

Future water demand for agriculture is in part determined by strategies for food security. Current growth in food production is only half of what is required to balance the population increase. It has been estimated that the growth needed in agricultural output in the region is a 3.3 percent per year increase—or a little more than three times between 1990 and 2025—to achieve food security objectives. If the area under irrigation were to grow by a factor of 3, to over 16 million hectares, this would only represent a 5 percent contribution to the required threefold food production increase needed by 2025. This makes rainfed agriculture important and creates the need for increasing cropping intensities and achieving higher yields using less water. Farmers must adopt production technologies that include soil and water conservation measures and that increases productivity significantly on a large scale to meet the more than tripling of food demand in the region by 2025.

Power: Hydroelectricity and Cooling. Approximately 95 percent of the energy consumption of the region is supplied from coal-based power production, and about 4 percent of the demand is covered by hydroelectricity. However, the region has considerable potential for hydropower generation, estimated to be about 1.4 million GWh per year— although the total hydro-electricity production in 1989 was only 41,000 GWh, less than 3 percent of the potential. Both potential and actual hydropower development varies greatly in different countries, with the best opportunities often on the main courses of the large rivers. About 39 percent of the hydropower potential of the region is found in Zaire, followed by Cameroon with 7 percent, and Ethiopia and Zambia with about 4 percent each. In some countries, potential hydropower production is very high in relation to current energy consumption, and Ethiopia, for instance, uses only 2 percent of its assessed potential (Ethiopia Country Paper 1996).

Considerable variations in flow often require the construction of large dams and storage reservoirs to regulate seasonal and periodical discharge variations. On the one hand, hydropower is less of a competitor for water use than irrigation, domestic, and industrial water abstraction since it consumes less water, although it does move water to lower downstream elevations. On the other hand, hydropower operations require a high degree of regularity and timing of flow control to meet power demand. This flow control does not necessarily match the demand for irrigation or other consumptive uses of water downstream. Hydropower demands become competitive with consumptive water uses, when substantial water volumes are withdrawn upstream of a hydropower plant, as has been the case in Pangani River Basin in Tanzania (Box 2.2).

Concerning water demand for cooling, coal-fired thermal power production is dependent on a highly reliable water supply. South Africa has by far the highest coal-fired power production in the region. The current cooling water consumption is about 1.5 million cubic meters per year - about 3 percent of the water demand in the country. The quantity of water consumed per unit of energy produced is approximately 0.005 m^3 per kWh. Due to increasing water scarcity, and hence water costs, South Africa is exploring opportunities for dry cooling, but these are resulting in somewhat increased coal consumption per produced energy unit. On the other hand, these increased production costs could be offset by lower water supply costs.

Navigation and the Transport Opportunity: Maintaining Waterborne Highways. River and lake transport has long been important in the region and will remain so as economies develop. Demand for water to maintain river flows for navigation therefore remains part of the complex web of demands to be met. In addition, estuary management is important to maintaining many harbors in the region. There are many examples where soil deposition in coastal areas has damaged port and harbor facilities and tourist infrastructure. In Madagascar the deposition of more than 100 million m^3 of sediment over twenty-five years in the port of Mahajanga has rendered the port useless. Mozambique's rivers deposit large volumes of sediments into the Indian Ocean and have formed huge sand banks and extended deltas, which are causing changes in ocean wave hydrodynamics and fluvial deposition. The resources of Niger and its tributaries have been substantially developed, with projects covering the whole range of water related purposes, such as flood control, hydropower generation, irrigation, water supply, and navigation. The lower Niger and the Benue are navigable, although commercial navigation on the Benue is restricted by the very low dry season flows.

Ecology: Water, an Essential Element. Along with water demands for the conventional sectors (e.g., water supply, agriculture, power), the water environment has substantial demands of its own as it is an integral part of the water resources system. The region is endowed with lakes, rivers, wetlands, and ground water resources, all of which have demands in terms of water quantity and quality. These demands are often in conflict with others, and allocating water to environmental needs now and in the future will require making conscious decisions which assess benefits foregone if water resources assets are degraded. Wetlands have always played an important role in the rural economy of the region, with an estimated 200 million hectares in the region. The floodplains of major rivers, the *dambos* (seasonally-inundated headwater swamps) of Southern Africa and the *fadamas* of Nigeria all provide highly productive agricultural land, dry season grazing for migrant herds, fish, fuelwood, timber needs, medicines and other products, in addition to important wildlife habitats and ground water recharge. All these functions bring direct economic and social benefits. Meeting environmental water demands must increasingly be seen more as maintaining the water resources system and less as just another competing demand center, as degradation of the water environment is often inextricably linked to increasing water costs to other sectors of the economy.

The Infrastructure Gap and Rising Costs

In most instances easily accessible surface and ground water resources have already been exploited in SSA. Exploiting water from new sources and transferring of water over vast areas and distances will increase costs significantly.

Rising Costs for Water Supply and Sanitation. The investment needed to ensure full coverage in water and sanitation services, even at a basic level, are enormous since many people do not have access to clean water and sanitation. An analysis of Average Incremental Costs (AIC) based on a sample of previous and new water supply projects financed by the World Bank in the Africa Region indicates that the unit cost of water would almost double and in some cases increase by three times under a new water development project, as shown in Figure 2.12.

Figure 2.12

Examples of Increasing Construction Costs

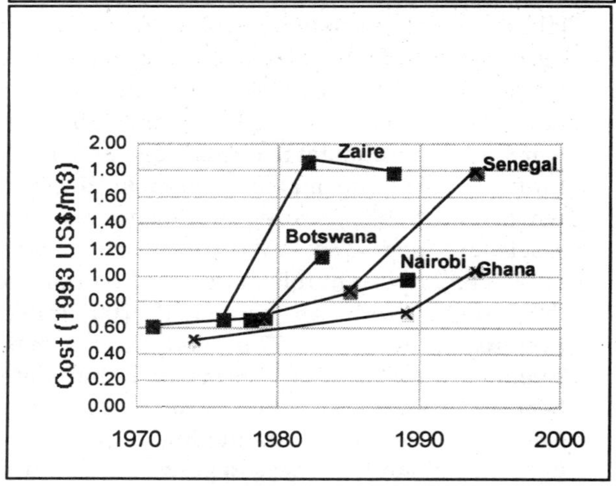

In this sample, the average incremental cost of water sources ranges from about $0.80 to about $1.80 per m^3. Among the most prominent reasons for these cost increases are more distant sources, more complex source works and treatments, and the lack of flexibility in reallocation of lower cost water from other users. Another reason for increased cost of water delivered to users is the absence of incentives for supply organisations to hold down investment costs and the amount of water which is not accounted for in sales. This has led to larger investments in supply capacity than are justified in terms of demand growth at the water prices charged.

Figure 2.13 shows the magnitude of meeting the demand for water and sanitation services during a ten-year period. It is important to note that the average costs used, given in Table 2.2, do not include either essential investments in rehabilitation of many existing schemes or individual connection and in-house plumbing costs, which could double the per capita investment. Scenario I shows the costs of providing 50 percent of the users with high level (water and sewer house-connections) and 50 percent with low level (standpipes or yard hydrants and on-site excreta disposal) services. Scenario II represents the investments needed if the ratio were to be reduced to 40/60 (high/low level). The enormous difference in costs demonstrates the importance of having a range of service levels for water and sanitation services in the urban areas in response to increased urbanization. Based on this calculation, the lower cost Scenario II would require an investment of US$36 billion to serve all people at the end of the year 2000. The higher-cost Scenario I would require some US$47 billion. Using a different method of calculation, the OAU and UNICEF have arrived at a smaller figure of US$47 billion in investment costs to serve all people by the year 2000 (WHO/UNICEF 1993).

Figure 2.13

Effect on Investment Need of Reducing the High Density Service Connections from 50% to 40% over a Decade

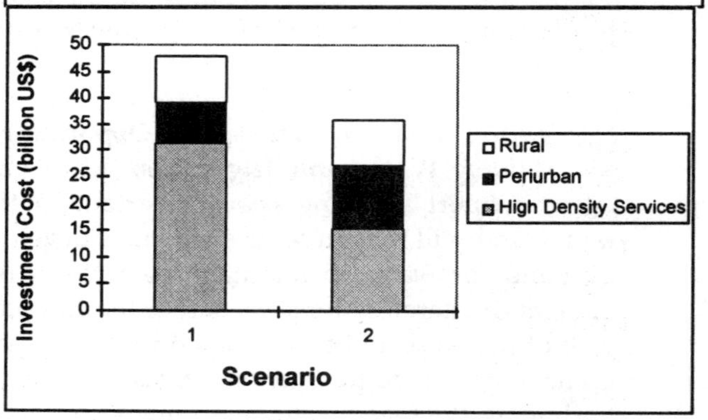

Table 2.2: Definition of Consumer Categories

Consumer Category	Water Service	Sanitation Service
High Income (high service level)	house connection, yard taps	Septic tanks, sewerage
Peri-urban (low service level)	yard taps, public standpipes, handpumps	VIP latrines, vaults, none
Rural	handpump wells, rainwater collection	Latrines

Population in Each Consumer Category:

	Million People			
Consumer Category	Scenario I		Scenario II	
	1990	2000	1990	2000
Income (high level)	69	113	69	90
Peri-urban (low level)	69	113	69	135
Rural	349	422	349	422
Total	487	647	487	647

Unit Investment Costs:

	US$/capita		
Consumer Category	Water Supply	Sanitation Sewerage	Treat-ment
Income (high level)	270	350	100
Peri-urban (low level)	120	50	10
Rural	80	40	0

Sensitivity to Sanitation Costs. The cost difference between the different scenarios reflects the investment needed for sewerage. High service levels not only represent substantially higher water demands, and associated costs, they also require follow-up investments for new sewerage systems and sewage treatment plants. With per capita sewerage investments exceeding those for water, high water supply service levels impose a financial burden on many consumers. The determination of effective demand investigations must therefore be based on the cost of both water supply and sewerage, even if sewerage facilities are temporarily postponed. This underscores the relevance of alternative—on-site or intermediate — sanitation solutions for a large proportion of the urban population. In Senegal, about 76 percent of the urban and peri-urban population is currently served by on-site sanitary solutions, and similar ratios are found in other countries in the region.

Rising Irrigation Costs. Irrigation investment costs have risen steadily over the past decades. Recent comparative studies show that the irrigation developments are generally cheaper in South and East Asia than in other regions of the world. In SSA, on the other hand, large- and medium-scale irrigation development is more expensive than in any other region, amounting to about US$ 8,000 per hectare on the average (1992 normalized prices). The reasons for the high costs are numerous, including the following: (a) schemes often include storage works to regulate river flow; (b) severe climate requiring high irrigation duties and expensive flood protection; (c) schemes in remote locations require high transportation costs and basic infrastructure: (d) insufficient local engineering expertise to design and supervise construction works; (e) infant local construction industry, resulting in the need to hire foreign contractors with high overhead costs; (f) small contracts; (g) lack of local manufacturing and service industries, necessitating import of materials and equipment; and, (h) overvalued exchange rates and poor project management.

However, possibilities exist to bring down irrigation investment costs to a threshold level of about US$ 3,000 per hectare. This begins with the realistic planning of irrigation schemes. Irrigation schemes cannot be designed without extensive geological, hydrological, and topographical data, nor can schemes be designed without simultaneous consideration of resettlement and the needs for infrastructure and social services. Second, designs should be simple. Primary (and perhaps secondary) water supply and drainage infrastructure should be provided, but farmers or farmer groups can use their own resources to construct tertiary distribution systems or to install pumps which lift water to their fields. Third, the management and implementation capacity of local construction companies should be utilized and built up. Companies require an economic environment that allows the purchase of supplies (e.g., through reduced tariffs), and benefit greatly from larger contracts (e.g., to construct a number of small schemes within a district) that guarantee continuous operation and reduce average costs. Finally, irrigation efforts should be encouraged by the private sector, NGOs, communities, or individuals. Ultimately, governments may move away from implementation of irrigation schemes, instead providing expensive infrastructure (e.g., roads, main drains, electricity supply) and an enabling environment of laws and policies that ensure equity and environmental protection.

D. Environmental Issues: Deteriorating Quality and Ecological Risk

Watershed Protection: Soil and Water Conservation

Catchment Protection. Water brings life to soil but can also destroy it. Soil can conserve water but, when mobile, can severely degrade water resources. Catchment management—through soil and water conservation, tree planting, and improved land use practices—is critical everywhere, but nowhere more than in those parts of Africa where soil and water resources are scarce and cannot be wasted. Soil erosion in areas which have lost their vegetation cover due to increased human activities, rapid increase in population, and widespread poverty can contribute to land degradation. It can also result in severe flooding, due to a reduction of the land capacity to absorb water. Ground water recharge is reduced, as is base-flow to streams, resulting in high but short peaks in flow and long periods of low flow. It is estimated that about 320 million hectares of vegetated lands have been degraded over the past several decades in SSA.

In Kenya, increased soil erosion is causing rapid siltation of major reservoirs, such as the Kamburu Dam and the Masinga Dam in the upper sections of the Tana Basin. The Ibohamane and Moulela Reservoirs on the Niger are said to have lost half their storage capacity over the last fifteen years. There is a dual loss which no country can afford—that of the soil, which will not regenerate in the foreseeable future, as well as costly infrastructure, with consequent impacts on downstream water users. It must, of course, be recognized that erosion is also a natural process, which can be attenuated through good land management. The impacts of poor land husbandry are described below and illustrated in Box 2.7.

Box 2.7: Impact of Land Degradation in Malawi

Soil erosion due to deforestation from tree felling for woodfuel and cultivation of maize, often on steep slopes, has increased substantially in most catchments in Malawi and is seriously affecting the water resources infrastructure. Degradation in the catchment of the upper Mulunguzi River on the Zomba Plateau would potentially affect the water supply for the city of Zomba. The poundage at Nkula on the Shire River supplies both the largest power plant in Malawi and the pumping station providing the entire water supply for Blantyre. Sediment accumulations in the Nkula poundage, including around the pumping station, are extensive. The sediment content of the water is very high. The likely source of the high turbidities in the river is sediment bedload from the Shire River transported during the wet season by its tributaries between Liwonde and Nkula poundage. Silting of the Nkula poundage, which has a live storage of 1,500,000 cubic meters, is affecting power output, and occasionally Blantyre's water supply, especially during periods of drought. As a short term measure, the power utility plans to dredge about 500,000 cubic meters at a cost ranging between US$1.5 and US$3 million.

Source: Busia 1995.

- ***Impacts of poor cultivation.*** In much of the region productive arable land is a scarce resource. Population pressures and agriculture policies have often resulted in small farmers abandoning their traditional patterns of cultivation and adopting unsustainable practices, such as using shorter fallow periods in areas where shifting cultivation and slash-and-burn are practiced. This does not allow regeneration of the necessary nutrients, thereby diminishing the productivity of the soil. Areas with steep slopes (greater than 15 degrees) or marginal areas receiving little rain or which were previously used for dry season grazing are now being cultivated. Such shifts in land use have caused serious land degradation in highlands and dryland areas and made soil erosion a major problem. In fact, in Ethiopia, based on projections of population growth and soil loss through the year 2010, it is possible that 75 percent of the country's highland region will be unsuitable for agricultural production (Ethiopia Country Paper 1996). Lesotho, meanwhile, loses 1320 tons of soil per square kilometer each year, for a total of 40 million tons per year (Lesotho Country Paper 1996).

- *Impacts of deforestation.* Deforestation for cultivation, construction timber, and woodfuel can also accelerate soil erosion. When cutting rates exceed replanting rates, soils in cleared areas become unstable and susceptible to erosion, particularly so in vulnerable areas, such as on steep slope or in arid or semi-arid regions. Madagascar, for example, is very vulnerable to soil erosion because about two-thirds of the country has steep slopes, much of which is very fragile and erosive soil. Deforestation, through the annual conversion of more than 100,000 hectares of forested areas of the eastern highlands for agricultural use, has significantly reduced the vegetative cover and increased the potential for soil degradation. In many watersheds, soil erosion rates of around 25-40 t/ha/yr. are typical, with highland areas having rates as high as 300 t/ha/yr. (UNEP 1992). An example of international problems caused by poor management practice is the increasing sediment loads caused by deforestation in Malawi, Tanzania, and Mozambique which are inhibiting fish reproduction in Lake Malawi.
- *Impacts of overgrazing.* Livestock rearing can also contribute to soil erosion. Cattle, sheep, goats, and pigs supply nutritional needs, generate foreign exchange, and in some societies, have important cultural significance as units of exchange. High livestock densities (exceeding the land's carrying capacity) can cause losses in top soil and vegetative cover. Overgrazing and repeated trampling by animals destabilize the soil structure. In arid or semi-arid areas, such consequences are magnified because the soil structures are weaker and more vulnerable to damage from the outset. Prior to the current unrest, Somalia used to derive almost 80 percent of its export earning from livestock products. The pastoralist practice of bringing animals down to the coastal areas from upland areas during the rainy season, in order to escape tsetse flies, has destabilized coastal sand dunes, enhancing the process of desertification and affecting more than 500,000 hectares of land subject to active dune movement. Overgrazing in the middle and lower sections of the Tana Basin in Kenya is also contributing to enormous top soil losses, increasing sediment loads carried into the ocean.
- ***Avoiding degradation of irrigated land.*** All irrigation carries the risk of soil degradation, with the degree of risk depending on soil composition, quality of irrigation water, water management, and natural drainage. Poor irrigation practices cause the water table to rise, leading to secondary salinization through capillary rise and evaporation of the ground water. This risk of salinization and sodication can be reduced through improving irrigation practices, construction of field drainage, and leaching of excess salts. Measures then must be taken for proper disposal of drainage water. With the concentration of salt often increasing downstream in rivers due to drainage inflows, special outfalls to the sea or evaporation ponds are needed.

Protecting Aquatic Systems

As noted earlier, SSA has many aquatic ecosystems that provide valuable ecological services for maintaining natural systems. Sociopolitical and economic factors have contributed to the degradation of some of these ecosystems. The scale and intensity of degradation is likely to increase with expanded economic activities and urbanization. Without measures to address the problems now, high concentrations of population and increasing poverty will exacerbate these problems as demonstrated in the cases of Lake Victoria and Lake Chad.

Lake Victoria is Africa's largest freshwater body extending into Rwanda, Kenya, Tanzania, and Uganda. The lake provides benefits to more than ten million people inhabiting its basin. In addition, urban centers around the lake and thousands of rural people draw water supplies from the lake. It also provides water for industrial and agricultural purposes and is an important source of food protein for the local people. Lake fisheries are vital to the regional economy. However, the lake is also used as a receptor for human, industrial, and agricultural waste for a population growing at the highest rate in the world. These multiple uses are endangering the integrity of the lake. Overfishing, industrial pollution, and untreated sewage are threatening the lake's resources and biodiversity. The situation of Lake Chad is described in Box 2.8.

Box 2.8: Lake Chad: An Ecosystem at Risk

Lake Chad is a very shallow lake shared by Chad, Niger, Nigeria, and Cameroon with a drainage area of 1.9 million square kilometers. The lake area has been fluctuating between 10,000 and 25,000 square kilometers due to unstable hydrological conditions, extended drought, and increased anthropogenic activities. In 1973, the lake level was reduced dramatically, and the lake system was split into three separate water bodies referred to as 'Lesser Chad.' Lake Chad and its perennial tributaries (including the Logone River and Chari River) are rich in fish with 1,305 species of fish. The pre-1973 'Normal Chad' was a tropical lake rich in phytoplankton.

The Yaeres floodplains of the Logone River support flood recession agriculture, pasture, fisheries, Waza National Park, and drought security. Irrigation development in the Lake Chad Basin has been carried out by and in all four riparian nations, much of which is uncoordinated and thus affecting flows into Lake Chad. The Maga Dam in Cameroon, has reduced the flow of the Logone River and the seasonal inundation of floodplains in the Waza National Park. As a consequence, the wetland functions have been diminished. Fisheries and livestock pasture have been seriously affected, and wildlife is infringing on cultivated land for forage and causing considerable damage to the agricultural fields. Unregulated migration and the resulting activities—such as over-cutting of trees for fuelwood or construction purposes, overgrazing and trampling by livestock, land clearing for agriculture, waterworks, or human settlements—have intensified soil degradation and put significant pressure on the basin resources. Lake water levels have declined below the threshold of reversible equilibrium. Reduced surface supplies have resulted in intensified ground water pumping for municipal and industrial water supply.

Source: SSA Hydrological Assessment 1992.

Potential Effects of Climate Change

Climate Change Impacts. Increasing concentrations of greenhouse gases in the atmosphere will lead to a steady increase in the global mean temperature over the next century. Such an increase will, in turn, have a profound effect on the local and regional climate regimes and hence on hydrological and water resources systems (Box 2.9). There is a great deal of uncertainty about the impacts that climate change will have locally on spatial and temporal changes to precipitation and evapotranspiration. While the scenarios for future climate change in the next century are uncertain, there are two practical reasons for studying their potential impacts. The first is to provide scientific information to policy-makers and managers responsible for managing water resource systems exposed to climatic variability over the next few decades. The second is to provide information for public debate and hence a basis for political decisions on the mitigation of global warming and its impacts. The region needs to build the capacity to manage the response to climate variability and drought. There is also a need for international review and collaboration between research institutes and monitoring programs.

Box 2.9: The Impact of Climate Change on Water Resources in East Africa.

An assessment of the impact of climate change on water resources in East Africa has been undertaken following a defined methodology for impact analyses (Carter and others 1992). The hydrological model was developed on a regular network of 0.5° x 0.5° cells (about 3000 km^2) over Eastern Africa, covering Somalia, Uganda, Kenya, Tanzania, Mozambique, and Madagascar, with each grid cell being treated as a 'catchment.' The water balance model used consists of a number of stores with parameters controlling the store size and the rate of removal of water from the stores. Inputs are daily rainfall and potential evaporation. The model was calibrated and validated using runoff data from 101 flow gauging stations across the region. The baseline period was selected as the period 1951-1980. Climate change scenarios were developed for the year 2050 for rainfall and potential evaporation from the output of several General Circulation Models (GCMs). Large areas of the region show an increase of up to 25 percent in the annual rainfall totals, with some decreases in southern Somalia, western Tanzania, and southern Mozambique and Madagascar. Potential evaporation increases throughout the region, particularly in western Tanzania and southern Madagascar. These climate changes translate into changes in annual runoff with very different potential impacts across the region. Much of Kenya and the coastal fringes have increased runoff in 2050 by up to 50 percent of the baseline annual total. In contrast, northern Somalia and southern Madagascar show decreases in the annual totals of up to 60 percent (although in some regions these are changes from low annual totals).

The impact of changes in runoff and the availability of water resources has been extended to the potential economic implications. This methodological approach attempts to assess the main economic impacts of climate change for market and non-market goods and services in the region. The analysis also takes account of the impact on the socially vulnerable and food scarce rural populations, where changes cannot be measured in monetary terms.

Source: Carter, et. al. 1992.

E. Capacity Issues: Awareness, Human Resources, and Institutions

Lack of Awareness. One factor impeding sustainable water resources management and stakeholder participation in SSA is the lack of awareness of the state of water resources in terms of availability and demand, as well as the economic, social, environmental, and management aspects relating to water use. People need to be aware that water is no longer a free good. It is a finite resource with supply constraints; it has a scarcity value, and there is a cost to using it . Similarly, people must be made aware that water quality cannot be degraded; water contamination leads to water-borne diseases, impacting human health and productivity. People also need to understand the consequences of deforestation and land degradation on the quantity and quality of water resources.

Thus, the challenge is to build awareness at the individual and national level, among all stakeholders. National policies need to focus on an integrated approach to water management, and a 'water culture' needs to be promoted that emphasizes conservation practices and better stewardship of this scarce resource.

Centralized Management and Low Capacity. The public sector plays a dominant role in the management of water resources. However, management is fragmented and involves multiple agencies. These agencies are involved in allocating water resources for different uses, investing in infrastructure, and providing services to the people. Generally, institutional and implementation capacities are weak, and the level of stakeholder (private sector, local communities, NGOs) participation in water management still remains limited.

Despite past efforts in SSA, the institutional capacity necessary for comprehensive and sustainable water resources management is still lacking. This holds for the public and private sector and within both formal and informal institutions. Capacity-related problems manifest themselves through poor sector performance: the lack of access by much of the urban and rural populations to water supply and sanitation services, poor service delivery, deteriorating water quality, and increasing conflicts for scarce resources. Such problems are caused by many factors, for example, poorly-designed policies and regulations, wasteful and inefficient practices, inadequate operation and maintenance, poor financial management, government actions that distort markets and undermine performance, and the insufficient number of skilled staff. An example from Zambia illustrates this last factor, where the Department of Water Affairs lists 1,800 personnel, of whom only 13 percent are permanent staff and 60 percent are temporary 'daily' employees (Zambia Country Paper, 1996).

African countries have continued to rely on technical assistance without adequately transferring know-how to local stakeholders, using indigenous knowledge and institutions, or creating a sense of ownership among the intended beneficiaries. This undermines project sustainability. Insufficient consideration to providing consumers with the services they demand and are willing to pay for, together with the failure to treat water as a scarce resource and economic good, has led to a vicious spiral of deteriorating service provision and infrastructure. Incentives based on political loyalties, which neither reward nor hold parties accountable for performance, have contributed to the erosion of the civil service, an undermining of professionalism, and the departure of qualified people to opportunities overseas. Policy frameworks too have been weak: budgetary and funding decisions have not been routinely linked to policies; policy objectives have not been well-articulated, and policies and plans have been overly ambitious, setting unattainable goals and inflexible service standards with 'blueprint' master planning (Box 2.10).

Box 2.10: Priority Functions Determine the Institutional Structure in Tanzania and Uganda

Historically, the *development of water resources* has been the focus of water management activities in Tanzania and Uganda. These activities, in turn, gave rise to specialized sub-sectoral development institutions for water supply, irrigation, and hydropower. These institutions, however, have lacked the capacity to address emerging issues, which require an intersectoral, comprehensive resource perspective.

In Tanzania, a recent Rapid Water Resources Assessment (1994) identified priority water resources issues in four of the country's nine major basins: conflicts between downstream hydro-power production and upstream uses in Pangani and Rufiji River Basins; pollution of Lake Victoria, which threatens the internationally-shared Lake Victoria Basin; and Dar es Salaam's inadequate water supply and sewerage, affecting the Coast and Ruvu River Basins. Depending on the functions to be performed, the Ministry of Water, Energy and Minerals is responding with different institutional changes. For example, Basin Water Offices and Boards have been established in the Pangani and Rufiji Basins, with cross-sectoral representation, with responsibility for *basin-wide allocation of water resources*. Similarly, detailed studies are underway on allocation and development of water from Ruvu and other smaller coastal basins to satisfy Dar es Salaam's requirements on a sustainable basis. Following these studies, the institutional structure will be determined.

According to the Uganda Water Action Plan (1994), the priority management issues requiring new institutional capacities are industrial point pollution, mainly of Lake Victoria coastal waters near Kampala and Jinja towns, and localized conflicts over allocation of the most accessible and thus cheaper water resources. Developing drinking water supplies and supplies for minor productive uses continue to be priorities. Consequently, the Water Action Plan emphasizes *water quality control* through the strengthening of the central water laboratory and the introduction of mixed regulatory and economic mechanisms to control industrial pollution. It also calls for the decentralization of water allocation permits and the deregulation of minor water uses, with formal recognition of the mitigating role of local informal institutions.

Source: Stone, Boesen, and Fye 1995.

Factors which have undermined capacity-building efforts also originate from the donor side, including a host of uncoordinated donor programs which lack coherency, consistency, and a results-orientation as well as projects and programs more in tune with donor objectives than with country needs, priorities, and capacities. There has also been little focus on creating sustainable, self-reliant national institutions.

The capacity-building implications of the new consensus for most SSA countries will be considerable. The content, process, and sustainability of capacity-building efforts will need to be addressed. This implies going beyond a project-by-project approach centered on training in order to address broader issues related to: (a) the management organization, including how organizations are structured, allocated responsibilities, and linked in order to carry out water management tasks; (b) information management and sharing, including both the incorporation of indigenous knowledge and the availability of the requisite hardware and software for carrying out tasks, (c) people, including how to educate, attract, retain, motivate, and train them, and (d) the institutional setting, including the policy and regulatory frameworks which establish the rules and incentives that govern (e.g., sanction and reward) behavior.

Creating an enabling environment for strengthening, selectively, centrally-held functions and moving towards decentralized management to the lowest appropriate levels and private sector participation will involve: (a) addressing the incentives underlying current policies and institutional arrangements; (b) improving governance so that decision-makers act openly and responsibly; (c) empowering the stakeholders closest to the source of problems to make decisions and assume responsibility; and (d) allowing demand to drive service provision. Capacity building is also required for regulation, drafting and enforcing contracts, and providing information on water availability, demands, and willingness to pay (Box 2.11).

Box 2.11: The Results of Insufficient Capacity

Since capacity for managing water resources comprises numerous components, it is often an oversimplification to say that a single component — human, financial, technical, organizational, institutional — is to blame for an apparent problem. Thus, each example below represents one, but not all, of the ways in which deficient capacity prevents sustainable water resources management.

- ***Human Capacity:*** In Botswana, individual pastoralists lack the education to understand the reasons behind government exhortations to raise fewer animals and draw less water from boreholes. The pastoralists ignore government limits because they are unaware of how their combined actions have disastrous consequences for the country.

- ***Technical Capacity:*** In Ethiopia, the government lacks the technical ability to measure and predict current and future withdrawals from tributaries in the upper Blue Nile. Without this capacity, the government refuses to enter agreements with other Nile riparians, particularly Sudan and Egypt.

- ***Financial Capacity:*** When cost-effective and appropriate technologies are available, local governments, water user groups, and individuals may only require short-term credit to implement rural water supply and sanitation projects themselves, but this financing is often unavailable.

- ***Organizational Capacity:*** In the Central African Republic, the state forestry agency (MEFCPT) was ill-equipped to manage the country's vast forest reserves, with serious effects on the upper watersheds of the Lake Chad and Congo River Basins. The World Bank is now supporting efforts to restructure MEFCPT and provide it with equipment, facilities, and training.

- ***Institutional Capacity:*** Urban water supply and sewerage in Uganda have been hampered by an inappropriate legal and regulatory framework. Underpricing and lack of monitoring and enforcement have created serious urban and downstream health risks. Since 1990, the World Bank has supported efforts to revise the institutional framework.

Source: World Bank 1990a and World Bank 1990c.

The challenge facing African countries is to move toward an integrated, multisectoral approach to water management. This will require African countries to utilize existing capacity effectively, build capacity in priority areas of institutional building and manpower development, and sustain improved capacity over time.

F. Policies and Regulation Issues: A Weak Enabling Environment

Few countries have adequate national water policy statements, national water plans, legislative and regulatory frameworks, or mechanisms for intersectoral coordination. Even if countries have been involved in the process of water policy reform, the implementation and long-term viability of these reforms have often been undermined by financial constraints and political instabilities.

Policy Failures. African countries have made some progress in formulating and implementing water policy and water laws, as shown in Table 5.1. The National Environmental Action Plan (NEAP) process has been important in promoting new water policy, laws and regulations or refining existing ones. However, there are a number of countries throughout the region that need to adopt a comprehensive water policy based on sound water assessments, establish an effective regulatory framework, and develop capacity for enforcement of approved laws, and legislation. Countries like Madagascar have laws still based on the French colonial system (Madagascar Country Paper 1996), while countries which have undergone rapid political change, such as Eritrea, have yet to put new laws in place (Eritrea Country Paper 1996).

It is important for African countries to link policies to people. Policy formulation and the setting of national priorities should occur with the involvement of all major water stakeholders (both users and managers). Stakeholders can be linked to policymakers through existing organizations and forums (e.g., community-based organizations in rural areas, neighborhood groups in urban areas, village councils, district governments, and elected officials in local, district, and national offices.) As popular participation increases with an effective, two-way flow of information, existing policies may need to be revisited.

Perverse Pricing Policy. As a consequence of excessive central government control, current water prices are too low, not reflecting true scarcity value. Throughout SSA, water use is highly subsidized as water tariffs are set below the supply costs and often below the operation and maintenance costs. This is particularly true for irrigation water and domestic uses, in both rural and urban areas. A study of water supply and sanitation projects in the later 1980s shows that average incremental costs (the appropriate basis for efficiency prices) and actual average prices in SSA countries were US$0.65 and US$0.29 (1988 prices), respectively. This implies even high levels of subsidies through the structure of prices for different user groups. The level of subsidy would be higher if the marginal production costs included environmental costs or opportunity cost of access to water resources, reflecting the full economic costs.

Pricing decisions are generally influenced by political considerations, preferred priority users, and equity reasons. However, the benefits (or subsidies) do not necessarily, or usually, go to the low-income groups. Commercial farmers engaged in irrigated agriculture and well-to-do domestic consumers capture a high proportion of those subsidies. Further, the absence of revenues undermines investments for expansion of services to those who need it most. Even with sound national pricing policies, it should be realized that objectives vary and require local approaches. Therefore, individual irrigation projects need to be managed differently, with decentralized control and efficient management at the project level.

Such a situation also leads to increased dependency of African countries on external financing. A recent study of Bank-supported water supply and sanitation projects for the period of FY87-90 shows that a much higher proportion of financing came from external sources in SSA than any other regions. In SSA, external financing amounted to 81 percent, compared to 65 percent in Asia, 58 percent in Latin America, and 54 percent in the Middle East and North Africa. In the case of SSA, less than 20 percent of financing is supported by local government and revenues of supply agencies. This pattern of dependency and financing is also prevalent in the irrigation sub-sector.

African countries need to increase cost recovery from various user groups through appropriate pricing of water supply for various uses. From optimum resource allocation considerations, efficiency pricing would be a desirable way to go, but since prices are so far below this level, a transition toward full cost recovery through changing average cost prices would be a move in the right direction.

Special attention needs to be given to poverty. To cater to the needs of the poor and marginal areas (e.g., peri-urban areas), the governments need to provide adequate supplies to the poor. Subsidies, as necessary and required, should be targeted to the poor or marginal areas. Tariffs on water to this group should be sensibly priced (for instance, governments could subsidize connection fees for the poor and appropriately price all other water costs). The subsidy to the poor could be cross-subsidized by other user groups or, preferably, financed from general revenues.

The Regulation Gap. The regulatory framework in many of the region's countries is inadequate and often weakly enforced due to overlapping institutional responsibilities and governance problems (as is true in some industrial countries). In most African countries, written water law is based on the water laws of colonizing/administering European powers. Responsibilities of key agencies are not clearly defined.

Most regulatory and enforcement agencies do not have the adequate technical and financial capacity to develop a system of monitoring the quantity and quality of sewage effluents discharged into waterways by treatment facilities. Without the implementation of such a system, such agencies cannot determine whether or not the treatment plants are in compliance with water pollution effluent standards.

Besides, political, technical, financial, and managerial problems have thwarted the regulatory and enforcement process. In particular, such problems have militated against the formulation and rigorous enforcement of standards (safe drinking water and clean water) and quality control requirements (e.g., The Gambia reports that its 1979 Water Act is largely unenforced). Handicapped by the lack of technological and scientific data, most regulatory agencies have failed to develop water quality standards for waterways or to formulate implementation plan for controlling water pollution. With the absence of subsidiary legislative standards, the responsible regulatory agency is unable to determine and identify the quantity and quality of compliance. The situation presents a major hindrance to enforcing regulatory measures since no specific standard may be shown to have been violated. A regulatory or enforcement agency is limited to making only vague claims against an alleged violator.

Even if relevant agencies acquire the required technical and managerial skills, there is still the danger that political considerations would continue to militate against rigorous enforcement and regulatory measures, particularly those against government violators. Like public regulatory and enforcement agencies, state institutions that provide sewage treatment services are an integral part of the government. By suing state institutions for not complying with environmental regulations, public enforcement and regulatory agencies are indirectly suing the government and themselves. Any penalties imposed on these institutions would pose some financial hardship to the government and its agencies, especially since the government is expected to provide funds to all its agencies involved in the provision of water and wastewater services.

Therefore, citizen suits and participation as a supplement to the role of public enforcement and regulatory agencies are crucial. Such participation would induce the government agencies to perform their respective functions effectively. However, in most countries, active citizen involvement cannot be achieved without increased environmental awareness and education.

It must first be emphasized that there is no 'correct' solution for creating an effective institutional framework for water resources management. Solutions evolve in an adaptive way in response to constitutional and cultural settings and to clear policy objectives and political commitment to policy enforcement. It must also be stressed that most industrial nations continue to have many tensions within their water resources management institutional framework, and many are in a dynamic process of radical change. Institutional development and reform are a long 'journey' which is embarked upon without clear knowledge of the eventual destination—which is as it should be. There is a wide range of regulatory agencies, including line ministries, autonomous bodies, and statutory councils. However, the determination of an appropriate form of regulatory and institutional framework would depend primarily on the prevailing socioeconomic, political, and local conditions.

The Water and Wastewater Utility Issue. Most countries in the region have local or national government-run or semi-autonomous public sector utilities. In many cases, such utilities are heavily under-investing and are saddled with many of the inefficiencies of the public sector—overstaffed and underpaid, central treasury control, and political interference. Full private ownership has been attempted in very few countries in the world.

Privatization across Africa requires a sophisticated legal framework and a role for government in regulation and the monitoring of compliance, requiring experienced and accountable public sector staff. Levels of governance needed for effective privatization are high. In addition, the political problems associated with privatization of public services can be severe, particularly where there is an informed public. Many industrial countries are only beginning to move in this direction. In the US, for example, there is resistance by labor unions and financial institutions (which raise municipal bond market funding) against privatizing the large number of municipal sewage treatment works.

Technical Assistance Trauma. More than any other developing region of the world, Africa has had a history of external intervention, initially by colonizing powers and more recently by donors, resident expatriate advisers, and international consultants. Within the region, there is only recent and still limited 'ownership' by many governments and their professional staff, as well as some of the public, of water resources concepts, policies, strategies, plans, standards, physical investments, and institutions. In the post-independence period, many countries set ambitious development targets in collaboration with external donors who pledged substantial external resources.

A good example is the 1967 Arusha Declaration in Tanzania which led to pledges for national coverage with water supply. Within a few years regional water master plans and water supply programs were under way across the country supported by the donor community. Consultant teams—often large—from Germany were in Tanga, from Finland in Mtwara and Lindi, from Denmark in Iringa and Mbeya, from Norway in Rukwa and Kigoma, from the Netherlands in Shinyaga and Morogoro, from Sweden in Mara, Mwanza, and Kagera. Too often, project camps became surrogates for government offices and project staff surrogates for local officials, thereby undermining the incipient institutions. Similar situations can be described from Kenya, Burkina Faso, Togo, and other countries. The long-term results of much of this investment include failed schemes, frustration, and dependency. In contrast, countries that did not see such aid largesse saw the gradual evolution of relatively strong water programs, such as the Malawi gravity-fed piped water program.

Building and Broadening the Skills Base. Effective water resources management requires many skills, a network of capable institutions and significant analytical capacity. Cross-sectoral management introduces new complexities, as does the interdisciplinary analysis needed. Developing, maintaining, and retaining these skills are costly and pose a problem in the region, as in many parts of the world. Much of the region's water resources management is being undertaken by the hydrologists, hydrogeologists, and engineers of public sector water institutions, who are monitoring, archiving, assessing, planning, regulating, and developing water resources for the many uses for which they are needed. Similarly, much of the water development is in the hands of the engineers of water utilities and irrigation agencies. Frequently well-trained, these professionals are often over-burdened, under-resourced, and poorly paid. They often have limited access to professional associations and peer review, mid-career training, books and journals, and other professional incentives. Limited capacity in the private consulting industry leads to the extensive use of international consultants and advisers, who rarely face these constraints. This may yield short-term solutions, but it also leads to long-term problems, through dependency and frustration. The problem is a serious one, widely recognized in other sectors and addressed, in part, in the African Capacity Building Initiative. In the case of water resources management, an added complexity is the need to go beyond hydrologists and engineers to incorporate social and economic skills.

G. Data and Information Gap: The Need for Knowledge and Knowledge Transfer

Data and information systems (physical, technical, socioeconomic, etc.) relating to water resources in terms of quantity, quality, accessibility, and use are generally inadequate throughout the region. Some South and West African countries have, to some extent, established data and information systems relating to climate, rainfall, hydrology, and soil. However, in most cases these systems need further improvements through better technology, trained human resources, strengthened capacity, and capital. Through the SSA Hydrological Assessment (SSAHA) Program, more than forty countries have completed hydrological assessments. This assessment shows that hydrological services are weak in the region, as shown in Box 2.12. Regional and local capacities need to be developed for the continuous updating of pertinent data for planning and monitoring.

Surface and ground water quality networks are not well-developed in SSA due to budgetary constraints, lack of analytical equipment, logistical limitations, as well a lack of appreciation of the importance of water monitoring. In some cases, such as Eritrea, historical data is completely lacking, while in countries like Mozambique, security of data collection stations is an issue. (Mozambique reports in its Country Paper that prior to 1975 there were 260 flow stations and 340 rainfall stations; today, there are only 60 flow stations and 75 rainfall stations.) Some ad hoc investigations of raw water quality are being carried out in connection with planning new water supply and irrigation projects, and some monitoring of treated water is undertaken by water utilities.

Lack of data has international implications as well, as discussed in the following section. For example, Lesotho reports that it believes that the Senque (Orange) River has a flow of approximately 115 cubic meters per year when flowing over the border into South Africa. However, without hard information, Lesotho is unwilling to make a firm international agreement guaranteeing a certain quantity of flow into South Africa (Lesotho Country Paper, 1996).

Box 2.12: Sub-Saharan Africa Hydrological Assessment

The Sub-Saharan Africa Hydrological Assessment (SSAHA), supported by the World Bank, UNDP, AfDB, EU and France (1988-1996), was developed to examine hydrological services in SSA, covering more than forty countries in SSA.

Findings: The deterioration of hydrological services in SSA is attributable to three major causes:

- Reduction of budgetary support to implementing agencies.
- Lack of awareness of the economic importance of hydrological information by policy and decision-makers.
- Numerous technical assistance projects have contributed to hydrological activities in SSA, with direct funding, expert assistance, and training of local staff. While many are quite successful, many encountered problems of sustainability. One problem associated with hydrological data collection programs is the data's lack of use for decision-makers, which in turn causes hydrological services to be seen as lower priority, thus exacerbating under-funding.

Operational and Manpower Problems: Operational hydrometric networks have generally declined in extent and quality over the last decade in almost all of SSA. The decline has been reflected in many aspects: abandonment of numerous hydrometric stations, reduction of maintenance and reading frequency due to acute problems of transport and difficulties in retaining qualified staff in the service. Working environments in most hydrological agencies are usually poor in terms of salary, job satisfaction and opportunities for advancement. Loss of staff, who have received special training in readily marketable areas, such as computer and instrument skills, is a common problem in many countries.

Security problems: Political instability and civil war in some countries of the region, intensified by deteriorating socioeconomic conditions, have contributed to the deterioration of hydrometric networks. This aggravation is normally due to damaged gauging facilities, lack of security personnel, or the destruction of offices, equipment, historical records and hydrological maps. Political instability has not only severely curtailed hydrological network directly, in some countries, but has also adversely influenced field activities in neighboring countries, causing significant loss of valuable data in border regions.

Source: Damhaug and Matthews 1995

Monitoring of water quality for inland water resources should be closely linked to hydrological services and recorded with reference to a river flow or water level in an aquifer. Furthermore, there is a need to monitor water quality and quantity at the pollution sources from major polluters— not only the piped discharges, but also from the diffuse sources, such as agriculture and forestry. The challenge for the future is to reconsider how water quality data are to be collected and used, and to take advantage of new developments within monitoring and information technology. There needs to be a strong link between the information base and the decision-making process.

African countries will need to improve their knowledge and data about management of water resources including protection of water ecosystems, the interaction of humans with water systems, the inter-relationships between water, land, and forest variables in a natural resource management framework, multisectoral considerations in water use, and the international characteristics of river basins and consequent implications for management. Without this base, water resources cannot be sustainably developed and managed. The generation of data should be demand-driven, reflecting the needs of the various stakeholders. Similarly, the agencies or firms that produce hydrological data should have the financial autonomy to market the information as a product. While data and knowledge have public good characteristics, some stakeholders (utilities, industries, commercial entrepreneurs) should contribute to costs of generating, processing, and disseminating data.

H. International Water Resource Issues: Recognizing Responsibility

The International Dimension. All of the countries in continental Sub-Saharan Africa share one or more international river basins. A river basin is the geographical unit determined by the watershed limits of a water system, including surface and underground water, flowing into a common terminus. There are at least fifty-four rivers or water bodies that cross or form international boundaries in the region, a greater number than in any other continent of the world. Ten river basins have drainage areas greater than 350,000 km^2, and these combine to affect thirty-three SSA countries and Egypt (Table 2.3).

Table 2.3: The Ten Largest Surface Water Bodies in Sub-Saharan Africa (Rangeley and others 1994)

Basin	№ of Countries	Basin Countries	Basin Area '000 km^2
Congo	9	Zaire, Central African Republic, Angola, Congo, Zambia, Tanzania, Cameroon, Burundi, Rwanda	3,720
Nile	10	Sudan, Ethiopia, Egypt, Uganda, Tanzania, Kenya, Zaire, Rwanda, Burundi	3,031
Niger	9	Mali, Nigeria, Niger, Guinea, Cameroon, Burkina Faso, Benin, Côte d'Ivoire, Chad	2,200
Lake Chad	6	Chad, Niger, Central African Republic, Nigeria, Sudan, Cameroon	1,910
Zambezi	8	Zambia, Angola, Zimbabwe, Mozambique, Malawi, Botswana, Tanzania, Namibia	1,420
Orange	4	South Africa, Namibia, Botswana, Lesotho	950
Okavango	4	Botswana, Angola, Namibia, Zimbabwe	529
Limpopo	4	South Africa, Botswana, Mozambique, Zimbabwe	385
Volta	6	Burkina Faso, Ghana, Togo, Côte d'Ivoire, Benin, Mali	379
Senegal	4	Mali, Mauritania, Senegal, Guinea	353

As shown above, ten major basins have more than four riparian countries each, and twelve countries are co-riparian on four or more basins (Table 2.4). The major rivers in sub-Saharan Africa have the following hydrological characteristics which both influence their mode of development and underscore the interdependence of co-riparian nations.

- Rainfall commonly predominates in headwaters in upstream countries, making downstream countries dependent on the actions of their upstream neighbors.
- Dry season river flows can be very low due to high seasonal and inter-annual rainfall variability, implying the need for water storage in areas without perennial surface water.
- Major perennial rivers are far apart, giving the region broad diversity in terms of being surface-water-rich or surface-water-poor, creating interdependencies.
- The most productive soils are typically found near water-courses, limiting the potential for large-scale irrigation far from major rivers.
- The main stems of the large rivers hold opportunities for water resource development, implying that large projects are necessary for economies of scale (Rangeley and others 1994).

Few of the transboundary river basins in the region are effectively jointly managed. To do so is a major challenge, requiring treaties and political commitment, institutions and capacity, information and finance. However, national interests often override regional objectives, and international treaties themselves are no guarantee of effective cooperation. Complicating matters, if joint management of one basin is a challenge, joint management of six, eight, or twelve basins by one country is almost unprecedented. A categorization of international river basins with its constituent countries tells us which basins will require particular attention in order to secure coordination and cooperation. In Table 2.4, the situation is reversed, telling us which countries need to address the issue. The implication is that such countries will be in particular need of capacity building and human resource development in order to achieve a level playing field for negotiation and coordination.

Table 2.4 Countries Belonging to Multiple International River and Lake Basins (Gleick 1993)

Country	No. of Basins	Basins
Guinea	12	Cavally, Corubal, Gambia, Geba, Kolenta, Little Scarcies, Loffa, Moa, Niger, Ntem, Senegal, St. John
Mozambique	9	Buzi, Imbuluzi, Incomati, Limpopo, Maputo, Ruvuma, Save, Pungue, Zambezii
Cameroon	6	Lake Chad, Congo, Cross River, Niger, Ntem, Ogooue,
Liberia	6	Cavally, Cestos, Loffa, Mano Rora, Moa, St. John
Angola	5	Congo, Cunene, Cuvelai-Etosha, Okavango, Zambezi
Gabon	5	Benito, Ntem, Nyanga, Ogooue, Utambori
Namibia	5	Cunene, Cuvelai-Ethosha, Okavango, Orange, Zambezi
South Africa	4	Incomati, Limpopo, Maputo, Orange
Tanzania	4	Congo, Nile, Ruvuma, Zambezi,
Zimbabwe	6	Buzi, Limpopo, Okavango, Save, Pungue, Zambezi
Botswana	4	Limpopo, Okavango, Orange, Zambezi
Ethiopia	4	Baraka, Gash, Juba-Shibeli, Nile, Gemle-Doma

Interdependencies and Risks. As noted previously, there are many downstream countries that depend on water imported through rivers from upstream (see Table 2.5). This dependency can create insecurity, misuse of water resources, or conflicts (see Boxes 2.13 and 2.14). Mozambique feels at risk in relation to its upstream neighbors, where over half of the country's water supply develops (Mozambique Country Paper 1996). Conversely, Angola has legitimate claims on the Cuvelai River in the country's southern region, yet can only proceed very slowly with development plans, as 50 percent of Namibia's population is dependent on this river (Angola Country Paper 1996).

Table 2.5 Dependence on External Surface Water, Selected Countries (Gleick 1993)

Country	% total flow originating outside border	External water supply : internal supply*
Egypt	97	32.3
Mauritania	95	17.5
Botswana	94	16.9
Gambia	86	6.4
Congo	77	3.4
Sudan	77	3.3
Niger	68	2.1
Senegal	34	0.5

**Note*: "External" represents river runoff originating outside national borders; "internal" includes average flows of rivers and aquifers from precipitation within the country.

This complexity can be illustrated by examining the Zambezi Basin. One must consider the relative importance of each state to the basin as a whole. Thus, while in terms of area, Zambia is the largest contributor to basin area, Malawi is the one country completely reliant upon basin surface water resources. In terms of population, Malawi and Zimbabwe have the greatest numbers relying on basin waters. However, while Angola, Namibia, and Botswana have small proportions of their populations within the basin, they still have strong vested interests in sustainable basin management. For example, perhaps only 0.8 percent of Botswana's population lives within the basin, but it is still possible that 100 percent of Botswana's population has hopes of using Zambezi Basin waters. In addition, Mozambique, as the furthest downstream riparian, stands to lose most by upstream developments—unilaterally by any one state or multilaterally by any group of states.

Another example of the complexity of managing international rivers is the Nile River Basin. Egypt and Sudan depend on the Nile for 97 percent and 77 percent of their water requirements, respectively. Egypt's water security depends on nine other African countries in the Nile Basin. Egypt and Sudan signed an agreement allocating the waters of the Nile, but other countries are not party to it. The riparian countries have development plans.

Ethiopia, source of the Blue Nile, needs more water for irrigation, industries, and hydropower. Kenya and Tanzania have plans to use Lake Victoria for irrigation expansion. Burundi, Tanzania, and Uganda are developing the Kagera River which links to Lake Victoria. Lake Victoria is now facing increasing levels of pollution and degradation of the catchment areas. The Nile watersheds are also being degraded with increased farming, grazing, and fuelwood gathering. Cooperation is required among the riparian countries to address pollution and protection of catchment areas, particularly upstream, in addition to dealing with water allocation issues. These actions have significant cost implications for each country as well as for the riparian countries collectively. Some of the costs relating to the protection of catchment areas would need to be shared among the riparian states.

Closing the Knowledge Gap. Information acquisition and sharing are critical to the development of transboundary waters. Without knowledge, riparian states are extremely nervous about threats to sovereignty, especially when another riparian (particularly, but not necessarily, upstream) is deemed to have that knowledge (and is therefore 'powerful'). Any attempts at rational negotiations are seriously hindered. It is in the interest of both powerful and less powerful riparians (a 'win-win') to strengthen capacities and databases. In addition, knowledge and information are essential elements in any efforts to develop international water resources for the mutual benefits of riparian states.

Africans and the world community have no choice but to respond to the issues and challenges described above. However, it is important that this response be based on existing solutions and practices that are generating positive results. To this end, the next chapter describes how African people, governments, NGOs, and cultural institutions have *responded to* and are *adapted for* meeting water resource management challenges in order to develop an integrated approach to water resources management, involving stakeholders and focusing on economic and social efficiency.

Box 2.13: Impacts of Uncoordinated Action

The consequences of uncoordinated management of river basins are important at all levels but particularly so with transboundary waters as co-riparians will see threats from any development. Projects can impose unplanned costs on various stakeholders; for example they can:

- ***Cause non-water sector side effects***: The construction of the Kariba Dam on the Zambezi River between Zambia and Zimbabwe caused the relocation of approximately 50,000 people in the 1950s (Scudder, 1994); the recent Ruzizi II Dam between Rwanda, Zaire, and Burundi caused the relocation of 12,000 people (Gleick 1993).
- ***Disrupt each other***. The dam at Diama on the Senegal River is unnecessary in light of its sister project, the much larger Manantali Dam upriver (LeMarquand 1990).
- ***Cause water-related health effects***: Schistosomiasis increased from low levels before projects to high levels after completion of the Volta Dam in Ghana (70 percent prevalence post project), sugar estate irrigation in Tanzania (85 percent), Kainji Dam in Nigeria (30-70 percent), Malumfashi irrigation project in Nigeria (65 percent), Aswan High Dam affecting Egypt and Sudan (100 percent), and Gezira irrigation project in Sudan (70 percent) (Gleick 1993).
- ***Be inappropriate***: the Manantali Dam was over-designed to supply power for a market that does not yet exist (LeMarquand 1990).
- ***Be short-sighted in their planning***: Efforts to eradicate onchocerciasis (river blindness) in the Niger, Senegal, and Volta River Basins may have been successful but did not include plans for potential immigration on to the newly inhabitable land (Scudder 1994).
- ***Waste money and water***. Zimbabwe removes water from the Zambezi River for its coal-fired Huangwe thermal stations despite the fact that neighboring Zambia has a hydropower surplus. Moreover, this causes Mozambique to receive less downstream water (Scudder 1994).
- ***Have high environmental costs in proportion to benefits***: For example, in the case of the Cabora Bassa Dam in Mozambique, the Kariba Dam in Zambia-Zimbabwe, and the Akosombo Dam in Ghana (Gleick 1993, Scudder 1994).

Box 2.14: Case Study: The Ruzizi II Regional Hydroelectric Project

In the early 1980s, with the support of the World Bank and other donors, an ambitious effort was undertaken by Rwanda, Burundi, and Zaire to jointly construct and operate a hydropower plant on the Ruzizi River (part of the Congo Basin) between Lake Kivu and Lake Tanganyika where the river forms the border between Rwanda and Zaire. The project also involved installation of transmission lines and the creation of SINELAC, a trilateral utility to own and operate the facilities. The project has not performed well, illustrating the difficulties in achieving co-riparian co-operation. At the time, the Ruzizi River represented an important resource for bringing electricity to a region where only 2-3 percent of the people had electric power. The three countries understood this and had good intentions, yet the project failed because:

- The three countries lacked the technical and organizational ability to implement the project. The information base that was sufficient for the feasibility study was insufficient for actual project design. Moreover, SINELAC drew high-quality personnel and resources *away* from water and power agencies within each country.

- Each country individually lacked the information it needed to trust the other two. The countries were wary of bearing project costs without assurances of secured benefits. Moreover, Burundi's commitment to the facility was limited because the power lines from the plant to Burundi were owned by Zaire. National pride was no small factor in Burundi's drive for a separate plant on its own Rwegura River.

Insufficient capacity for implementation led to serious externalities. Upstream, many people were displaced by the dam-created reservoir, and operation of the Ruzizi II facility required changes in operations of the upstream Ruzizi I plant. Downstream, Zambia and Tanzania, the two other countries on Lake Tanganyika, were not consulted. The Ruzizi River still represents a vital resource to the region. Its coordinated management will require stability within the three basin countries, followed by major investments in human, technical, and organizational resources at a national level. At that point, the three countries will have the ability to both work together and trust each other.

Source: World Bank 1993b

3. *Results on the Ground: Achievements and Opportunities*

People in Sub-Saharan Africa clearly need more and better access to clean water and sanitation – and a great deal must be done to reduce water degradation and pollution, improve local capacity, and enhance the efficient use of water for agriculture and commerce. Yet, along with these problem issues, there have been significant achievements at the local level, and there are great opportunities for the sustainable use of water resources. SSA countries must now use these achievements as a base to build strategies, develop investment programs, and involve diverse stakeholders in the better long-term management of water resources.

A. ACHIEVEMENTS

Growing National Awareness and Commitment

A Transformation is Under Way. Any discussion of achievements in water resources management in Africa must first recognize the transformation which has been taking place in recent years at the national level in many of the region's countries. Many governments have undertaken National Environmental Action Plans (NEAPs), highlighting the importance of water in environmental management. Water resources assessments and the reform of water policies and institutions have been carried out—or are under way—in many countries. National programs for water supply and sanitation are being developed and implemented across the region, incorporating 'new' ideas that focus on beneficiary assessment and participation. Awareness of the need for effective water resources management is becoming increasingly widespread among national policymakers, in part because of increasing scarcity (caused by rising demand and drought) and in part by deteriorating quality (caused by rapid urbanization and degrading watersheds). In addition, there is more and better dialogue between countries on issues of international water resources. As economies grow, the benefits of regional economic cooperation are recognized, and the potential constraints posed by scarce and valuable water resources that are shared but not jointly managed begin to emerge. This chapter presents some illustrations of this transformation, drawing from across the region and across different sectors. In examining the achievements, lessons can be drawn, pinpointing some of the underlying factors behind success. Some of these factors are listed in Box 3.1.

Box 3.1: Success factors

Some underlying factors common to success include:

- Political commitment by the leadership, signaling the importance of managing natural resources.
- Stability and maturity in the civil service, with incentives ensuring retention of experienced professional staff who have risen through the system.
- Decentralization of responsibility, increasing accountability to primary stakeholders.
- Participation, involving primary stakeholders in choices and actions that affect them.
- Greater engagement of national expertise and corresponding ownership of principles and practices.
- Greater recognition of and pride in indigenous and traditional strengths, of special significance to water management.
- Better coordinated, less fragmented donor support, with less and better technical assistance.

Extending Water and Sanitation Services to the Poor

Learning from Experience. One of Africa's most important priorities is to ensure sustained water and sanitation services to the hundreds of millions of unserved people. The International Drinking Water Supply and Sanitation Decade (1981-1990) disappointed many when it failed to achieve the ambitious targets of full coverage set at the outset. The targets were set at a time when many agreed that central government could best provide services to poor communities. This approach was quickly established as being unsustainable, with several African countries taking the lead in demonstrating sustainable ways to close the enormous service gap. Significant lessons have been learned and achievements registered in both rural and urban water supply and sanitation. These achievements, which provide the foundation to build successful programs, are described here.

Rural Water Supply. In many African countries, there was first a determined move towards increased community participation in RWSS projects early in the decade. This was followed by a gradual but significant move beyond participation to 'community management', accompanying— and to some extent leading — the broader move in development programs to greater stakeholder consultation and involvement. In the RWSS context, community participation may include community contributions in cash or kind, committee formation and training, hygiene and user education, and some responsibility for operations and maintenance. The community management of RWSS can be seen as the community determining its priorities and assuming the responsibility, authority, and control over improvements in and operation of its services. Such efforts have resulted in examples like The Gambia, where 70 percent of the rural population has access to safe water supply. Box 3.2 describes a review of community participation in seven RWSS projects in Togo, Burkina Faso, and Mali, and Box 3.3 describes the best practices in the Mali Rural Water Supply Project.

Box 3.2: Community participation in RWSS

A review of community participation in seven relatively successful projects in Togo, Burkina Faso, and Mali (featuring drilled wells with handpumps) illustrates the shift towards developing community management:

- Initially limited participation in management with choice of waterpoint location but no choice of service levels.
- Pre-designed management systems (mandating inclusion of women) generally imposed, limiting spontaneous and voluntary initiatives.
- Extension services important and inexpensive in successful implementation; rarely planned for beyond construction phase.
- Other important elements: simple handpumps, local mechanics (ideally community-chosen), independent spares distribution networks, and willingness to pay for maintenance.
- All communities made investment contributions, in three cases ex-post, to give ownership sense.
- Review concluded communities willing and able to manage facilities, if skills, tools, spares available.

Source: World Bank 1991

Box 3.3: Mali Rural Water Supply Project

The project was designed with the participation of the beneficiary population and focused on improving water supply in 230 villages through handpump wells, setting up a user-based O&M system, and strengthening project preparation and management capacity at the national level.

The project design and costing proved conservative: compared to expectations at appraisal, the credit was adequate to construct about 85 percent more wells and double the beneficiary population to 228,000 versus the 110,000 estimated at appraisal.

The project's policy objective—to transfer the responsibility of O&M of wells to beneficiary communities—was implemented successfully. Further proof of sustainability is the fact that all handpumps are still in good operating condition, four to seven years after their installation.

Source: World Bank 1995c

Rural Sanitation. Two of the most successful rural sanitation programs in the region— and, in fact, in the developing world— are in Lesotho and Zimbabwe (see Box 3.4 for the Lesotho case). Sanitation and improved hygiene components of RWSS programs are often marginalized, as 'water and sanitation' programs are developed to respond to the population's high demand for water and due to the political visibility of improved water supplies. Demand for sanitation is generally much lower. Despite the conventional wisdom that good programs integrate water, sanitation, and health education, one option of avoiding such marginalization is to consider a free-standing sanitation and hygiene program. Thus, although a RWSS program may have a full range of activities, the sanitation component could be managed and delivered separately, creating incentives for its successful promotion. Provision of sanitation in rural areas is an individual responsibility, with families meeting all or most of the cost, although public subsidies can be and are successfully employed in community programs, where widespread individual household support is demonstrated. As successful results show, effective demand must be the guiding principle in sanitation because the objective is to provide facilities that people want and will use. Rural sanitation programs can create jobs, and then leave promotion to local private sector 'marketing,' as demonstrated with the Lesotho rural sanitation program. Results in the field show that good sanitation/hygiene programs first identify the needs of the population (privacy, convenience, status, etc.), as well as the constraints within the community to widespread adoption of improved sanitation and hygiene behavior. Public awareness programs, using a wide range of media, can play a key role in changing perceptions and have been successful in sanitation programs in several parts of the world.

Box 3.4: The Lesotho Sanitation Program

The program maximizes private sector involvement in planning, financing, and implementation, including involvement of local latrine builders (LLB), credit unions, and building materials suppliers. Experience gained includes:

- slower initial progress with privatized, non-subsidized approach to sanitation;
- once under way, program continues partly independent of external inputs;
- greater health impact when household invests in latrine than in externally-driven program;
- general builders now pre-dominate over program LLBs, due to demand/ supply stimulation by program; public investment in extension remains important.

Source: Damhaug 1995.

Urban Water Supply. Although many of the region's water utilities are weak and delivering unreliable services, there are striking examples of good practices. There is increasing evidence from across the world that the commercial practice required of water utility is often better managed by the private sector, with government setting the rules and ensuring compliance. The roles of regulation and supply are thus clearly separated. However, relatively high levels of governance are required for effective regulation. Côte d'Ivoire's SODECI, described in Box 3.5, is an example of a successful private utility which today delivers water supply to three-quarters of the country's urban inhabitants. Another interesting case is in Guinea, where the privatization of the delivery of urban water supplies in 1989 has led to marked increases in service reliability and in billing and collection. However, extension of coverage and reduction in unaccounted-for water have not had the same success and will be addressed in the second project under preparation. Well-performing utilities are not only private—for example, the Botswana Water Utilities Corporation (Box 3.6) is a well-managed public utility with many of the characteristics of a private firm, including financial autonomy, good salaries, and efficient staff. Successful public water utilities can be found in several other countries, including Togo and Malawi.

Box 3.5: Côte d'Ivoire: Successful Private Concession For Water Supply

SODECI is a thirty year old Ivoirian company whose capital (about $15 million) is owned 52 percent by local interests; 46 percent by Saur, the French water distributor; and 2 percent by a government investment fund.

- All urban water supply services are now a national concession contract for the entire country.
- Today the company has 300,000 connections serving 70 percent of Côte d'Ivoire's 4.5 million urban residents -- 2 million in Abidjan.
- Under a policy to provide low-income households with direct access to water, 75 percent of SODECI's domestic connections have been provided with no direct connection charge.
- Connections are growing by 5-6 percent a year. Full cost recovery is the rule, and revenues from water sales fully cover capital and operation and maintenance costs.
- During the past 10 years, unaccounted-for water never exceeded 15 percent, and collection from private consumers never fell below 98 percent (collection from government agencies is more problematic).
- Only 4 staff per 1000 connections, reflecting best practice standards; expatriate staff reduced while expanding operations.
- Retains part of rates collected to cover operating costs, depreciate assets, extend and rehabilitate distribution networks, and pay dividends to shareholders. Pays government a rental fee to service the debt attached to earlier projects.
- Provides service close to the standards of industrial countries, with the costs to consumer no higher than in neighboring countries in similar economic conditions or in members of CFA franc zone, where tariffs rarely cover capital and operation and maintenance costs, and service lags behind.
- Private Ivoirian interests now own a majority of SODECI's shares. Its bonds are one of the main items traded on Abidjan's financial market, and it has distributed dividends to its shareholders. The company has also paid taxes since its inception.

Source: World Bank 1995e

Box 3.6: The Botswana Water Utilities Corporation: Effective Public Sector Delivery

The Botswana Water Utilities Corporation (WUC) has made that country one of the few in Africa with a safe urban water supply supported by a semi-autonomous public agency. It has done so through strict recognition of water as a scarce economic good, while still considering equity concerns.

- WUC: a public utility with many features of a private firm.
- Urban areas have 24-hour supply and high-quality water treatment.
- Overall losses [of unaccounted-for water] relatively low at 25 percent.
- Commercially-oriented tariffs, monthly billing, enforced disconnection policy for nonpayment.
- High monthly tariffs, but progressive rate structure does not exceed ability-to-pay of poorest customers.

Source: World Bank 1995c.

Urban Sanitation. The high costs of conventional water-borne sewerage and the management requirements for effective treatment and disposal mean that relatively few of the urban inhabitants are served by sewerage systems, and those systems in place often have unreliable or poorly operated treatment plants, resulting in the serious risk of polluting water courses. Unconventional, and particularly on-site, sanitation systems have been pioneered in many countries in Africa. Strategic sanitation planning, a technique which has been developed largely in Africa for resolving the urban sanitation problem, focuses on effective demand (i.e., willingness to pay), and the informed choice of households for different sanitation systems. This has been well demonstrated in Kumasi, Ghana (Box 3.7).

Financing Water and Sanitation Services. The widespread provision of grants or very high levels of subsidy for water supply and sanitation services provision are a major issue. With grants, some poor people receive a much-needed basic service. On the other hand, limited resources cover only a small percentage of those in need, and most remain unserved. The self-reliance essential to sustain services in remote rural areas can be positively discouraged; and the sub-sector is perceived as uncreditworthy by the major potential financing institutions. Both the scaling-up of service coverage and the need to increase the perception of community ownership of the service would greatly benefit from access to credit facilities, rarely available in developing countries for the purpose of constructing water supply and sanitation services.

Box 3.7: Sanitation Planning in Kumasi, Ghana

Through the Kumasi Project, the Metropolitan Authority (MA) developed a city-wide plan that matches supply to demand and emphasizes cost-effective solutions that benefit people quickly. While individuals can install any technology which is technically viable on their property, the plan calls for:

- Sewers in the high density, low-income areas where they are the only viable technology, with MA financing off-site sewers and treatment facilities.
- Household latrines in medium-density, low-income areas under an introductory 50:50 cost sharing formula.
- Septic tanks in low-density, high-income areas where homeowners pay the full cost.

The Sanitation Plan places particular emphasis on the institutional and financial arrangements needed for implementation. Key features include:

- The MA to stop direct delivery of sanitation services and focus on planning, mobilization of financial resources, and management of private sector contracts.
- Sewers to be operated by lease contractors, selected through competitive bidding, who would pay 'rental fee' to city with revenue collected from individual households set according to utility water bills.
- Household latrines to be constructed by local contractors trained in marketing and design. Local management intermediaries paid on commission, to train contractors, accept applications through contractors, check authenticity and design at site, and pay 25 percent advance and 25 percent on acceptance.

With this arrangement the cost to government would be about US$10 million to serve the entire 750,000 population, compared to US$40 million if sewers were employed universally.

Source: Grey 1995.

The development of purpose-designed financial intermediation and, most important, the associated regulatory framework that will ensure adequate credit-worthiness and promote sound financial management and appropriate institutional structures at the community level pose a challenge that the Mvula Trust in South Africa addresses (see Box 3.8). A particularly interesting feature of the Trust is the 'barriers to entry' created by administrative demands on the community applying for funds. These barriers can be designed as hurdles of various heights geared to build the appropriate capacity level (e.g., in accounting) to manage the level of service funded by the credit.

Box 3.8: South Africa: The Trust

The Mvula Trust was founded by three parastatal development finance institutions in 1993, with seed funding of R150m, as a financing window for water and sanitation development in disadvantaged rural and peri-urban settlements.

- Documented policies/procedures, including targeting basic service provision, grant application and appraisal, subsidies and cost ceilings, contracting, and performance incentives.
- Applicants need to hold community meeting, form association, open bank account, complete application forms, prepare plan, collect 8 percent capital contribution, negotiate contracts, etc.
- 'Hurdles' created by administrative procedures create capacity to manage service for which support is sought.
- Risk that easy entry to grants from others (NGOs etc.) will negate capacity building.

Source: Grey 1995.

Basin Approaches. Again in South Africa—a country with the enormous challenge of overcoming decades of slow economic and social progress of the poor, largely black community—Umgeni Water Board, in Kwa-Zulu Natal, is demonstrating that cross-subsidization from urban to peri-urban and rural areas is justified not only on the grounds of equity, but also on the basis of efficiency and effectiveness in providing formal urban services as well (see Box 3.9). Poor people often live at the headwaters of basins, upstream of major settlements. Water that falls on the land of which they are guardians becomes the life blood of a city downstream. Yet, water supply projects that target the rural population rarely take account of their stewardship role, and they receive little benefit. If peri-urban and rural areas are not provided for, the future costs to urban users will rise rapidly due to the environmental degradation of water sources. In the Umgeni service area, informal settlement in the catchment areas is causing pollution and siltation of headwaters, seriously affecting downstream reservoirs.

Box 3.9: South Africa: Umgeni Water

Umgeni Water in Natal covers an area of 24000 km2 with 5.5 million people: 1.5 million rural and 4.0 million people in formal and informal urban settlements, projected to increase to 13 million by 2030. In 1987, Umgeni Water began to invest in rural and peri-urban water supply and sanitation in the headwaters of the catchment; these investments increased fourfold in the last financial year. Sound economic reasons for this investment illustrate the interdependencies in rural and urban services.

- Water resources threatened by sewage from informal settlement and soil erosion, with growing treatment needs escalating the costs of urban water, justifying service expansion to rural areas on economic and environmental grounds.
- Full cost recovery for operation and maintenance, with small cross-subsidy from urban to rural areas for the capital cost: Rl.36/cu.m. for rural, Rl.85/cu.m. for urban, latter including 2.35 cents capital subsidy for rural areas.
- Demonstrates service provision jointly to rural and peri-urban areas, spreading the benefits from economies of scale and considering overall management of the river basin.
- Umgeni receives no subsidies, issuing triple A rated bonds on the capital market.

Source: Grey 1995.

Thus, an important synergy arises from environmental considerations which calls for examining costs and financing issues in water resources development on a catchment basis, leading to a 'one basin' approach. Such an approach still requires looking at technology choice, consumer preferences, affordability, costs and cost recovery—but from the perspective of water resources management within a coherent service area or basin. The interdependencies arising from the underlying economic principles of water resources development call not so much for a choice in the allocation of resources between urban and rural areas but rather suggest that both can be delivered efficiently and cost-effectively if appropriate institutional structures and financing mechanisms are adopted. The Umgeni Water Board experience shows that if the costs of urban water supply are fully recovered and calculated not on a project basis but in relation to the costs of water resources management within the basin, then services can be improved in rural and peri-urban areas in a rational and cost-effective manner. Cost allocation and cost-recovery in a basin management approach are thus not necessarily a cross-subsidy from urban to rural areas. This is because of the long-term benefits to the providers of the 'subsidy' in terms of the environmental impacts and effects on long-run costs.

Impacts on Health. There have been important achievements in improving health through water and sanitation interventions in localized areas throughout the region. One success story is the near eradication of dracunculiasis (Guinea worm) in countries where it is endemic and where it has severely affected the quality of life and economic status of villages (see Box 3.10).

Box 3.10: Dramatic Reduction in Guinea Worm

In the past ten years, West Africa has seen a 90 percent reduction in Guinea worm cases. This was achieved with balanced complementary strategies, and points to opportunities to capitalize on this experience.

- Approximately one million cases in 1980s; 100,000 cases in 1994.
- Water supply and hygiene education for affected population.
- High-level advocacy from the Presidents of Nigeria and Ghana.
- Community-based surveillance and systematic reporting on progress.
- Service Delivery strategies (e.g., provision of safe water, distribution of filters, chemical treatment of traditional sources, and case containment).

Source: Listorti 1996.

A second success is the sustainable settlement and development of West African riparian areas formerly suffering from endemic onchocerciasis, or river blindness. As Box 3.11 shows, the coordinated actions of neighboring African countries and multiple donor agencies resulted in not only the sharp decline of this water-related disease, but also a subsequent increase in economic activity and food production.

Box 3.11: Sustainable Settlement and Development of the Onchocerciasis Control Programme (OCP) Area

The OCP was initiated in 1974 to control river blindness in Benin, Burkina Faso, Côte d'Ivoire, Ghana, Mali, Niger, and Togo, and later in Guinea, Guinea-Bissau, Senegal, and Sierra Leone. Two decades after inception of the program, the OCP is regarded as a model, effective regional health program. River blindness is no longer a public health threat in the original control zone, and many of the river basins are being resettled. Moreover, the OCP represents the power of donor collaboration, for it was jointly sponsored by FAO, UNDP, WHO, the World Bank, and nineteen other agencies.

River blindness had major socioeconomic consequences, including the uneven distribution of populations away from fertile river valleys, declining agricultural yields due to overcultivation, proliferation of unsustainable micro-plots, decreased household productivity, and low incomes for farmers. In afflicted areas, it was not unusual to find 60 percent of the adults suffering from the disease, with 3 - 5 percent completely blind. However, through intersectoral cooperation between agencies for public health, economic development, and water resources management, afflicted countries were able to stop the disease. The challenge now is to manage the results of success; namely, resettlement into the newly inhabitable areas.

Source: Elder and Cooley 1995.

Achieving Consensus. Recently, there has been a fundamental shift in the way of doing business, with governments disentangling themselves from providing RWSS. Instead, they promote RWSS by providing credits (and grants where appropriate) and both technical assistance and long-term extension services to rural communities as well as by providing incentives to the private sector to ensure the availability of competitively-priced goods and services needed for sector development.

This shift presupposes that rural people who perceive a need for improved water supply and sanitation (this perception may be promoted through hygiene education) can and will repay part of at least the capital cost and all of the recurrent cost of these services. It also assumes that people can organize themselves to manage the services, on the essential condition that appropriate service levels and technologies are employed to meet demand. The 'promotion vs. provision' debate was a central feature of the 1990 Abidjan meeting (see Box 3.12) and was at the core of the conclusions of the working groups. The shift to promotion has been adopted in several national strategies in the region and is being incorporated in major projects in several countries, such as in Benin's national rural water supply and sanitation project (see Box 3.13).

Box 3.12: The 1990 Abidjan Meeting: Laying the Foundation for the 1990s

This highly successful regional policy meeting drew on rich experience from across the continent, achieving a remarkable degree of consensus on the way forward.

- Delegates were all high-level government policymakers and sector specialists, from 45 African countries.
- Observers came from thirty-three external support agencies and NGOs.
- Co-sponsored by ADB, UNDP, World Bank, and supported by nine bilateral agencies.
- Three-day RWS workshop followed by two day sector-wide conference.

Key conclusions included:

- Change in role of government needed, from providing services to promoting service provision by local agencies and community organizations.
- Major commitment needed to building capacity of local government, formal/informal private sector, and communities.
- Women, primary users of water, particular targets for training and participation.
- Service levels to reflect effective demand and high levels of cost sharing (especially of operation and maintenance costs) needed to achieve sustainability.
- Appropriate sector development policies and strategies needed to be defined.

Source: World Bank 1991.

Box 3.13: Benin: Rural Water Supply and Sanitation Project

Benin has a population of 5 million, with 3 million in rural settlements of less than 5000, a 3.2 percent population growth rate, and a per capita income of $400. To date, RWSS services have been delivered in major construction programs, with boreholes and protected dug wells equipped with handpumps serving a theoretical 44 percent of the rural population. However, about 25 percent of the pumps are not functioning, and wet season usage is low. Only 12 percent of the rural population have pit latrines, mostly unimproved. The Benin IDA-supported rural water supply and sanitation project (total $15 m) has recently been launched, adopting the government's 1992 sector strategy, whose main principles are:

- Decentralization and community participation, with communities identifying needs/priorities and managing facilities; prequalified local NGOs acting as intermediaries/trainers; and line department regional offices promoting services, bulking civil works, and managing contracts.
- Cost recovery, with communities bearing full costs of maintenance and contributing to capital costs of basic services; higher service levels encouraged, but 'substantial' recovery of incremental costs.
- Cost reduction, targeting reduction of drilling costs (local contractors, simpler technologies, reduced administration) and the rationalization of pump supply.
- Promotion of the local private sector to undertake 'provision' functions, leaving 'promotion' roles only to government, thus ensuring an enabling environment for effective construction, operation, and maintenance.

The RWSS project includes: support to water supply for rural communities in two provinces, in response to demand and community choice; promotion of on-site sanitation in the same provinces, using 'marketing' techniques and materials, demonstration at key centers, and artisan training; supply of village level operation and maintenance (VLOM) pumps for national RWSS programs, with private outlets; and capacity building across the public and private sectors. The project seeks 6 percent of water supply capital costs and 100 percent of water supply O&M costs and household latrine capital costs from beneficiaries. Procurement arrangements promote local private sector involvement and NGO participation as agents of the community.

Source: Damhaug 1995.

Making Irrigation Work

Local experiences throughout SSA show that irrigation in high-potential areas yields significantly higher levels of productivity than rainfed agriculture. Particularly notable successes have been achieved in small and medium-scale irrigation schemes that involve water user associations in project planning and implementation or that use low-cost technologies and less costly infrastructure and distribution systems. The success of these irrigation schemes is also enhanced by clearly-defined water rights, land security, improved agricultural services (credit, extension, transport, and marketing), and cropping patterns that include both food crops and higher-value products.

Three success stories highlighted here come from small-scale irrigation efforts (less than 200 hectares) in Nigeria, Kenya, and Ethiopia. In Nigeria, *fadama* development has shown the potential impact of individual farmers if given access to relatively simple technology (Box 3.14). In Kenya, small-scale water harvesting efforts in combination with improved market conditions and infrastructure have increased food production (Box 3.15). In Ethiopia, farmers have initiated irrigation schemes that do not require sophisticated design, equipment, or skilled labor. Rather, they utilize indigenous capacity while using existing water more efficiently (Box 3.16).

Box 3.14: Fadama Irrigation in Nigeria

Fadama are river valley areas which are seasonally flooded or have high water tables for all, or a large part, of the year. Fadama are important dry season farming locations in Northern Nigeria, where soil moisture is the principal constraint on crop production. Fadama area development was a project component of World Bank Nigerian Agricultural Development Projects (ADPs) in the 1980s. While initially the ADP performance was, on the whole, disappointing, the Fadama components were successful. The projects made available motor pumps at subsidized prices, and drilled tubewells, which enabled farmers to greatly increase water use for dry season crop production. These systems each allowed irrigation on 1-2 hectares at a cost of US$ 350-700 per hectare. Individually owned and maintained, 70 percent of farmers in project areas use the pump systems, and the schemes have a 90 percent success rate. They have increased both food security (through increased yields of rice and maize) and market-crop production (i.e., onions, peppers, garlic, tomatoes) in project areas. Finally, with over 50,000 pumps operating nationwide, a strong service industry has developed to maintain them, ensuring sustainability.

Project success is attributable to farmer demand for increased crop output, incentives for adoption of the pump systems, the appropriateness and relative simplicity of the pump system technology, and gradual improvement in pump systems with project experience. If African nations seek to emulate Nigeria's success, they can look to these factors, as well as the domestic market demand for higher value-added farm products (e.g., garlic, peppers) than just basic food products. When farmers have the technology, and the market exists, even small amounts of water may be used efficiently to increase rural welfare.

Source: World Bank 1995b.

Medium-scale irrigation schemes (approximately 1,000 hectares) have also been implemented and operated in a cost-effective manner, as shown in Box 3.17 on Madagascar. The message from Madagascar's experience is that key steps all take place at the beginning of a project, with the most important being the use of balanced criteria for site selection and participation of all stakeholders.

While the majority of irrigation success has come with small and medium-scale schemes, this does not mean governments should completely ignore the value of large-scale irrigation projects. Through a coordinated effort, Nigeria has irrigated 70,000 hectares of land (Nigeria Country Paper 1996), and Sudan, through careful upstream management to control sedimentation, has operated its Sennar dam for seventy-six years with only a 56 percent loss in total capacity (Sudan Country Paper 1996). As Box 3.18 shows, in the 1980s the Office Du Niger in Mali showed a spectacular turnaround after fifty years of dismal performance. Factors which hold true for other development efforts also hold true for irrigation projects of such magnitude: the availability and extension of a comprehensive package of improved technological messages, liberalization of crop marketing and processing, land tenure security, improved roads, bureaucratic reform, government commitment, focus on well-defined goals (in this case, water management), partnership with the individual farmer-producers, and donor coordination.

Box 3.15: Small-Scale Water Harvesting in Machakos District in Kenya

As a technique for increasing water supply, water harvesting methods work in the Machakos District in Kenya. Even if little seems to be known about traditional water harvesting practices in the region, experience in the Machakos District over the past two or three decades may be an exception, as the District underwent a transformation of its agricultural sector in that period. The essence of this transformation was substantial improvement in management of the region's land and water resources. An important component of the improvement was the building of terraces to control soil erosion and to slow runoff, thus increasing the supply of water in the crop root zone. These measures have increased crop yields and production. Perhaps the most significant feature of this achievement was that it resulted almost entirely from farmers' decisions to invest their own resources in improving the natural resource base and other aspects of the farm enterprise. The government contribution - by no means trivial - was to improve farm-to-market roads, both within the region and between the region and Nairobi.

Source: Brown, Grimble, and Morton 1995.

Box 3.16: Ethiopia's Success With Small-Scale Participatory Irrigation

The Ethiopian highland areas of Arsi, Bale, Sidama, and Hararghe have an estimated 20,000-35,000 hectares that meet the hydrological, economic, agricultural, and technical criteria necessary for successful small-scale irrigation. Initiated in 1987, the World Bank's Special Country Program was aimed at the 25,000 families who depend on this land for subsistence and income. The Program's objective was to enable farmers to produce marketable surplus crops in years of normal rainfall and to produce subsistence amounts in drought years. Specifically, the project provided funds for rehabilitation and construction of 4,400 hectares of small-scale irrigation schemes (with average investment costs of approximately $1200 per hectare) in the four regions, and technical assistance support to the Irrigation Development Department at national and regional levels. In total, the project was designed to benefit 18,000 farmers.

Eight years after initiation, Ethiopia has shown quite satisfactory performance in implementation of the project. Over 40 water user groups voluntarily formed at the time of initiation then fully participated in scheme identification and construction. These groups have also assumed total responsibility for operation and maintenance. Income generation and growth have resulted in project areas, and 100 personnel have been provided with training. Lastly, the project met its 1994/1995 target of 2,000 hectares of irrigated land.

Source: World Bank 1987.

Box 3.17: The Achievements and Lessons of Irrigation Rehabilitation in Madagascar

In 1985, Madagascar had 116 medium-size irrigation schemes representing 140,000 hectares of irrigated rice fields. The need to operate these schemes at higher efficiency led to the creation of a partnership between the World Bank and Malagasy Government, with the main objective being to develop a systematic approach to rehabilitation with increased involvement of beneficiaries, as an alternative to reliance on Government for management and maintenance. The specific goals were to rehabilitate 16 schemes comprising 17,000 hectares and to provide management support for the Ministry of Agriculture. Despite delays, the project has been largely successful, with an average cost of US$1,730/hectare and increased yields on all schemes to date. Based on this success, 140 medium and small-scale schemes have been pre-selected for the follow-on project.

The project delays and schemes which performed below expectations point to some important lessons. For instance, rehabilitation costs will at times be high due to environmental factors (e.g., siltation, lack of water, cyclones). Such physical characteristics should be part of criteria that also include social cohesiveness and financial potential. Secondly, beneficiaries should be prepared to pay for or provide maintenance and management services, most often through water user associations (WUAs). Finally, regulatory changes should become effective prior to scheme completion to allow for timely management transfer to WUAs.

Source: World Bank 1995a.

Box 3.18 Spectacular Success in the Office du Niger

The Office du Niger (O.N.) in Mali began in 1932 as a French scheme to produce cotton and rice in a one million hectare area over a fifty year period. However, in 1982, the project was far from meeting its objectives: only 6 percent of the target area had been developed (60,000 ha), infrastructure was poorly maintained, cotton production had been discontinued, average paddy yield was at a low point, and settlers were unhappy. However, after 10 years of careful preparation and implementation, the O.N. is on its way to becoming a success.

The success of these efforts is marked by the following changes between 1983-1994: average paddy yields have tripled, 10,000 ha of abandoned land have been rehabilitated, the settler population grew by 222 percent, and per capita production of paddy rose from 0.9 tons to 1.6 tons. The combination of settler population and productivity increases thereby made an important contribution to poverty alleviation and food security for the overall country.

Success has been achieved due to technical and institutional/economic factors. Improved water management (both delivery and disposal of excess) in combination with high yielding varieties were the first step. This was combined with a proper extension package for farmers and appropriate agricultural mechanization. On the institutional side, regulations for the marketing of rice were liberalized, tenure was improved, roads maintenance increased, and farmers were allowed to participate more fully with the O.N. (e.g., through the setting of fees and collection of payments). Additionally , the O.N. itself has been restructured and streamlined, and fee collection has reached a level of 97 percent (even with an increase of 43 percent over the last two years).

Source: Aw and Dejou 1996.

Learning from Resettlement

Providing water and energy for expanding cities and urban areas will require that large hydropower and water diversion projects be undertaken in SSA. These projects often have significant environmental and social costs. The most common adverse social impact is the involuntary relocation of project-affected persons. Adversely-affected populations should not become victims of development intervention. Rather, through participatory planning, the incomes and sources of livelihood of persons affected through water-related development projects should be restored if not improved. Good practices and experience accumulated through past projects suggest that pre-project planning with the affected communities provides ample opportunities to transform a resettlement project into a development program which is beneficial to both displaced persons and host communities. The Ziga Dam project in Burkina Faso is a case in point. Project authorities organized an elaborate workshop with all the stakeholders to distill from the technical documents a community-based development program for the project impact region. Similarly, the authorities for the Lesotho Highland Water Project have been working closely with the stakeholders during the revision of the compensation policy and in the preparation of the rural development program. Such consultation is now commonplace due to the lessons learned from past projects, like the ones reported in Box 3.19. They highlight the importance of turning involuntary resettlement into an opportunity for setting up a development program.

Successful Approaches to Water Resources Management

New Approaches to Water Resources Management. There is a move in several countries across the region to strengthen the legal, institutional, and policy framework for water resources. This is happening for several reasons. In response to serious droughts at the beginning of the 1980s and 1990s, as well as in recognition of the need for more equitable distribution of scarce water, Zimbabwe is in the process of major water resources management reform. A reform process is also under way in Senegal, as described in Box 3.20. Also, Ghana, South Africa, and Zambia are all currently reviewing the status of water resources management. Tanzania is conducting a water sector review and rapid water resources assessment. Mozambique completed its national water policy in 1995 (emphasizing, among other things, popular participation and water as an economic good). Eritrea plans to have a water law by 1996 that promotes systemic management. Ethiopia is preparing a water resources management policy (to complement similar national policies on conservation, population, and science and technology); Malawi is emphasizing community service and environmental protection in its future policies. Guinea is conducting a regional project for integrated management of the Massif du Fouta Djallon.

Box 3.19: Resettlement in Zaire Due to Hydroelectric Projects

Large hydropower and water diversion projects may be relatively few in the future of Sub-Saharan Africa, but such projects will take place. One of the inevitable repercussions of such projects is the involuntary resettlement and livelihood disruption of local people. Although the experience of governments and agencies engaged in managing resettlement in the past has been largely negative, lessons learned and some successful efforts offer directions for the future.

Ruzizi II Hydroelectric Facility

- Built by Rwanda, Burundi, and Zaire between 1983-1989, negatively impacting 15,000 people.
- Lessons learned include need for effective pre-project planning, government commitment to resettled people, and institutional capacity to undertake resettlement activities.

Kpong Hydroelectric Project

- Built by Ghana along the Volta River between 1977-1982, negatively impacting over 5,500 people.
- Resettlement efforts were positive in providing replacement housing using traditional architecture and social infrastructure like schools.
- Maintained women's pottery industry.
- Showed need for strong implementation agency, community involvement, and resettlement funding.

Source: Fisiy 1996

With increasing emphasis on water resources management, there is a commensurate need for a government role in regulation -- both 'economic' regulation of prices in an otherwise essentially non-competitive and monopolistic industry, as well as environmental regulation (abstraction licensing and pollution protection), compliance monitoring, and enforcement through prosecution and other instruments (such as license revocation). Over the last three decades, many (but not all) western countries have rewritten water laws to vest ownership rights of all waters in the State. Recent legislation in Niger (Ordinance No 93-014 of March 1994) vested all waters in the public domain, *except* for many categories of water on private land. Permits for water abstraction in Ethiopia have been introduced for the first time under Proclamation No. 92 of 1994, with the regional environmental protection bureau granting permits for waters entirely within the region and the central ministry issuing permits for transregional waters.

Box 3.20: Progress with Water Resources Management in Senegal

The Senegal government's immediate strategy includes:

- Creation of an Institutional Framework: Water Resources Planning and Management Service (Service de Gestion et de Planification des Ressources en Eau, SGPRE) created, responsible for managing and allocating all water resources and for issuing abstraction permits. Water Advisory Board (Conseil Supérieur de l'Eau) proposed as steering committee for water resources policy-making and management, with membership including representatives of consumers' associations, farmers' and livestock breeders' associations, industries, water and forestry associations, rural communities, mayors, the national water supply holding company (SONES), as well as the Ministries of Hydraulics, Health, Rural Development, and Environment. Technical Water Committee (Comité Technique de l'Eau) proposed for preparation of water resource development and conservation projects.
- Improvements in Data Collection: Databases created to track the volume and quality of water resources, identify water uses and users, and collate information for water-related projects within seven planned water management zones.
- Improving the Efficiency of Urban Water Use: Urban water losses reduced to 23 percent, to be reduced further to 15 percent in five years under planned private lease contract. Tariffs increasing gradually to cover full costs. Repairs and metering to reduce waste in public buildings. Use of potable water by market gardeners near Dakar discouraged by full cost tariff. Feasibility of substituting wastewater reuse for irrigation is being explored.

Source: Senegal Country Paper 1996.

Drought Management. Key elements of drought management include prediction and information, both of which benefit from a regional and not a country approach. At the same time, capacity to manage drought at the country level can often be enhanced by participation in regional or even global climate and agricultural management systems. In the Sahel, the AGRHYMET program (Agronomy - Hydrology - Meteorology), located in Niamey, was established in the mid-1970s to strengthen the national meteorological and hydrological services in the CILSS (Inter-state Committee to Combat Drought in the Sahel) countries. AGRHYMET collects data to monitor weather, crops, grassland, and surface water; stores and analyzes the data it collects; assists in national and regional efforts to increase agricultural production; and trains specialists to strengthen national services. Most Eastern and Southern African countries are now cooperating under the Drought Monitoring Project, supported by UNDP/WMO. This project spans twenty-one participating countries through their meteorological and hydrological services to support a three-year project. Two drought centers have been established in Nairobi and Harare to monitor the intensity, extent, duration, and impact of drought and provide data for drought prediction. Yet another project, also based in Niamey, is to be a continent-wide effort. Among relevant global projects is ENSO (the El Niño-Southern Oscillation) which is one part of the Tropical and Ocean and Global Atmosphere Program, monitoring climatic changes and patterns and assessing their implications for rainfall, floods, droughts, and agricultural production. While these various regional and global programs are valuable, they must be supplemented by national programs within a broader framework of water resources management. Namibia's drought mitigation plans, described in Box 3.21, provide one such example.

Box 3.21: Drought Mitigation in Namibia

In response to the severe droughts of the early 1980s and early 1990s, Namibia has implemented drought mitigation plans which demonstrate the importance of public support and decisive action. Namibia is a sparsely populated country with 70 percent of its population dependent upon agriculture. Average rainfall stands at 356 mm/year (ranging across the country from 50 - 700 mm/year). The 1991-93 drought caused 70 percent drop in cereal production and livestock loss of approximately 50 percent.

- Raise in consumer tariffs did not alter behavior due to many disincentives against water conservation.
- Wide public campaign for water conservation raised savings from 18 percent to 46 percent over the period between 1981-1982.
- Water supply authorities cooperated.
- Pricing and supply measures designed to avoid undue hardship on vulnerable groups.
- Drought Relief Plan included livestock subsidies, food for work programs, free food for vulnerable groups, and an Emergency Water Supply Unit.

Source: Namibia Country Paper 1996.

Transboundary Waters

Leveling the Playing Field. An excellent example of sub-regional cooperation in hydrological information is the FRIEND project, described in Box 3.22. This concept started in Europe, where a well-established network now exists. The Southern Africa FRIEND is now a well-functioning indigenous network of professional hydrologists and water resources institutions. The justification for such initiatives are numerous: a substantial proportion of the region's water resources are transboundary, so there is no alternative to cooperation and shared data for effective water resources management; major gaps in national water data archives can be filled through statistical analysis of data-sets from neighboring countries; hydrological capacity building is probably best handled at the sub-regional level, providing a critical mass of professional staff for effective training and, at the same time, creating confidence among institutions from neighboring countries. The confidence building that such a network program will promote will help avoid disputes and develop rational solutions as pressures grow on the water resources in international basins. Activities are needed which build capacity, share experiences, and create camaraderie and trust among the people who brief the Ministers engaged in international negotiations. Without a level playing field in terms of skills and information, rational and fruitful negotiation will be impossible. A related program for cost-effective freshwater quality monitoring in the region is being developed within the UNEP/WHO/GEMS/Water Program framework, in cooperation with WMO and UNESCO. The program is active in several regions of Sub-Saharan Africa, providing education, logistical support, and a flexible delivery system. The key strategy is targeted water quality monitoring, adapted to each country's priorities and needs.

Box 3.22: Flow Regimes from International Experimental and Network Data (FRIEND)

The southern African FRIEND project is increasing the multinational cooperation essential for optimal use of water resources, as well as building capacity and the knowledge base, through:

- ***Standardization.*** Simple, standard hydrometric database systems adopted by seven SADC states, overcoming availability/compatibility of computer software/hardware facilities for river flow data.
- ***Training.*** High cost and poor availability of training courses in hydrology and computing addressed through participation in FRIEND and through regional training centers (e.g. IMTR-Nairobi).
- ***Research activities.*** Spatial and temporal characteristics of low flow periods, droughts, and floods are being researched by FRIEND participants.

Source: Andrews undated

Achieving Basin-Wide Cooperation. Although international river basin organizations have a long history in the region, only a few have a successful track record in effective management of transboundary waters. Some, like the organization for the cooperative management of the Gambia River, the OMVG, are now taking concerted measures to streamline their objectives and workforce. Meanwhile, there are several important new initiatives in the region that represent serious attempts to bring co-riparians together to resolve questions of international water resources allocation and management and to examine opportunities for joint development programs. Swaziland, Mozambique, and South Africa maintain a Tripartite Permanent Technical Committee, and commissions exist for the cooperative management of the Okavango, Inkomati, Orange, and Limpopo Rivers. Guinea and Mali are undertaking a pilot cooperative project for hydro-ecological evaluation and monitoring. Finally, the Nile Basin Action Plan (TECCONILE) and the SADC Protocol on International Waters are described in Boxes 3.23 and 3.24.

Box 3.23: The Nile Basin Action Plan

The Technical Cooperation Committee for the Promotion of the Development and Environmental Protection of the Nile Basin (TECCONILE) issued an action plan in 1994 promoting a comprehensive and cooperative framework for water management on a river basin level. The plan proposes twenty-one projects at a cost of US$100 million, with five main components.

- Integrated water resources planning and management for efficient water use.
- Capacity building, including design of an executing agency.
- Training, with a comprehensive needs assessment and short-term priority training programs.
- Regional cooperation, including harmonization of legislation and identification of large projects for joint operation.
- Environmental protection and enhancement, including control of land degradation, siltation, pollution, and water weeds, development of environmental protection policies for major lake regions, and diagnostic studies.

Source: Hirji 1996

Box 3.24: The Southern Africa Development Community (SADC) Protocol

On May 16, 1995, most SADC states signed the Protocol on Shared Water Course Systems in the SADC Region. The Protocol's affirmation of the need for equitable use of shared waters, river basin commissions, and dispute resolution mechanisms places Southern African states at the forefront of a global trend toward the cooperative management of regional environmental resources. The Protocol has the following elements.

- Adoption and recognition of general principles (Article 2), including: respect for the customary international law principle of equitable use; promotion of information exchange; maintaining balance between resource development and environmental conservation; and requirement of national permits for waste discharge.
- Establishment of RBOs and delineation of objectives and functions (Articles 3, 4, 5), entailing: a unit to support SADC in its role in respect to water; RBOs in multinational basins which implement protocol and multilateral projects, harmonize national legislation, and undertake research and data collection.
- Dispute settlement (Article. 7) facilitated by SADC tribunal for adjudication, with final and binding authority.

Despite shortcomings, the SADC Protocol is an important step in a region which is highly dependent on shared surface waters.

Source: Okaru 1995.

B. STRENGTHS AND OPPORTUNITIES

Stewardship

Coping Strategies. Country experiences in the region show that building upon tradition brings good results. For generations, African society has been in harmony with its environment, with cultural practices and lifestyles which incorporate coping strategies for climatic variability and endemic drought. Traditional farming systems conserved water and soil in arid lands, and people and livestock moved to locate water and grazing areas. Population pressures and rapid political changes are breaking down many of these coping strategies, resulting in human hardship (and occasional tragedy) and environmental degradation.

Protecting existing water resources is crucial because water is scarce and tapping new supplies is becoming increasingly costly. Watershed protection measures include enhancing and controlling land use through soil and water conservation methods. Box 3.25 describes successful watershed protection programs in the region. Unlike in many parts of the industrial world, coping strategies remain rooted in society and are a great strength. Preserving and building upon them is a feature of initiatives across the region.

Participation

A Tradition of Participation. Across the region there is evidence of a rich tradition of participation in water management. Examples of this include community rainwater harvesting on the Makonde Plateau of southern Tanzania, ancient and very deep village dug wells in northern Nigeria, community sand river dams in the Botswana, *tontine,* and traditional revolving fund mechanisms in West Africa to finance domestic infrastructure. More recently, the Green Belt Movement in Kenya has been mobilizing women's groups to protect catchments and conserve soils. This participatory capacity is firmly embedded in the culture of many parts of the region and is a valuable resource. However, building on indigenous skills and cultural traditions can only be successful where there is awareness of the problem and identification of solutions.

Community Management. Participation in water resources management and development can take many forms, ranging from active consultation to stakeholder involvement as a watchdog (e.g., in democratic form, or on a utility board) to full community ownership and management of process and product. A specific area where participation is central to sustainability is discussed in the section on rural water supply and sanitation.

Box 3.25: Watershed Protection in Guinea, Niger, and Lesotho

Africans can look to their own achievements at the local level and in the national policy arena to see how a water-based land management approach can lead to sustainable water resources management. The emphasis is consistently on the importance of watershed protection in the successes cited here.

Watershed protection programs in the Fouta Djallon Mountains of Guinea.

- Government-initiated watershed rehabilitation and afforestation.
- Programs based on detailed studies and mapping of human and livestock densities, climate, land use, and susceptibility to erosion.
- Success was dependent upon confidence and participation of farmers.

Combating desertification in the Keita Valley of Southern Niger.

- Cultivable land reduced to one-fifth of total area.
- Integrated projects encourage farmers to combine traditional production systems with water harvesting, preventing rapid runoff over degraded land.

Lesotho's proposed National Plan for Agricultural Development.

- Plan is to have cabinet-level endorsement.
- District-level components focus on agency strengthening and provision of field services.
- Local level plans group villages, informal organizations, and individuals along watershed lines.

Source: FAO ARC/90/4 and Hirji 1996

Here, community management of services can be the only viable solution where there are inadequate incentives for formal public or private institutions to provide and sustain services. Participation at a higher level in water resources management, with 'water parliaments' at the watershed (basin) level, is being considered in Zimbabwe, and also in South Africa, where the imperatives to accelerate the democratization process makes enhanced participation a policy goal. Broadening the ownership of apex water resources management institutions to incorporate community members should create the right incentives for ensuring local responsibility and 'stewardship.'

Gender and Success. Several programs in Africa have demonstrated that the active involvement and empowerment of women improves sustainability of water and sanitation services. The work of the Kenya Water for Health Organization (KWAHO) is an important example of this (see Box 3.26). However, projects must also bring net benefits to women by not adding to their already substantial overall burden. In poor communities where water availability is limited, the important task of ensuring adequate water for the family almost invariably falls on the woman. As long as women and girls continue to spend a major portion of their time and energy on water collection while being excluded from the overall development process, human and economic development suffers. By easing this burden and removing other barriers to entry into the decision-making and management process of water and sanitation development, the risks to sustainability of services are substantially lowered.

Box 3.26: Successes in Involving Women: The Example of KWAHO, Kenya

Women are key stakeholders in rural water-supply and sanitation projects, given their roles as users, collectors, and protectors of water. They are, however, often overlooked. The priority of the KWAHO is to facilitate women's involvement in project activities.

- Provides intensive training to women in operation and maintenance, leadership skills, organization and management, and health and hygiene education.
- Registers water projects in names of women's groups, thus making women responsible for management of new facilities.
- Initial emphasis solely on women, but as female participation became more accepted, KWAHO modified strategy to include men as well.

Source: Stone and Fye 1995; Patorni 1995

Customary Law

A Great Strength. Customary law plays a critical role across SSA. Customary laws and practices are still applicable, especially at the local level, in and outside traditional courts. This largely unwritten law is anchored in societal tradition and culture, with the additional influence of Islamic water law across much of West Africa (as well as in countries like Tanzania). The customs and local traditions governing the management, use, ownership of, and dispute resolution over water resources continue to vary from place to place and from time to time. However, most of the customary principles governing use, management, and ownership of land and water were based primarily on 'community interest.' Individuals, including those residing along the bank of the river, had only a right to use and not to own water resources. Water was unanimously perceived as a basic essential and social commodity. Water had spiritual and social value as opposed to a purely economic one. Besides, most of the varied customs shared a common theme of empowering a local chief or respected elder to administer the water resource on behalf of the community, including the settlement of disputes that would arise (Lesotho, Box 3.27, Ghana, Tanzania, riverine Ibo community-Ossomalla and Oguta, Nigeria). To ensure the impartiality and accountability of authority, sanctions—in the way of dismissal—were imposed on a chief or an elder who abused his power. The presence of customary water law represents a great strength in many countries of the region since it blends well with the participatory approaches required by new thinking in water resources management.

Box 3.27: Customary and Statutory Law in Lesotho

Basotho culture is characterized by its customary law, which vests the rights to land and water in the office of the local chief, as guardian and trustee for the community. The 1978 Water Act incorporated some customary rules and practices, bringing together the advantages of both.

- Chief allocates three fields (two to three acres) to resident married males, together with domestic water use rights.
- Water Use Permits for greater areas and other water uses issued by Water Affairs Minister.
- Customary law widely respected, allows for local settlement of dispute and backed by ritual sanctions, including ostracism.
- Customary law allows communal access (with some exclusion of non-residents), accommodates various demands (e.g., for livestock), and induces locally efficient and sustainable water use.
- Statutory and common law provides national perspectives, five year water use permits, and exclusionary rights.

Source: Okaru 1995.

Water Availability and Use

Using Water Wisely. Although water resources are scarce across the region as a whole, there are important opportunities that should be recognized. First, the great lakes of the East African rift system are an extraordinary resource which, if wisely managed and protected, can be developed to meet the needs of human society as well as of their unique ecosystems. While interbasin transfers from the lakes are not being considered due to the international accords needed and the high investment costs, it is possible that such solutions will be developed in the coming decades as least cost solutions to meet the needs of major cities whose water demands will be increasingly difficult to meet from local sources. However, environmental impacts will need to be assessed and managed carefully. On a very different scale, the 'basement' aquifer also provides the opportunity for widespread small-scale development, including for industry and for micro-irrigation (Box 3.28). Weathered granites and gneisses that make up the basement aquifer, although low yielding, outcrop across large areas of the region, recharge rapidly during the wet season, and provide a valuable buffer against drought. Recent experience in Zimbabwe has demonstrated the use of 'collector wells' — large diameter wells with horizontal bores drilled tens of meters out from the base of the well — to provide remarkably drought resistant supplies of water from the basement for small-scale irrigation schemes, with water delivery directly to plants through porous clay pipes giving very high efficiencies on small private plots. Meanwhile, Botswana and Namibia are at the forefront of nations trying to use alternative or unconventional water resources, such as wastewater reuse, reclamation of brackish water, solar driven pumps, and desalinization for local consumption. Thus, the region's water resources have largely unrecognized strengths, which present opportunities for development.

Box 3.28: Opportunities for Ground Water Development for Small Scale Irrigation

Ground water has great potential for farmer-managed, single-holder irrigation plots using appropriate technology. Ground water is easily used in an incremental fashion, expanded as farmer funds and needs increase. Capital costs for drilling can be low with suitable drilling technologies, and recurrent costs are lower than those for schemes requiring transfer of surface water over a large distance. Ground water can also be developed so that single farmers control their own sources, thus lowering the transaction costs of cooperation. Ground water also tends to have greater seasonal and annual stability in drought-prone areas. The main risk in its use, of course, is the ease with which it can be depleted without proper legislation, pricing, or control measures. Opportunities exist for small scale ground water irrigation in Nigeria, Zimbabwe, and Angola, and some estimates say that 10 percent of Africa's land (i.e., 200 million hectares) is underlain by high yielding aquifers.

Source: Carter undated.

Valuing Environmental Assets

New Ideas in Environmental Economics. Rationalization of national economic policies adopting the principles of environmental economics should lead to the efficient and sustainable use of water resources in the region. Many African (and other) nations have undervalued their water resources and continued on a non-sustainable path of exploitation. The lessons of environmental economics point to significant opportunities for managing African water resources in a new and sustainable manner. Essentially, there are multiple 'values' (use and non-use) of environmental goods and services. If African nations can account for all these values, they can manage their water resources sustainably while avoiding the past mistakes of the more developed countries. African nations have the opportunity to re-value these resources using the newest economic tools (Box 3.29).

Box 3.29: Considering All the Values and Costs of Water for National and Regional Planning

Efficient, equitable, and sustainable management of water resources requires 'environmental accounting' of the true value of water resources, going beyond the typical approach for assigning costs to the use of water. While direct-use values are commonly used, indirect-use and non-use values are often ignored. If all these values are considered, the cost of water will more accurately reflect its scarcity, thereby allowing market-oriented mechanisms to allocate water fairly among many current and future stakeholders.

- Direct-use value, or the traditional means of determining water costs. A reflection of extraction costs (e.g., pumps, piping, canals), even these are not fully recovered when subsidies exist (e.g., for large-scale agriculture and utilities).
- Indirect use values, which include the maintenance of downstream ecosystem processes (e.g., flood regimes, riparian habitats). Disruption of these processes has environmental costs. One method of covering these costs is via 'polluter pays' regulations.
- Non-use values, which are a function of the value people place on water through knowledge of its existence (and the habitats, species, and human cultures that water supports) and a function of the ability to bequeath the services water provides to future generations. Degradation of such services are user costs, the value of foregone benefits. Determination of these costs may require sophisticated economic tools, but even an approximation may alter or rationalize current activities.

Source: Munasinghe 1993.

Research in Irrigation

Priorities for Investment. The catchment area provides the most appropriate framework for conducting R&D in irrigation in SSA. A uniform method for measuring performance and efficiency is needed to consider more than just yield per unit of water but also the effects on competing uses of water, declining water quality, overall ecosystem health. In this context, there are opportunities for R&D in four areas.

- Increased productivity can be achieved with further study into supplemental precision irrigation in areas of acute water shortage and study into alternatives methods for inland valleys (i.e., alternatives to ponds or tanks).
- Sustainability can be improved by preventing or reversing soil degradation through utilization of crop varieties that tolerate salinity and alkalinity in the course of soil rehabilitation. Improved scheme design and management, including adequate drainage, also present strong opportunities.
- Management transfer is needed from governments and to farmers or the private sector. Thus, more study is needed into the role of land and water rights, and into management of irrigation systems in the context of traditional cultural values.
- Expansion of irrigated area is a necessity in SSA. Research is needed into how this may best be accomplished, either through improved use of surface and ground water, improved scheme designs, or lower construction costs. Lastly, there is an opportunity for improved donor collaboration in R&D itself. With our new understanding of the catchment area approach, the Consultative Group on International Agricultural Research (CGIAR) and its seventeen research centers can expand their focus beyond improving the productivity of agricultural commodities to also include research on environmental sustainability in irrigated areas (Barker 1996).

Regional Cooperation: from Threats to Opportunities

Seeking Win-Win Solutions. The international character of river basins in the Region seems to present multiple situations ripe for conflict. Yet, these very same geographic traits present opportunities for win-win solutions. The fundamental step is that co-basin states accept the principle of equitable and sustainable use. Upstream and downstream states must acknowledge each other's rights to use water resources for national development, as well as each nation's responsibility to prevent the pollution and degradation of water. Once this step is taken, potential relationships exist that will yield higher benefits for all parties. For example, Ghana has surplus power from its Volta Dam that it may consider selling to Burkina Faso, and Box 3.30 illustrates a potential win-win solution in the Lake Chad Basin.

Starting Early

Avoiding the Mistakes of Others. In many parts of the industrial world, the scale of environmental damage caused through the lack of protection of water resources during the period of industrialization has only recently been recognized. The resulting investment implications of remediation are enormous, as with the Superfund in the USA. In consequence, the 'precautionary principle' is now widely adopted, meaning that, where knowledge is absent or limited, no action is taken that puts the environment at risk. Catchment protection is the solution of choice, even where this means limits on economic activity — such as farming or industrial development — in vulnerable areas. In Africa, there is the opportunity to take action now and prevent the massive damage (e.g., water pollution, degradation of aquatic ecosystems, and destruction of watersheds) that so much of the world now has to face. For example, the nitrate and pesticide legacy in European ground waters is causing enormous concern and substantial investment. The situation in Africa is unlikely to be as serious anywhere yet, and action taken now can prevent it from ever being so. If this opportunity is missed, then future generations of Africans will have to pay the price.

Box 3.30: From Political-Economy Theory to Reality: C.A.R and the Other Lake Chad Riparians

A win-win solution is available for basin-wide cooperation in the Lake Chad basin, whereby the Central African Republic (CAR) receives resource management assistance while the four shoreline states (Niger, Nigeria, Cameroon, and Chad) are assured of the stewardship of basin headwaters. While 90 percent of total lake inflow comes from the Chari-Logone system, which rises in CAR and flows through Chad, the organization of shoreline states (the Lake Chad Basin Commission, or LCBC) has mandate over only 19 percent of the 'conventional basin,' which does not include the CAR. This sub-basin management, combined with droughts and over-extraction of lake waters by the riparian states, has created disastrous falls in lake levels.

The win-win solution is one that entails inclusion of the CAR in the LCBC and cooperation on the part of all five basin states. CAR specifically needs some positive inducement for taking efforts to preserve the Chari-Logone headwaters. It needs information on current and future water supply and demand, reasonable and public long-term development plans, and an understanding of the costs and benefits of water-use schemes. Building of such capacity requires a long-term set of actions, but in the near future, the win-win scenario is as follows:

- The four shoreline states require water flow in the Chari-Logone system that is of high quantity, quality, and consistency. Simultaneously, CAR requires forestry assistance for national income and local development.
- If the shoreline states offer human, technical, financial, and organizational resources towards CAR's sustainable forest management of the Chari-Logone headwaters area, all five states benefit. CAR sees continuous income from its forests, while the shoreline states see reduced flooding and sedimentation and increased river flows.

Source: Rothberg 1995.

African nations should build on these achievements and opportunities in formulating strategies for sustainable water resources management. The next chapter integrates these 'indigenous' African strengths into key strategic interventions that use a long-term vision and systemic approach. The best practices learned in other parts of the world, such as treating water as a scarce good and using a cross-sectoral approach, are combined with African strengths to propose strategies for the consideration of African peoples and governments.

4. Strategies: Transition To Better Resources Management

African countries must develop and manage their scarce water resources efficiently in order to meet present and future needs. Integrated water resources management is the message of the World Bank's WATER RESOURCES MANAGEMENT POLICY PAPER. *Nations and groups of nations need to share and use water resources rationally, ensuring clean water and sanitation services for all people and providing water for food production and economic development. This vision includes achieving poverty reduction and economic growth through wise allocation of water resources and achieving environmental aims through the effective conservation and protection of these same scarce resources.*

A. STRATEGIC IMPERATIVES

Long-Term Vision

The long-term strategy includes social, economic, and environmental objectives which reflect the scale of the issues in individual countries and the capacity to address those issues. Despite the region's diversity, African countries must deal with five priority challenges: providing access to safe water and sanitation services, addressing water quality problems, enhancing food production with the efficient use of water, protecting catchment areas, and developing mechanisms for dealing with conflicts in water use.

African countries must give priority to closing the services gap, ensuring that a large number of rural and urban poor have access to at least the basic level of acceptable water and sanitation services at affordable prices. Without this, people's health will be compromised, and economic productivity will be constrained. Integrated water resources development plans must aim to close this gap as a central policy platform. Otherwise, increased water pollution and degradation will continue to threaten human health. Emphasis on environmental objectives through the protection and rehabilitation of catchment areas must increase significantly to avoid further water scarcity and quality problems. And with increasing demands for scarce water resources will come tension and conflict within countries and among riparian states. This potentially serious problem needs to be addressed by the African countries through improved mechanisms to resolve conflicts and promote cooperation among stakeholders.

In developing a regional perspective it is important to (a) recognize that there are few 'prescriptions' for the region, due to physical and cultural diversity, and that sustainable basin- and country-level solutions will need to evolve gradually from different starting points, although this process can clearly be actively promoted; (b) avoid two opposing extremes: promoting ideals which are hard to achieve, even in the industrial world, or relying on the notion that everything can be left to indigenous skill and cultural strengths, which will be insufficient in a rapidly changing environment—a correct balance needs to be struck; (c) promote change which results from conscious decisions by stakeholders within the region and its individual countries, as a result of raising awareness, consultation, and adoption, and not as a result of imposed strategies and conditionalities; and (d) recognize that while building sustainable water resources management will be slow and difficult, the process of strengthening water resources management must begin quickly.

Strategic Underpinning

As water is becoming increasingly scarce in many areas in SSA and as the costs of extracting water from new supply sources are escalating, countries in the region will need to focus on both supply and demand sides. Water can no longer be supply driven or managed through technical and engineering solutions to capture, store, and deliver it. Policymakers need to give more attention to demand management and changing the behavior of people through incentives, regulations, and education to reallocate existing supplies to higher-value uses, promote efficient use through conservation and water-saving technologies, and facilitate more equitable access. On the supply side, African countries need to modernize infrastructure, improve management practices, reduce costs, and make the delivery of water more efficient from existing supplies.

There are roles for both the state as well as the market in water utilization and management. Countries in the region need to make a concerted effort to make a transition from an administrative command and control approach to a more participatory approach that treats water as a scarce valuable resource. Treating water as a scarce resource or economic good can provide a coherent and comprehensive policy framework. SSA countries should -- whenever feasible and appropriate -- develop market-like solutions and adopt policies which favor the use of economic instruments and analysis in the management of water allocations, in making investment choices for water development, and in the management and operation of water service delivery systems. The main economic instruments which could be considered are: (a) market-related and demand-oriented laws, policies, regulations, and incentive structures; (b) water markets with tradable water rights; (c) more extensive utilization of the private sector; and (d) economic pricing of access to water, raw water (whether surface or ground water), and water for specific uses (such as irrigation, industrial, and domestic use). The markets, as they develop in African countries, will be important coordinating devices that will promote the more efficient allocation of water resources and efficient behavior from its participants, both among suppliers and those who demand water services.

Even in the more advanced industrial countries, 'new approaches' that integrate these economic instruments are not yet fully adopted and are difficult to adopt, for diverse reasons, reflecting political, social, and cultural considerations. Presently, there is no single country in SSA which applies all of those instruments, although in a number of countries (e.g., Malawi, Senegal, Tanzania, South Africa, Côte d'Ivoire, and Guinea) some movement in adopting market-oriented solutions is on-going or is being put into place. In reality, it is unrealistic to assume that other factors, such as ecological and equity considerations, would not be taken into account in a market-oriented approach through public sector interventions. Moreover, it is reasonable to assume that some portion of costs associated with water utilization (watershed protection, pollution clean-up) should be shared by the government and paid out of general taxation.

By and large, the role of the government will remain important in creating and helping to implement laws, rules, and regulations which provide incentives to use water more efficiently and flexibly in response to changing demands and costs of water for different uses. The government can also play an important role in reinforcing the incentives for improved coordination of demand and supply, and protection of the public interest in the process. Furthermore, the government also needs to play an important role in ensuring protection of watersheds, conservation of biological resources in aquatic ecosystems, and cooperation among riparian countries sharing waters from international rivers, ground water aquifers, and lakes.

Systemic Approach and Cross-Sectoral Coordination

Water utilization is often fragmented and addressed along sectoral lines. Conventional approaches often fail to take into account competing demands and interrelated variables in the assessment of water resources in the context of a river basin, drainage area, watershed, or catchment area. These approaches often fail (a) to recognize the spatial and temporal dimensions of water resources supply and demand, interests of stakeholders, and transboundary considerations; and (b) to assign proper roles for the market and public sector to promote more efficient use of this finite resource.

As illustrated in Box 4.1, African countries need to adopt a systemic approach to water resources management that reflects socioeconomic, ecological, and equity considerations. A call for a more systemic approach should not be interpreted as requiring a more extensive and rigorous central planning role and the establishment of administrative arrangements that will increase the government's control of water resources. A systemic approach requires a broad-based partnership including all stakeholders, from the public sector to farmers, to local communities, and to the private sector to participate in water resources management. Such a comprehensive and coordinated approach will allow each sovereign country to assess water needs in a multi-sectoral framework and take into account transboundary considerations.

Box 4.1: Systemic Approach to Water Resources Management

A systemic approach based on a river basin or watershed facilitates the development of water resources in an integrated, multisectoral framework taking into account the political economy. This approach requires sovereign countries and users of water resources to think holistically and to make local and sectoral actions which are consistent with long-term development goals. It promotes a more objective assessment of water resources and better understanding of the interconnectedness and interdependencies among various components, such as land, water, and forests, of an ecosystem. Land use and changes in land use patterns, deforestation, degradation of vegetation, soil erosion, decreased river flows, climate change, and development programs are all interrelated and have an impact on water utilization. A systemic approach also facilitates an understanding of interactions among economic sectors, such as agriculture, industry, energy, and commercial, as well as the role of various stakeholders, such as farmers, local communities, and domestic users. Further, a systemic approach provides a regional perspective that transcends political boundaries.

Countries in Sub-Saharan Africa are diverse in terms of their natural resource base, level of development, human capital, institutional arrangements, and local capacity. Therefore, a holistic approach to water management must be tailored in keeping with each country's circumstances, needs, and priorities. A number of countries (e.g., South Africa, Tanzania, Zimbabwe, Senegal, Malawi, Côte d'Ivoire, Ghana, Benin, Botswana, Namibia) have the necessary conditions to adopt a more integrated approach to water management. In other countries, in which more needs to be done in terms of capacity building and development of human resources, the transition to a more comprehensive approach would be gradual and incremental. However, even in these cases, cross-sectoral, socioeconomic, and environmental considerations will allow countries to implement better policies and investments for the sustainable management of water resources.

Source: Sharma 1995

Key Strategic Interventions

In defining strategies for water resources management in SSA, both threats to water resources (e.g., water scarcity and water pollution) and the capacity to manage those threats need to be considered. An overarching priority in the region is to build capacity and an enabling policy environment. The challenge is greatest where threats are great and capacity is low, since actions are unlikely to succeed without prior efforts to build capacity. Building capacity implies good governance and the involvement of diverse stakeholders. Further, it includes human resource development, improvement of data and information systems, and mechanisms for regional cooperation and conflict resolution. Figure 4.1 illustrates the key strategic interventions needed by African countries to promote the sustainable and equitable use of water resources. These interventions integrate the important roles of the public sector, the market, and the people at large. However, these roles require a sound legal and regulatory framework, as well as a policy and enforcement framework to assess operational efficiency and external consequences.

More importantly, many countries in the region continue to have a pressing need to build the capacity necessary to manage their water resources in a comprehensive and sustainable manner. Capacity building is required to address not only the traditional management agenda of providing adequate household water and sanitation services, but also the new agenda of environmentally sustainable development. The capacity building implications of the new consensus for most SSA countries are considerable. Capacity building will need to be defined broadly to include not only traditional approaches—e.g., training, provision of equipment, and organizational restructuring—but also more broadly the policy, regulatory, and administrative frameworks that establish, implement, and enforce rules and incentives to spur efficient decision-making, investments, and operational performance. For SSA, capacity building choices should be based on a systematic assessment of what capacity exists, how well existing capacities perform, and what capacities do not exist. Various kinds of capacity building efforts will be called for to address the complexities inherent in managing integrated, interdependent, and increasingly scarce water resource systems. In general, efforts should start small, be rigorously selective on priority management functions, take a long-term perspective, and be given the time they need to take hold.

Key Strategic Interventions

Figure 4.1

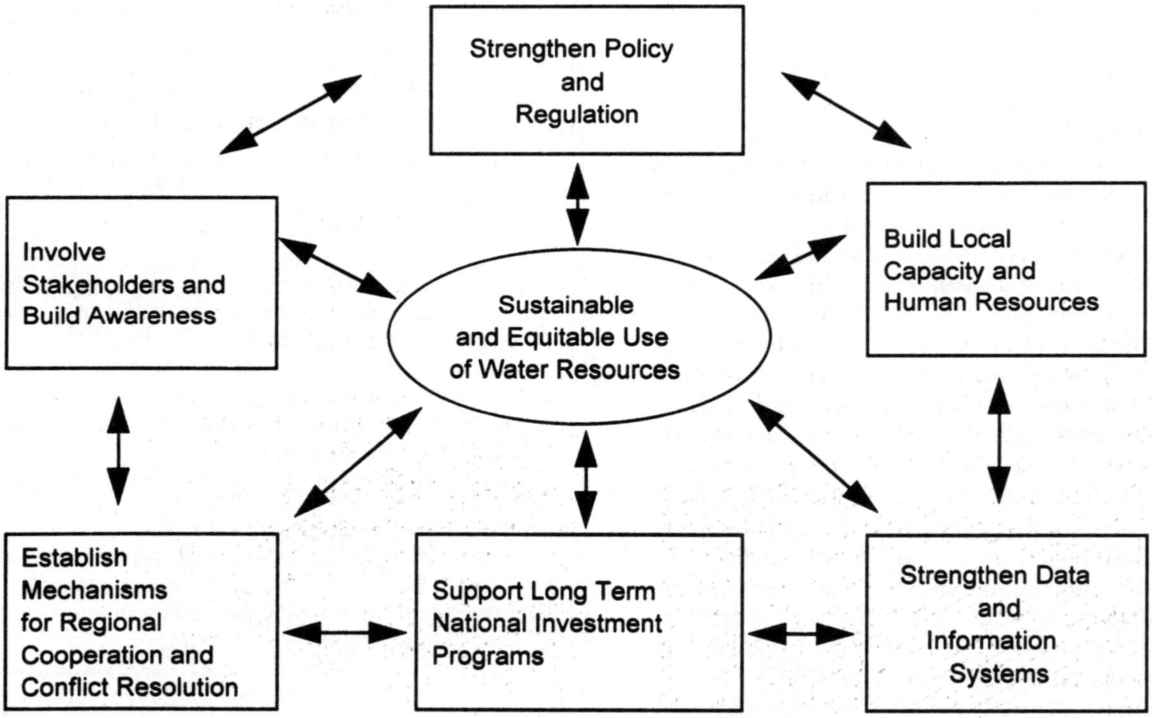

B. A Strategy For Building Awareness*

Strategy: Build Awareness

Awareness of water resources challenges, issues, and opportunities is an essential starting point for improving water resources management and needs to be enhanced:

- *at the regional, sub-regional, and basin level, to create a climate of mutual understanding and knowledge;*
- *at the national political level, to create commitment;*
- *at the executive level, as part of building capacity; and*
- *among the public, to create society-wide stewardship.*

Building political and public awareness in African countries about water conservation and protection is crucial, particularly where scarcity, unreliability of rainfall, and water pollution are common. At the regional and national political level, advocacy is needed to stimulate interest in water resources issues and create commitment and political will. For building public awareness, social marketing techniques—namely, understanding behavioral and cultural norms and using them appropriately to engender the right responses in the target groups— can change perceptions and create a sense of communal responsibility for a scarce resource at both societal and policymaking levels. Growing awareness will encourage public support of policy initiatives, such as tariff reforms, good governance, and decentralization of public decision-making.

**Note*: In sections B through G of this chapter, the key strategies for improving water resources management are described. With each description, a list of strategic actions to be considered is presented to the right. The lists should be viewed as options to be considered.

Strategic actions to be considered include:

Fostering regional, sub-regional, and basin-level dialogue among countries, based on broad participation and promoted through:

- building awareness of the need for joint management and development of transboundary resources, particularly where scarcity and pollution are serious threats;
- stimulating the exchange of experiences, best practice, and models among countries;
- achieving these goals through the use of seminars, peer groups (such as of leading African advisers) , networks, regional entities such as the Global Coalition for Africa GCA, and targeted publications.

Promoting national political commitment to integrated water resources management through policy review, seminars, and targeted publications, all at the national level.

Promoting public awareness through campaigns which employ social marketing techniques and a range of media to:

- encourage water conservation and quality protection;
- encourage watershed management and soil conservation;
- encourage other aspects of community-level stewardship of the water environment, including allocation and conflict resolution.

Integrating awareness of the social, economic, and environmental importance of water into a wide range of other activities, including:

- primary and secondary education;
- community development strategies;
- health education programs;
- local government training.

C. A Strategy For Building Capacity

While technical and professional capacity across the region is generally weak, there is a richness of relevant skills in African society - for example those related to custom and culture - and a level of commitment— for example among women and local communities—which can be tapped to strengthen water resources management. This section examines strategies for building capacity in water resources management institutions as well as through broader public and private participation.

Water Resources Management Skills and Institutions

***Strategy:* Build capacity: develop water resources management skills and institutions**

Enhancement of human, technical, financial, organizational, and institutional capacity is the key strategy for solving the critical water resources issues facing Africa -- individual and household access to water, growing scarcity and the potential for conflict, and environmental degradation. Both the international and the cross-sectoral dimensions of the issues demand a sophisticated and unprecedented -- yet feasible -- effort to build capacity.

Ultimately, the capacity building challenge for each locality, nation, and even international river basin will require identification of water management functions, delineation of management structures, design and adoption of appropriate operational policies and practices, and the development of appropriate skills. Capacity building -- and the choices and demand which drive it -- must come from the stakeholders themselves, implying that neither a single capacity building solution, nor a fixed time-table, exists for the region or any group of countries. Nevertheless, there are valuable guidelines, developed largely by the 1993 Delft Agenda on capacity building, to be considered in developing capacity building initiatives.

Strategic actions to be considered include:

Promoting a sound policy and regulatory framework through:

- promoting internal analysis so that policies, strategies, and programs emerge from and are not prescribed to local institutions;
- adopting inter-sectoral approaches to water resources use and development, including consistent water legislation;
- strengthening capacity to manage and develop shared river basins; and,
- improving donor coordination, ensuring that every effort is made to work with and build on local capacity, accepting possible short-term costs to achieve long-term benefits.

Promoting institutional development through:

- working with existing indigenous structures, experiences and cultural values, recognizing gender issues, and building upon existing capacity rather than creating new institutions in the public, private and NGO sectors;
- seeking ways to retain qualified staff through improved career management and incentives;
- promoting development of well-managed, financially independent and accountable water and sanitation utilities;
- promoting stakeholder involvement to the extent feasible, emphasizing community involvement from earliest stages of planning.

Improving education, training, and research through:

- supporting regional and national centers of excellence to promote experience and information exchange;
- exploiting the demonstration effect of technical cooperation between neighboring countries, to illustrate the benefits of specific policies, strategies, and actions; and
- mobilizing and focusing research capacity at the regional and national levels to address priority issues.

People's Participation

Strategy: Build capacity: promote people's participation

Promoting and enabling popular participation in water resources management is a fundamental strategy for achieving sustainable development, with public involvement as 'watchdogs' monitoring performance of public and private institutions; community ownership of assets (such as water supplies and irrigation systems); and community management of the water environment. A particular focus on women and children is called for since they stand to gain most from 'household water security,' and to lose most from a lack of it.

Across much of the region, community participation is a cultural tradition, rooted perhaps in coping strategies for collective survival under harsh conditions. Harnessing this tradition, without overexploiting it, to build awareness and instill water resources responsibility and management in society at large is a central strategy for water resources management. Examples of existing and 'hidden' capacities may be found among women (who traditionally have primary responsibility for the daily management of water), among indigenous groups (who have highly adapted water-management practices in balance with local environments), and among youth and the urban poor (where many examples exist of the informal sector providing reliable hand-carried water delivery).

Participation in water resources management and development can take many guises, ranging from active consultation and stakeholder involvement as a watchdog (e.g., in democratic fora or on a utility board) to full community ownership and manage-ment (such as with rural water supplies). Participation at a higher level in water resources management, with 'water parliaments' at the catchment level including public servants, local elected officials, and community members, is being considered in South Africa, where the democratization process underway makes enhanced participation a policy goal. Broadening the ownership of apex water resources management institutions to incorporate community members should create the right incentives for ensuring local 'stewardship.'

Strategic actions to be considered include:

Enabling and encouraging people's participation through:

- providing basic education and technical training at the lowest stakeholder levels;
- legitimizing, through legal and institutional means, indigenous water management practices;
- supporting, as intermediaries and representatives, NGOs with human, technical, financial, and organizational resources;
- devoting time and resources to the processes necessary to ensure active stakeholder participation.

Promoting stakeholder representation and consultation in all aspects of water resources management through:

- adopting institutional frameworks which provide for public representation in water resources regulation and allocation;
- promote accountability of water services agencies and utilities through community representation on boards.

Promoting 'community management of the water environment' at the local level as a first line of action in water resources management (think globally, but act locally), through:

- supporting community associations with small project funds (e.g., for soil conservation, artificial recharge, clean-up, waste disposal, etc.);
- building awareness of the importance of community-level stewardship.

Private Sector Participation

Strategy: Build capacity: promote private sector participation

The private sector – both formal and informal – can be a major contributor to achieving water resources management objectives, playing a major role in, among other things, financing and delivery of water supply and sanitation services, irrigation and agriculture development, and power generation. Promoting private sector participation will require an enabling environment of appropriate regulations and incentives as well as targeted efforts to build entrepreneurial capacity.

The private sector can and should be a major player in water resources development efforts. It has a permanent obligation (in the sense that it wants to profit from its activities), is more flexible than the public sector in its investments, and has a vested interest in using the latest research and the best-trained employees. But in SSA countries, the level of development of the private sector varies enormously. In countries where the private sector is weak, efforts will be needed to develop an enabling environment. On the other hand, in countries where there is a sound enabling environment, the private sector can improve economic productivity, the quality of service, the level of receipts, and the budget for water services. For example, there are clear incentives for private water companies to continuously improve their engineering techniques, design and management techniques, operation and maintenance activities, and responsiveness to customers. The private sector is motivated to reduce operating expenses, improve the efficiency of installations, prevent deterioration of equipment through regular maintenance, and limit the amount of outstanding payments. Its success is predicated on political and economic stability and guaranteed returns on investments. Also, private sector involvement will often - although not necessarily - entail higher costs for some constituency. A gradualist approach to private-sector participation in the water sector in SSA countries may prove the most realistic approach given the many considerations and required steps.

Strategic actions to be considered include:

Enabling and encouraging effective private sector participation through:

- defining clearly property rights and access to water or water rights;
- establishing clear contractual and regulatory laws, and applying them predictably and uniformly;
- allowing free and fair competition and eliminating political privilege;
- developing financial and capital markets to encourage investment;
- in the case of water supply, creating clear incentives and mandates for water services delivery, eliminating government interference, and allowing managerial autonomy;
- in coordination with donors, channeling foreign aid so it does not subsidize public sector competition with the private sector.

Building private sector capacity through:

- supporting trade training and certification and management training;
- promoting trade and professional associations;
- promoting joint ventures.

Resolving the social impacts (e.g., unemployment, increased prices) likely to accompany private sector strengthening.

D. A STRATEGY FOR AN ENABLING ENVIRONMENT

Creating awareness and building capacity are necessary strategies for effective water resources management. In addition, it is essential to provide an enabling environment within which aware and capable individuals and institutions can perform. Inappropriate laws, regulations, and policies and poor information are often serious constraints.

Water Laws and Rules

Strategy: Promote an enabling environment: ensure an effective legal and regulatory framework

Appropriate and enforceable water resource legislation is a pre-requisite for the effective management of water resources in countries throughout SSA, together with (and not as a substitute for) market-based incentives. The effectiveness and enforceability of water laws and regulations depend to a great extent on not only the adequacy of the scope and content of such laws/regulations but also on the soundness, reliability, competence, transparency, and accountability of the relevant institutions.

Effective regulations are the key to effective enforcement, and without standards, a responsible agency is unable to determine and identify the quantity and quality of compliance. Without technically capable institutions operating within clearly delineated laws and a transparent system of checks and balances, adequately drafted laws and regulations would not be enforceable. Challenges that need to be overcome include combating the technical, financial, and political considerations that militate against the formulation and/or rigorous enforcement of effective environmental standards (safe drinking water and clean water).

Strategic actions to be considered include:

Formulating water laws that reflect realistic country goals and social, economic, cultural, political, and technical conditions through:

- defining and allocating land and water resources property rights, based on prevailing co-existing legal systems, interests, and demands;
- defining the use, exploitation, allocation, and management of water resources;
- reconciling co-existing and conflicting laws, particularly statutory/common laws and customary law;
- establishing regional/ international environmental standards and subsidiary legislation (regulations) setting standards for water quality and safe drinking water;
- waiving the right of state immunity from suits, e.g., when government is a polluter.

Enforcing adequately drafted and enacted laws/regulations through:

- defining responsibilities of relevant institutions, separating regulator and service provider functions;
- formulating and implementing an effective system of checks and balances, particularly separation of powers of government (executive, legislative, judicial arm), and mobilizing public and media participation to ensure transparency and accountability;
- promoting environmental awareness, training, and education of the public, the media, lawyers, and judges;
- utilizing not only the stick of regulation but also the carrot of market-based incentives to induce compliance;
- enhancing the technical and financial capacity of relevant institutions to establish and monitor relevant environmental standards;
- establishing effective inter- and intra-state domestic water dispute resolution mechanisms.

Regulatory Functions

Strategy: Promote an effective enabling environment: ensure effective regulation

An important strategy is to promote separation of the regulatory ('gamekeeper') functions from the supply ('poacher') functions of water supply and wastewater collection and delivery in order to avoid conflicts of interest and ensure compliance. For regulation to be fully successful, good governance is important as are experienced and accountable public sector staff.

Separating regulation from supply is a first rule of water resources management. In SSA countries, many agencies are involved in water integration and management with both supply and regulatory functions. However, there is no 'correct' solution for the institutional framework for effective water resources management; solutions evolve in an adaptive way in response to constitutional and cultural settings and to clear policy objectives and political commitment to policy enforcement. It must also be stressed that most industrialized nations continue to have many tensions within their water resources management institutional framework, and many are in a dynamic process of radical change. Institutional development and reform are a long 'journey' which is generally embarked upon without clear knowledge of the eventual destination. Nevertheless, the separation of regulation functions from those of supply is an important principle. Some countries make water resources management the responsibility of an agriculture ministry, or they have a water ministry also responsible for municipal water supply and wastewater services; both preclude effective water resources management.

Strategic actions to be considered include:

Promoting the clear definition of the objectives of regulation, which could include all or some of the following:

- protecting water resources from over-exploitation, through issuing abstraction licenses, with license fees signaling the value of water;
- protecting water resources from pollution, through setting water quality standards and issuing discharge licenses, with fees signaling potential environmental risk;
- regulating prices, through setting tariff guidelines and reviewing tariffs;
- protecting and informing the public, through consumers' representation and consultation and public awareness programs;
- establishing national policies including: water allocation between uses/users; standards; legal framework; and policy goals (such as universal access to services and/or economically efficient allocation);
- strategic planning, through the assessment of water quantity and quality and developing national plans for water management;
- ensuring inter-sectoral coordination on water, linking the health, agriculture, energy, infrastructure, and industry sectors;
- maintaining international relations and negotiations on riparian water rights, management of transboundary waters, and cross-boundary water transfers.

Meeting these objectives within an organizational framework covering the following functions:

- *Policy and planning*: draft legislation and standards; establish policies; determine sector strategies; prepare strategic plans; undertake coordination functions; and manage international relations.
- *Regulation*: financial regulation (tariff review and audit); environmental regulation (licensing/ monitoring of abstraction quantity; licensing/ monitoring of discharge and quality); and enforcement.
- *Hydrological assessment*: mapping and monitoring, hydrometric data archiving; and analysis and modeling.
- *Public information*: dissemination of water data; public education and awareness; and public consultation.
- *Research and development.*

Allocation Strategies, Prices, and Incentives

Strategy: Promote an enabling environment: adopt appropriate allocation strategies

Economic instruments which serve to allocate water among users are complementary to laws and regulations and are a key element of the enabling environment for sustainable water resources management. Specific allocation strategies, based on the assessment of water resources and demands, must be developed, which will then determine appropriate pricing and incentive structures.

As water is an economic, social, and environmental good, allocation strategies must balance these objectives: (a) water is a good which needs to be allocated efficiently and whose price should increase with scarcity; and (b) water is fundamental to human life and culture and should be equally available to all people—individuals have inalienable rights to water for survival. These apparently opposing objectives require clear political choices. The balancing of these objectives allows for water allocation in a *market-oriented,* as opposed to a pure market, fashion. Cost-recovery can be consistent with equity if countries establish progressive, tiered pricing schemes with increased prices for increasing water consumption. In SSA countries, price discrimination can allow those with less ability to pay to continue to receive services while ensuring that wealthier users are not subsidized by the state.

Strategic actions to be considered include:

Seeking to ensure economic efficiency through:

- pricing water to reflect the opportunity cost of providing it;
- using volumetric monitoring to establish appropriate pricing and induce efficient use;
- progressively lowering and ending subsidies to water for low value uses, which may sometimes be the case for agriculture and irrigation;
- operating water utilities, whether public or private, in an efficient and competitive manner -- use prices and tariffs that recover operation and maintenance costs, at least partially make up opportunity costs, and over time, recover investment costs;
- establishing water markets for water trading with tradable water rights.

At the same time ensuring that equity concerns are reflected through:

- recognizing that the demand for subsistence levels of water by the poor is quite inelastic and, therefore, cost-recovery pricing will place a higher burden on them than on the wealthy;
- preventing the cutting of water services to the poor in the name of efficiency and considering lifeline tariffs if necessary;
- identifying and supporting traditional water uses (e.g., to grow certain crops) outside of the 'use-value' framework;
- allowing for the conservation of important natural areas; where, again, value is not determined through 'use' and normal markets.

Adopting demand management as a principle through:

- ending subsidies to water service providers;
- basing development of new works on demonstrated consumer willingness-to-pay;
- not using gross targets (e.g., like those of the IDWSSD); rather, identifying which communities are ready for and want new development.

Water Resources Information: Monitoring and Assessment

Strategy: Promote an enabling environment: sustain hydrological information systems

Water information, both historic and current, is essential for water resource management and for the planning and implementation of water resource projects. Hydrometric networks and information services are needed to underpin the formulation of policies, regulations, public investment plans, public and private sector activities, environmental management, and the management of international water resources.

In SSA, hydrological monitoring and assessment are an undervalued but essential activity, and high priority needs to be given to improving water resources information systems. Improved hydrological services will provide crucial information to planners in African countries, linking water resources and their related natural processes and human development. Well conceived and targeted monitoring of freshwater resources can ensure more efficient use of scarce resources through improved decision making. It can provide the necessary information for priority setting, planning, and impact evaluation, enabling corrective action to be taken. It is important not to consider water data in isolation. Socio-economic activities impacting on water quality, institutional and legal settings, surrounding ecosystems, climatological and geomorphological conditions, land use practices, etc., all have to be considered. Water information services have to work along a broad range of parameters, measuring frequencies, monitoring locations etc., to meet the needs of the different users. However, data collection for its own sake is of no value, and the first requirement for a successful monitoring and assessment program is to define its purpose.

Strategic actions to be considered include:

- Stimulating interest in and commitment to monitoring and assessment among politicians, government agencies, public and private water users, local municipalities, private organizations, and external assistance agencies.
- Rehabilitating and strengthening hydrological networks and water information services linked to the development of national water resources management strategies, which will provide the motivation for enhanced services.
- Upgrading national hydrological institutions, including developing manpower at professional and technical levels.
- Promoting development of regional water resource information systems, in support of equitable use of shared water resources and the creation and administration of international water treaty protocols.
- Investigating the reinforcement of conventional hydrological monitoring networks with regional telemetric systems, where appropriate, to give real-time data where needed and to enhance international partnership in hydrological information.
- Establishing protocols, standards, and guidelines for water data at the national and international levels for river basins and sub-catchments.
- Arranging combined sub-regional workshops and training courses on water resources management which include discussion of hydrological services and inviting principal decision makers, information users, and other stakeholders.

Coping with Drought

Strategy: Promote an enabling environment: institutionalize coping strategies for drought

The recurring long-term droughts of the 1970s, 1980s, and the recent severe drought across Southern Africa make 'drought proofing' a particular objective of the enabling environment in many countries of the region. Strategies for coping with drought need to be developed, institutionalized, implemented, and continuously refined in society-wide efforts to mitigate the consequences of unpredictable, but certain, occasional drought.

Drought is a recurrent phenomenon which will continue to threaten social and economic development in the region. A pro-active, rather than reflexive, approach to drought management is already being adopted by some countries. This includes the assessment of potential for drought and estimation of duration and severity, as well as the definition of policies and strategies for action to be taken both before and during drought. Public participation in water management and conservation must become a central strategy for coping with drought. In addition, regional cooperation and collaboration in monitoring and data-sharing can make an important contribution to drought prediction and management.

***Strategic actions to be considered include*:**

- Formulating a system of pre-established national and regional water use priorities, identifying both normal use patterns and emergency allocation procedures.
- Establishing a permanent, but regularly revised, national level drought management plan (with appropriate legislation), following widespread user and public consultation.
- Operating a committed hydrometric monitoring system, covering key resources and storage facilities, e.g., precipitation, ground water levels, streamflow, reservoirs.
- Promoting regional co-operation in monitoring, and possibly in linked emergency action plans.
- Establishing priorities for drawdown of available water sources, and financing and maintaining emergency water supply units, including mobile tankers and well drilling teams.
- Developing agriculture and livestock programs to respond to specific water shortages, including:
  - herd-warning, moving, and relocation plans;
  - drought insurance, fodder emergency plans, and stocks;
  - food-for-work programs to cope during drought;
  - diversification of agricultural crops to favor water efficient varieties.
- Improving the efficiency of municipal supplies, promoting conservation through demand management and loss reduction, and developing individual drought plans.
- Building public awareness of societal strategies for drought-proofing, including soil and water management, and recognizing the importance of promoting traditional coping strategies (e.g., the sand rivers of Botswana).

E. SECTORAL STRATEGIES: KEY ELEMENTS

This section summarizes the key elements of the strategies for the major water-related sectors, especially as they relate to the overall goal of sustainable water resources management. It is not the purpose to give a comprehensive statement of sector strategies as each country will focus only on certain key elements reflecting its prevailing conditions, needs, and priorities. However, it is imperative that effective coordination take place among the key sectors dealing with water resources.

Rural Water Supply and Sanitation

Strategy: Extend rural water and sanitation services sustainably

The key strategy for rural water and sanitation development is to promote a fundamental change in the role of central and local government, from being direct providers of services to becoming promoters of service provision, equipping local organizations to implement and manage schemes. In addition, beneficiaries must shoulder costs, at least of operation and maintenance, if services are to be sustained.

The Abidjan Rural Water Supply and Sanitation Workshop (1990) recommended strategies for sector development which are proving relevant and durable, as different countries adapt the strategies to their own circumstances in the development of national sector policies. This section draws heavily on the Abidjan findings, which have the legitimacy of being developed and endorsed by representatives of the governments of forty-five African countries.

While the urban and the rural water and sanitation sub-sectors are generally regarded to be very different and are therefore treated differently, there are marked interdependencies, as rural areas are collectors of water for urban supplies and receivers of urban wastewaters, justifying integrated planing and financing. Similarly, RWSS planning needs to be integrated into broader rural infrastructure development, recognizing the important role of local government in demand assessment and local planning and priority setting. Thus, while the sub-sectors are described separately here, the synergies that can greatly facilitate sector development are also emphasized.

Strategic actions to be considered include:

Promoting a shift in the role of government from provider to promoter through:

- creating appropriate enabling environment; mobilization of finance; appropriate policies and legislation; donor coordination;
- building management capacity of local government, NGOs and communities;
- supporting the formal and informal private sector through appropriate training, incentives and market conditions, focusing on local artisans and on privatization of drilling and other works;
- emphasizing promotional activities such as health education and community development and training.

Promoting progressive adoption of greater cost recovery, linked to effective demand, through:

- beneficiaries assuming all of the recurrent costs of operation and maintenance;
- subsidizing capital costs only to ensure widespread provision of basic service to the very poor, recovering full capital costs of incremental improvements to service levels;
- promoting user charges by permitting funds management by communities themselves and by linking income generating activities;
- reducing unit costs by promoting a choice of technology options and increasing efficiency in public and private institutions;
- exploring new financing sources, including mutual credit unions and private banks.

Improving sector management through:

- developing national sector policy and regulatory frameworks, within which external assistance must be coordinated;
- building national professional and technical capacity in public, private, and NGO sectors;
- channeling financial support directly to local level, encouraging direct contracts for the delivery of goods and services.

Urban Water Supply and Sanitation

Strategy: Meet the rapidly growing demand for urban water supply and sanitation services sustainably

Strategies to address and overcome the unprecedented urban water supply and sanitation challenge include: financial autonomy of utilities; recovery of costs; enhancing efficiency through greater use of the private sector; demand management; innovative institutional arrangements in peri-urban areas; and promoting a range of technical choices and financing options, reflected in different service levels.

The rate of urbanization, the scale of the urban water and sanitation gap, and the generally weak economic performance in SSA set an unprecedented challenge. Cities in African countries are relatively low volume users of high quality, high cost water and producers of equal volumes of wastewater. Meeting the needs for rapidly growing volumes of potable supplies is itself compromised by the wastes (liquid and solid) that the city produces, often resulting in rapidly rising marginal costs of supply. The range of urban water supply and sanitation issues relevant to management of water resources is enormous, incorporating public health and environmental aspects; infrastructure development; social and cultural concerns; and questions of governance, such as the legal and institutional framework.

Strategic actions to be considered include:

Promoting urban water supply and sanitation policies that integrate into national water resources management strategies, including:

- separating the roles of regulator and supplier, allowing effective regulation of urban water and wastewater services;
- defining clear institutional framework, covering excreta and wastewater services;
- conserving water through demand management and reduction of unaccounted-for-water, using incentives and sanctions;
- controlling pollution from solid waste, wastewater, and stormwater with discharge regulation, sanctions, and incentives;
- seeking innovative solutions, such as wastewater reuse, solid waste recycling, etc., to conserve and protect water resources (recognizing cross-sectoral linkages - e.g. with agriculture);
- promoting public participation through consultation and representation;
- using market instruments for allocation and protection and seeking full cost recovery, ensuring 'lifeline' solutions for the poor.

Improving the performance of water and wastewater utilities through:

- ensuring financial and political autonomy, allowing commercialization;
- considering, where appropriate, options for private sector participation to increase efficiency and raise capital;
- employing performance indicators, using them as comparators between utilities to set incentives for efficiency gains.

Identifying alternative - possible interim - solutions for settlement, including:

- using a range of technical options, particularly for sanitation, at different prices, reflecting demand and service level choices to be made by consumers;
- promoting the application of 'community management', where there is insufficient incentive for utilities to provide services;
- recognizing the very high costs of informal water vending and seeking more effective use of the informal and formal private sector in service delivery;
- marketing services and hygiene education.

Agriculture: Dryland and Irrigated

Strategy: Increase agricultural productivity and food production to meet growing demand

Agricultural production must increase by at least 4 percent annually to make African countries food secure. Sustainable production systems are closely associated with water and soil management in a land use framework. Water will continue to be a critical factor in food production in Africa. Agricultural growth must come from both rainfed and irrigated agriculture through intensification, improved technology, improved farming practices, the efficient use of water resources, and the restoration and maintenance of soil fertility.

Agricultural development is closely associated with economic growth, food security, poverty reduction, and environmental protection. Effective management and utilization of scarce water resources in both rainfed and irrigated agriculture are necessary for African countries to increase crop yields and food production and to reduce crop loss. Bringing in an additional 6 million hectares into irrigated agriculture could increase cereal and grain production by 25 million to 30 million metric tons annually. However, the use of water in agriculture, the single largest user of water, should become more efficient through proper pricing and conservation measures.

The strategic actions recommended for consideration here will be successful only in an enabling political and macroeconomic environment with sufficient budgetary commitment to agriculture, and appropriate pricing, marketing, land use, and trade policies to facilitate agricultural growth and food security.

Strategic actions to be considered include:

Promoting increased productivity (per unit of land and water) in rainfed agriculture by:

- improving moisture conservation and water harvesting in rainfed areas;
- supporting water and soil conservation (contour farming, minimum tillage and mulching, crop rotation and intercropping, vegetative and soil bunding, etc.);
- improving water management and supply for livestock;
- adopting improved technologies (improved and drought resistant varieties, fertilizers, husbandry practices) to increase yields;
- improving access to services, such as credit, marketing, extension, and rural roads;
- promoting agricultural research and extension services focusing on sustainable production systems, water conservation technologies, and soil fertility;
- supporting an integrated, participatory approach to natural resource management and watershed protection.

Expanding irrigated areas and improving efficiency of water use in irrigated farming by:

- expanding irrigated areas through small and medium-scale irrigation;
- increasing water use efficiency in existing irrigation schemes;
- ensuring that water legislation addresses water rights, customary practices, security of land tenure, water pricing, and organization of water users associations;
- supporting use of irrigated water for higher value products;
- increasing productivity in irrigated areas through improved technology and farm management practices;
- improving maintenance of existing irrigation infrastructure and reducing irrigation development costs;
- promoting private irrigation and stakeholder participation in small-holder irrigation schemes;
- establishing adequate levels of water charges and improving cost recovery;
- strengthening irrigation institutions at national, regional, and local levels.

Establishing drought proofing of management strategies by:

- establishing drought monitoring, forecasting, policies and action plan;
- using stress tolerant production systems.

Power

Strategy: Key water-related elements of a power sector strategy

There are substantial opportunities to develop the under-utilized hydropower potential of the region, but the investment costs are high and many of the basins are transboundary. Hydropower is not a consumptive water user, but its operations require reliable flows which are often affected by upstream use. The key strategy is to seek international consortia approaches to developing basin hydropower potential and to ensuring appropriate flow regulation.

The combined energy resource endowment in the region is substantial with considerable hydropower potential, coal and uranium deposits, and large crude oil reserves. Only 0.1 percent of the hydropower potential is exploited; the cost of harnessing the untapped potential is high, with notable exceptions such as hydropower in Zaire and Guinea, which call for large-scale projects which could exceed the absorptive capacity of the country. Coal-fired thermal energy production, which is the main (95 percent) source of energy in the region, is a consumptive user of water for cooling, also requiring a reliable supply of water.

Strategic actions to be considered include:

- Promoting sound sector policies, including transparent regulation, commercialization and corporatization, imports of services, commitment to reform, and private investment, seeking to promote demand-side and supply-side efficiency and the use of cleaner energy sources and technologies.
- Investigating the potential for international development of hydropower on transboundary rivers, providing economies of scale, markets, and investment potential needed; capacity building among co-riparians may be a pre-requisite, as may be upgrading of hydrological monitoring and river basin management.
- Examining cross-sectoral impacts of hydropower schemes and encouraging comprehensive water resources management and watershed protection.
- Investigating the relative merits of hydropower and coal-fired energy, taking account of environmental issues such as the non-consumptive water use of the first and the consumptive use of the second.

Environmental and other in-stream needs

Strategy: Mainstream the environment into water resources management

The strategy is to recognize the environment as not just another consumptive user of water, but the water resource itself, and that degrading the quantity and quality of water in rivers, lakes, wetlands, and aquifers can inextricably alter the water resources system and its associated biota, affecting present and future generations. Development decisions must recognize the trade-offs.

Elements of many of the strategies set out here include explicit and implicit environmental objectives, and it is not the intention to repeat them here. It is, however, important to emphasize that water resources management is one central element of environmental management.

Strategic actions to be considered include:

Promoting mainstreaming of environmental aspects into overall water development and planning as a demand driven process based on local participation through:

- promoting tighter integration of environmental impact assessment and mitigation plans and national environmental action plans into project design, budgeting, and implementation;
- monitoring and evaluating of WRM projects with potentially significant environmental impacts to capture lessons;
- incorporating relevant aspects of environmental policies into water programs;
- instituting new measures, such as artificial floods, to restore damaged ecosystems or to protect vulnerable ones, e.g., wetlands;
- integrating environmental concerns into transboundary basin conventions and promoting international environmental action.

F. A STRATEGY FOR REGIONAL COOPERATION

Regional cooperation is the best strategy for raising net benefits within international river basins in sub-Saharan Africa. At first glance, this actually complicates the job of balancing the multiple demands on water resources. In the typical unilateral approach, a sector competes with other sectors *within* the same country. Regional cooperation dictates that a sector must compete with other sectors *in all the countries in the river basin*. As complex as this may seem, it is the only approach for sustainability. Africans can look to their achievements in basin planning, data exchange, and use of RBOs to suggest strategies for an unprecedented level of co-basin state cooperation, leading to 'win-win' situations for water management.

A Basin-Wide Approach

Strategy: Promote regional cooperation: adopt a systemic or basin-wide approach

Sustainable water resources management mandates a basin-wide approach to planning and action. This requires co-basin states to adopt strategies involving varying degrees of co-operation, from coordinated behavior (e.g., harmonized legislation, exchange of data), to actual joint action (e.g., multi-lateral investment and implementation of projects). The result will be a more efficient use, on the whole, of basin waters that benefits all basin states.

Many countries in Africa depend on water from outside their political boundaries. There are competing local and national interests over water rights and allocations. Although it might be easier, politically, to base river basin management on the notion of single, sovereign nation-states, the physical reality is that hydrological boundaries often do not coincide with political boundaries; therefore, basin-wide analysis and planning are essential for sustainability. Questions concerning the use of shared water resources, distribution of benefits, and responsibility of costs associated with protecting catchment areas and pollution control are highly complex. To this end, policymakers must understand the connections between catchments, control systems, hydraulic problems, and human land use practices. Underlying the policies of co-basin states, both unilaterally and collectively, must be an ecological approach that emphasizes conservation of natural riparian functions, intensified (i.e., *not* expanded) land use, and adaptation to existing social systems.

Strategic actions to be considered include:

- On a national basis, determining the size of populations within shared basins, their growth rates, migration trends, and needs for the shared water resource; then formulating clear and feasible plans for agriculture and forestry, industry, rural and urban water supply and sanitation, health improvement, and environmental conservation.
- Exchanging the information generated in the action above between co-riparians.
- Promoting harmonization of water use regulations in the shorter term, to allow for an equitable apportionment of shared waters on a basin-wide basis.
- Investigating opportunities for multilateral action for river development to achieve economies of scale over the longer-term and on a basin-wide basis; (e.g., hydropower projects for region-wide power grids), with the caveat that capacity must first exist within each partner state.
- Identifying and adapting/replicating successful co-riparian experiences (e.g. the 1995 SADC Protocol on Shared Water Courses, and the GEF-sponsored projects for cooperative biodiversity protection on Lakes Tanganyika and Malawi/Nyasa).

Facilitating Exchange

***Strategy:* Promote regional co-operation: facilitate exchange between riparians**

For cooperation to occur, co-basin states must meet on a 'level playing field' within a climate of trust. The pre-requisites to such efforts, however, are that each basin state has internal political stability and that national leaders have demonstrated political commitment to shared river basin issues.

Nations can engender trust and achieve a level field by sharing information. Capacity building steps exist that can facilitate this information exchange. As capacity building activities progress and trust is reached, co-basin states will be able to make agreements, coordinate water use activities, and even act cooperatively on joint projects.

Strategic actions to be considered include:

- Promoting regional cooperation in hydrological services and data collection, and in training of water technicians, engineers, and economists (e.g., following up on the SSA Hydrological Assessment and replication of the Southern Africa FRIEND project).
- Promoting exchange and confidence-building through workshops and conferences, targeted training (e.g. in negotiation skills) and information-sharing networks throughout basins.
- Promoting establishment of dispute resolution bodies and mechanisms and adherence to the equitable use principle of international law.

River Basin Organizations (RBOs)

***Strategy:* Promote regional cooperation: develop/strengthen river basin organizations**

Depending on the capacity of co-basin states, RBOs are part of the near- or long-term solutions to cooperative basin management. Organizational theory and empirical evidence from existing African RBOs show that when these bodies are carefully designed, with modest and clear mandates, they can serve the needs of all basin states and foster sustainable use of water resources.

RBOs are not a panacea for transboundary water management, as no country will cede control over its vital water resources to a supranational authority. In the case of SSA, RBOs can emerge as vehicles by which co-basin states can express and implement their collective will. Lessons of the past show that, *as organizations,* international RBOs have certain comparative advantages over national agencies. If RBOs are well-designed by African countries, they can create 'win-win' situations, implementing projects that no basin state would undertake unilaterally but that would benefit all basin states in the aggregate.

Strategic actions to be considered include:

- Promoting consensus within each basin state that transboundary water problems truly are urgent and that an international RBO would be part of the solution.
- Promoting identification by each nation of the functions where an RBO would have comparative advantage, such as standardized data collection and processing, independent monitoring (to ensure equitable use, pollution control, and environmental protection), or dispute arbitration between co-riparians.
- Undertaking organizational design or redesign of the RBO and national agencies to develop satisfactory institutional interfaces, thereby ensuring efficient human and financial resource allocation and maintaining the motivation of the national agencies.

G. Financing The Strategies For Water Resources Management

Strategy: Finance the strategies for water resources management

Implementing the strategies for effective water resources management, some of which have been described previously, will have substantial short-run costs, which, although offset by long-run benefits, will need to be financed through a range of instruments, some of which will be innovative.

The ability to meet those costs will require commitment and innovative financing arrangements by governments, donors, and society at large. The specific interventions proposed previously have been suggested within the locus of African nations or groups of nations. If this strategy is followed by African nations, then the World Bank, as a major donor, will need to tailor its actions to facilitate African priorities. In other words, the Bank requires a strategy as well, which internalizes African needs and aspirations. The next chapter describes how the Bank can proceed, following a New Agenda in promotion of sustainable water resources management in SSA.

Strategic actions to be considered include:

Promoting domestic resource mobilization, wherever possible, as the key to sustainability, through:

- striving for cost recovery, while taking account of 'lifeline' tariffs for the poor;
- using price as an instrument for allocation, incorporating opportunity cost pricing of raw water resources to the extent possible, reflecting environmental value and scarcity; and marginal cost pricing of water supply services, reflecting rising infrastructure costs of meeting demand;
- ensuring that the 'polluter pays' through setting environmental charges for polluters;
- recovering water resources management costs - including environmental protection costs - through license fees;
- promoting the use of local saving and credit institutions and practices to finance household and farm water infrastructure.

Seeking to reduce costs where possible through:

- controlling new investments within sectors by emphasizing rehabilitation and demand management instead of supply expansion;
- maximizing net present value in investment selection between sectors;
- promoting a range of technology choices, including low-cost solutions that will provide basic but adequate service levels for the poor;
- adopting a policy of 'upstream' catchment protection rather than 'downstream' water treatment, taking account of the potential constraints that this may place on economic activity in areas of vulnerability to pollution.

Investigating supra-national financing opportunities where appropriate, including:

- regional financing of investments that improve water resources management or develop water resource infrastructure in transboundary basins;
- wider international financing (for example from the Global Environment Fund) for managing global commons, such as biodiversity in lakes;
- cost-sharing in the protection of watersheds and pollution clean-up.

5. *An Integrated, Multisectoral Approach to Water Resources Management in SSA: An Agenda for the World Bank*

The World Bank is an active partner in the development of water resources in SSA. It does this through policy dialogue, technical assistance, and investment support in the irrigation, water supply and sanitation, and hydropower sectors. The cumulative World Bank lending to these sectors is now approaching US$4.6 billion, supporting investments in over thirty countries. Overall, the World Bank's assistance has evolved in response to growing demands for increasingly scarce water resources by competing sectors, as well as the need for capacity building and infrastructure, reflecting the changing socioeconomic and environmental realities of African countries.

During the next ten years, the Bank's principal objective will be poverty reduction. To this end, the Bank will assist African countries to focus on both the supply and demand sides of water management, with increased emphasis on demand management. This means that the Bank will help African countries achieve some combination of efficient public sector interventions, market-oriented solutions, and popular participation as a critical element of its poverty reduction objective. The Bank will also help committed countries to move towards an integrated approach to water resources management involving major stakeholders, to promote private sector development, and toward a pricing system which reflects the scarcity value of water resources. Furthermore, the Bank will give more attention to the needs of peri-urban and rural areas, where most of the poor live. It will also help foster regional cooperation in managing international rivers. Capacity building, utilization, and retention – including policy changes, institutional strengthening, human resource development, and resource mobilization -- will be the cornerstone of Bank water sector operations in Sub-Saharan Africa.

A. BACKGROUND

Based on an assessment of 115 completed and 44 ongoing projects, World Bank operational support between FY61 and FY95 focused on infrastructure development (irrigation systems, water delivery systems for domestic use, and power plants) and technical assistance. As shown in Figure 5.1, (US$ billions) the Bank has directed a high proportion of total lending to the water supply and sanitation sector. The results of the completed projects were broadly positive as 65 percent of the operations succeeded in providing the needed physical infrastructure. Since FY86, projects in SSA have been shifting from providing new infrastructure to institutional strengthening, human resource development, and the rehabilitation and expansion of existing facilities. In more recent years, projects are beginning to respond to new challenges: an integrated approach to water management, private sector development, environmental considerations, and stakeholder participation.

Key Lessons Learned

World Bank-supported operations have helped African countries achieve several sectoral objectives, such as providing safe water and sanitation services to many households—both in urban and rural areas—expanding irrigated areas to augment food production, and increasing energy supply through hydropower development. Some progress is also being made in several other ways, including beneficiary participation, private sector development, and environmental assessment. However, there has been less

Figure 5.1 World Bank Cumulative Lending, FY 61-95

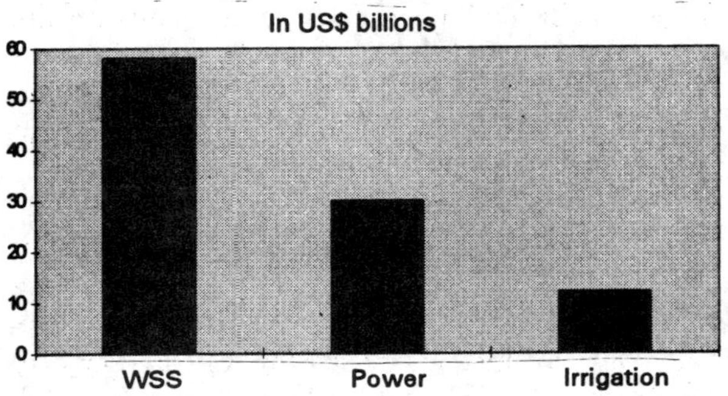

progress in (a) sustainable management of the water sector based on an integrated, multisectoral approach which rationalizes water use among various competing sectors; (b) capacity building, legal and regulatory framework; (c) integration of health concerns in project design and components; (d) cost recovery through the sensible pricing of water services; (e) technology development to improve use efficiency and reduce cost of water supply; and, (f) data and information systems. Based on lessons learned, the World Bank will emphasize the following:

Place More Emphasis on Rural and Peri-Urban Areas Where Most of the Poor Live. A strong slant is evident in the Bank's investment pattern in SSA, with 83 percent of the combined investments of completed projects in the water supply and sanitation sub-sector directed to urban areas, which account for about 30 percent of the region's total population. This strong urban focus continues for on-going projects, with over 80 percent of the water supply and sanitation projects directed to the urban population. In addition, a recent Bank study showed that since 1975, 20 percent (or US$ 494 million) of total Bank commitment in rural infrastructure in SSA supported rural water supply and sanitation investments (RWSS). The lending during the International Drinking Water Supply and Sanitation Decade of the 1980s amounted to only US$ 640 million in current dollars, providing coverage to some 60 million people.

In terms of coverage, by 1990 only 30 percent of the rural population had access to clean drinking water and 25 percent to adequate sanitation. Under existing trends, by 2020 about 250 million people in rural areas could be without adequate water supply and 350 million without sanitation services. Therefore, the Bank needs to pay more attention to the needs of the rural areas. Peri-urban areas are also important and require attention. These areas will continue to grow attracting significant numbers of people from rural areas. Generally, there is little or no water and sanitation facilities in peri-urban areas which are increasingly becoming breeding grounds for diseases.

Focus on Local Capacity. African countries need to use existing capacity and indigenous institutions, as well as to build capacity. Once established, local capacity must be retained. African countries have limited capacity to implement comprehensive water resources management programs. Results in the field show that inadequate capacity often undermines the sustainability of externally funded operations as donor support terminates. Capacity building components under Bank financed projects have tended to emphasize training, technical assistance, equipment, and organizational restructuring. However, the scope of capacity building activities must expand and go beyond the water sector to tackle issues related to good governance, strategic choices and planning, a conducive institutional environment, and incentives. Capacity building components need to emphasize the use of existing capacity, human resource development through training, information management, decentralization and stakeholder involvement, sound financial management, and policies and legislation.

In general, capacity building and utilization will focus on local institutions, traditional practices, values, skills, and knowledge, especially at the grassroots level. Often, responsibility for project preparation and implementation has rested with government agencies and technical assistance provided under the projects. While, in some instances, this technical assistance has helped, past lessons show that dependence on long-term expatriate technical assistance should be replaced with local consultancies and African expertise with support from short-term foreign professionals.

Emphasize Water as a Scarce Good with Economic Value. African experiences indicate that most countries have approached water management and allocation issues primarily as administrative and coordination problems for public sector entities rather than problems of efficiently allocating water and prudently investing in water development in ways that are ecologically sound and socially desirable. This approach has contributed to high costs and high subsidy levels for those having access to services as well as low cost recovery (prices are often less than half the cost, which does not reflect the environmental or opportunity cost of access).

In SSA countries, water prices are generally established by the public sector. The bases of these prices are an unclear combination of social choices — encouragement to preferred priority uses defined by government and judgments about affordability of the prices. The net effects are large subsides through the price level and structure of prices for different user groups. Often, these subsidies do not go to low-income populations. It is imperative that these distortions be addressed through economic instruments and incentive systems (pricing, property rights, etc.) and regulations, as appropriate. African countries need to increase cost recovery from various user groups through the appropriate pricing of water supply for various uses. This is because supply costs and the financial sustainability of key agencies become more critical issues as demand for scarce water resources increases.

Promote Regional Cooperation. Lessons learned from completed water projects and on-going operations indicate that transboundary issues and potential conflicts among riparian states need special attention in order to deal with issues such as water allocation, control of water pollution, and protection of catchment areas. These lessons also show that mechanisms (institutional and legal) to resolve and prevent conflicts are needed along with lending instruments to facilitate multi-country investment programs.

Implications for Future Operations

Future operations must build on best practices (in policy adoption, regulatory framework, use of indigenous practices, community participation, local capacity building, investment programs) and actions which have generated good results on the ground (see examples in Chapter 3). A number of World Bank-financed projects already show positive approaches and results, as shown in Annex A.

At the same time, the lessons learned from field experiences imply that more needs to be done in assisting African countries to link operations in the water sector to (a) poverty reduction; (b) stakeholder participation (involvement of beneficiaries, local communities, NGOs); (c) private sector involvement (delivery of public services); and (d) institutional reforms (managerial, financial, operational, incentives, flow of information, accountability, decentralization, etc.). Also, more needs to be done to incorporate health concerns in development projects and take into account the international dimension of water resources use. Furthermore, completed projects show the need to include social and environmental considerations in project design and implementation.

Drawing from past experience and best practices, the following key principles will guide World Bank interventions.

Key Principles

- Promote a systemic approach as a long-term objective for the integrated management of water resources, reflecting cross-sectoral, ecological, and multi-riparian considerations.

- Support an appropriate legal and regulatory framework and appropriate institutional structure at the national, regional, and local levels.

- Enhance policies and demand management principles that treat water as an economic good (or scarce resource) while meeting economic growth, environmental, and equity concerns.

- Foster a participatory and consultative approach that involves all the stakeholders (women, communities, NGOs, the public and private sectors) to promote economic growth, food security, and poverty reduction.

- Encourage the management of international waters (through local and national actions and regional cooperation), including their protection and development and strengthening of international river basin organizations.

- Build the water environment, emphasizing both pollution control and the meeting of environmental water demands.

- Support decentralization of functions to the grassroots level, with responsibilities vested in local government and service delivery functions in autonomous private, public, or community institutions.

New Projects: The Evolving Response

The current program consists of forty-four free-standing projects approved between FY87 and FY95. A number of these projects have incorporated lessons from private sector development, beneficiary participation, resettlement, and institutional strengthening. In these projects technical assistance is employed selectively (e.g., establishing computerized systems, developing public relations and education programs, identifying roles for private sector participation, etc.). In several countries (Senegal, Guinea, Malawi, Zambia), measures are being taken to ensure pricing for water services and electricity through tariffs and user fees. As shown in Annex A, a number of innovative features are incorporated in new Bank lending activities.

The future pipeline (FY96-98, with a proposed lending of US$700 million) includes about twenty operations in the water sector. These operations continue to emphasize private sector involvement, beneficiaries participation, institutional strengthening, and human resources development. In a few cases, they propose broadening their scope to include international aspects of water use as well as highlighting the need for efficient water resources management. Incentives, such as pricing of water, are discussed in a few instances but are not yet fully part of future project objectives. About eleven additional operations in other sectors (such as agriculture, public health, nutrition, and infrastructure) include water components, supporting rural water supply, and irrigation schemes (at a total amount of about US$ 340 million). While water components support social objectives, their dispersion across several sectors requires coordination and cross-sectoral considerations in the framework of an integrated approach to water resources management. In this connection, special attention needs to be given to Social Funds Projects which support water resources activities in various sectors in order to ensure consistency in overall water assessment and management strategies.

B. PRIORITY AREAS FOR WORLD BANK SUPPORT

Long-Term Vision

The World Bank will continue assisting African countries in the rational and efficient use of water resources to meet basic human needs, food security, and economic development, while maintaining the integrity of aquatic ecosystems. To meet their social objectives—and to take advantage of successes and opportunities, as discussed in previous chapters—African countries will increasingly need to (a) manage and reconcile many concerns and interests at the local, national, and regional levels relating to water resources use; (b) treat water as a scarce good with economic value, thus requiring changes in people's attitudes and behavior; (c) address important choices and trade-offs in how water is used and managed, balancing between short-term gains and long-term benefits from conservation and the sustainable use of water resources; and (d) define the roles of the market, public sector, and people in the management of water resources in a way that takes into account economic, ecological, and equity considerations. The World Bank, in collaboration with other donor agencies, can assist African countries to tackle these challenges to benefit present and future generations.

High Priority Areas

In the context of its **overarching objective of poverty reduction** in assisting African countries, the World Bank will direct its efforts to five priority areas:

- Household water security: ensuring that a large number of rural and urban poor have access to clean water and sanitation services at affordable prices.
- Food security and water: supporting measures that lead to increased productivity and food production through using and conserving water efficiently, improving technology and farming practices, and providing small-scale irrigation.
- Water quality and human health: supporting actions (policies, regulation, investments, etc.) that reduce water pollution and degradation which threaten human health.
- Environmental stewardship: promoting programs that protect and rehabilitate important watersheds, wetlands, and drainage areas.
- Regional cooperation: promoting mechanisms for conflict resolution and prevention among countries sharing water resources, multinational investment programs for the development of water resources, including hydropower, pollution control, and protection of catchment areas.

By concentrating on these objectives, the Bank will move toward its goal of assisting its member governments in poverty reduction, economic growth, food security, and environmental protection. Further, the Bank's interventions will focus on both the supply and demand sides, especially as water becomes more scarce and extraction costs from new supply sources rise sharply. To this end, the Bank will give special attention to: (a) demand management measures which can change people's behavior. Such measures—including incentives, regulation, and education—can lead to a reallocation of existing supplies to higher-value uses, promote efficient use through conservation and water-saving technologies, and facilitate more equitable access; (b) measures to improve the supply or delivery of services and reduce costs by supporting modernization and the rehabilitation of existing infrastructure (including bulk infrastructure providing large storage and inter-basin transfer), improvement of management practices, reduction of supply costs, and efficiency of water delivery from existing supplies; and (c) domestic resource mobilization to generate capital for the maintenance of existing systems and expansion of infrastructure.

Country and Sectoral Focus: Need for Selectivity

There are many stakeholders involved in the water sector: local people, the private sector, and governments at the country level, as well as multilaterals, bilateral agencies, and national and international NGOs. Also, as noted earlier, many African countries are now facing more water scarcity, potential conflicts among riparian states over shared water, and rising supply costs of extracting water from new sources. African countries are confronting five critical threats:

i. Scarce water resources: inadequate access to clean water and sanitation services -- health risks, and rapidly increasing costs.

ii. Deteriorating water quality: increases water-borne or water related diseases and increases costs of supply.

iii. Droughts: decreases food production and increases food insecurity, and can threaten domestic water supply.

iv. Deforestation and land degradation: affects both water quantity (river flows and water tables) and quality.

v. Regional conflicts: lowers option for water use among riparian states.

While African countries must -- individually and collectively, depending on the river basins -- deal with these threats by involving the stakeholders, the international community must also help African countries accelerate the transition toward the sustainable management of water resources.

In this context, the World Bank should be very selective in its assistance and concentrate on its areas of comparative advantage: policy changes, capacity building and human resource development, investment operations that promote sustainable development and poverty reduction, and improvements in donor partnership and collaboration. The extent and effectiveness of Bank involvement and assistance in promoting sustainable water resources management at a national level will be a function of each country's long-term commitment to sustainable development.

Nevertheless, the operational implications of this concentration imply a country priority focus. The Bank will **focus selectively on countries** which display strong commitment and ownership and in which development impact can be maximized by supporting long-term national programs. Country performance indicators have been developed in Table 5.1. To determine the level and extent of Bank country focus, the following points are critical:

i. The extent of political stability, African ownership of development efforts, and commitment to sustainable water resources management existing in each country. Without this, Bank support for specific water sector activities will not generate results on the ground, nor be sustainable. If conditions are unfavorable, Bank support and diplomacy will instead be used to establish the basic conditions needed for good governance and socio-economic development.

ii. The extent to which an enabling environment exists. This consists of transparent and accountable governance in the water sector, clear legislation and policy, strategies and investment programs, stakeholder participation, and the capacity for water resources management at all levels. These are fundamental to the success and sustainability of integrated water sector efforts.

iii. The extent to which information and knowledge exist. Data are needed to gauge water availability and quality, consumer demand, and sectoral needs (e.g., sanitation coverage, irrigation, hydropower). Knowledge is needed about the multiple cross-sectoral linkages relating to a nation's water development (e.g., competing demands for water from agriculture, industry, and municipalities; reliance upon international waters). Such information and knowledge are necessary as countries take the critical steps towards sustainable resource use.

With these points in mind, the information in Table 5.1 is very relevant. Columns 4-7 describe the enabling environment, while columns 1 and 2 are poverty indicators which are relevant to countries described in the context of any of the above three points. Columns 1, 2, and 3 can be seen as risk indicators, where problems will call for either more water or the more efficient management of existing stocks. Combining the three points with the information in the table, African nations can be placed in one of three **loosely defined groups,** each calling for different Bank interventions:

The first group of countries. These countries, described by point (i) above, lack political stability or visible commitment to comprehensive management and the sustainable use of water resources. This group includes Somalia, Sudan, Angola, Zaire, and Liberia. Despite the obvious need for improvements in capacity and human resources development in the water sector, investments will not be sustainable in countries lacking effective leadership and political stability. However, the Bank can effect change towards sustainable water management by including these nations within regional initiatives. Specifically, the Bank could help these countries by:

- Asking co-basin states to 'reserve a seat at the table' for the eventual participation of these countries in basin-wide efforts.
- Supporting water and hydrological assessment efforts which produce strategies and data useful for eventual project efforts.
- Supporting the training of nationals at regional capacity building centers.
- Promoting efforts of smaller groups and NGOs that are strong on advocacy and then developing constituency for good governance at the local levels.

The second group. As described in point (ii), these countries are emerging from periods of instability, undergoing political transformation toward a market economy, or have very low levels of capacity. The group includes, for example, Mozambique, Eritrea, Central African Republic, Congo, Chad, Guinea, Burundi, Rwanda, Zaire, The Gambia, and Sierra Leone. These countries must reach a capacity level at which more traditional Bank interventions will lead to sustained water sector improvements. In these cases, the Bank could design projects with the following components:

- Investment to improve water supply and sanitation services, as well as other investments supporting food production through the efficient use of water resources, protection of watersheds, and hydropower, as appropriate.

- Development of national water policy and strategy, legal and regulatory frameworks, and prioritized investment programs through the involvement of all stakeholders.

- Focus on capacity building at local, regional, and national levels, and human resource development.

- Implementation of economic policies for cost-recovery and equitable pricing of water services.

- Support for existing and indigenous institutions as a whole, and human resource development.

- Development of data and information systems, including the assessment of water resources.

The third group. These countries, described in point (iii), have already made some progress towards instituting a systemic approach to water resources management. Thus, the Bank can use the most targeted investments with this group of countries, which, for example, includes Tanzania, Ethiopia, Lesotho, Namibia, Swaziland, Zimbabwe, Uganda, Madagascar, Benin, Burkina Faso, Ghana, Niger, Togo, Guinea-Bissau, Mali, Mauritania, Kenya, and Senegal. Each of these nations requires investments for increased access to either safe drinking water or sanitation. The Bank could support actions that, for example, broaden and deepen policy reforms, legal and regulatory frameworks, capacity building, and private sector development. This support could be as follows:

- Support the integrated sector investments and national programs.

- Strengthen participation of local governments, the private sector, NGOs, and community organizations in water resources management.

- Promote the adoption of economic instruments and other demand management mechanisms.

- Improve sector management through an integrated, multisectoral approach and ensure wider integration in a river basin context.

- Strengthen data and information systems.

- Strengthen regulatory capacity, separating this from service functions of water supply and use.

Table 5.1: Sub-Saharan Africa: Country Indicators

	% Pop. with safe drink. water[1]	% Pop. with sanitation[2]	Irrigated area as % of potential[3]	Governance Environ-ment[4]	Capacity for resource management[5]	Status of water legislation[6]	Status of water plan/ policy[7]
Southern Africa							
Angola	Low	Low	Low	Low	Low	Available	Nonavailable
Botswana	High	High	Low	High	High	Available	Available
Lesotho	Medium	Low	Low	Medium	High	Available	Available
Malawi	Medium	High	Low	High	Medium	Available	Available
Mozambique	Low	Low	Low	Low		Available	Nonavailable
Namibia		Low		High		Available	Available
South Africa				High	Medium	Available	Available
Swaziland	Low	Medium	High	High		Available	Nonavailable
Zambia	Medium	Medium	Low	Medium		Available	Partial
Zimbabwe	Medium	Low	Medium	High	High	Available	Available
Eastern Africa							
Djibouti	Medium	Medium		Low	Low		
Eritrea				Medium			
Ethiopia	Low	Low	Low	Medium	Medium	Available	Available
Kenya	Medium	Medium	Low	Low	Medium	Available	Available
Somalia	Low	Low	High	Low	Low		
Sudan	Medium	Low	Medium	Low	Low		
Tanzania	Medium	High	Low	Medium	Low	Available	Available
Uganda	Low	Low	Low	Medium		Nonavailable	Available
Central Africa							
Burundi	Low	Medium	High	Low	Low		
Cameroon	Medium	Medium	Low	Low	Low	Available	Nonavailable
Central African Republic	Low	Medium	Low	Low	Low	Available	Nonavailable
Chad	Low		Low	Medium	Low		
Comoros	High			Low			
Congo	Low	Low	Low	Medium	Low		
Equatorial Guinea	Medium	Medium		Low	Low		
Gabon	High		Low	Medium	Medium	Available	Nonavailable
Madagascar	Low	Low	High	Medium	Low		
Mauritius	High	High		High	Medium		
Rwanda	Medium	Medium	Medium	Low	Low		
Seychelles	High			High			
Zaire	Medium	Low	Low	Low	Low		
West-Central Africa							
Benin	Medium	Low	Low	Medium	Medium	Available	Nonavailable
Burkina Faso	High	Low	Low	High	Medium	Available	Nonavailable
Cote d'Ivoire	High	High	Medium	Medium	Medium	Partial	Partial
Ghana	Medium	Low	Low	Medium	Medium	Available	Nonavailable
Niger	Medium	Low	Medium	Medium		Nonavailable	Nonavailable
Nigeria	Medium	Low	Medium	Low	Low	Nonavailable	Nonavailable
Togo	Medium	Low	Low	Low			
Western Africa							
Cape Verde	Medium	Low		Medium		Available	Available
Gambia	Medium	Medium	Medium	Low	Low	Available	Available
Guinea	Low	Medium	Medium	Low	Low	Nonavailable	Nonavailable
Guinea-Bissau	Low	Low		Medium		Available	Nonavailable
Liberia	Medium	Low		Low	Low		
Mali	Low	Low	Medium	Medium			
Mauritania	Medium	Low	Medium	Medium			
Sao Tome and Principe	Medium	Low		Low	Low		
Senegal	Medium	Medium	Medium	Medium		Partial	Partial
Sierra Leone	Low	Low	Medium	Low	Low		

Blank boxes indicate no data available. **Columns 1 and 2**: Low = 0-33%, Medium = 34-66%, High = 67-100%. **Column 3**: Low = 0-29%, Medium = 30 - 60%, High = 61 - 100%. **Column 4** based on political and social stability. **Column 5** based on efficiency of domestic resource mobilization and allocation. In **Column 6 and 7**, "partial" indicates draft bill/policy or obsolete laws.

Multiple Country Focus: Need for Regional Cooperation

River basin management and regional cooperation are vital if African nations are to meet their priority challenges for sustainable water resources management, and the Bank will support such efforts through its key strategic interventions. International river basins link the challenges of pollution, environmental degradation, and national water security across co-riparian countries. The externalities of uncoordinated basin management can increase localized poverty, negatively impact entire sectors of national economies (e.g., agriculture, energy, and industry), and even destabilize the political situation of an entire region.

The challenge of conflict prevention and international negotiation must be met by countries which are highly reliant upon international waters and which face the threat of water scarcity, pollution, and degradation of catchment areas. As discussed in Chapter 2, Mauritania, Botswana, The Gambia, Congo, Sudan, Niger, and Senegal have between 33 percent and 95 percent of total water flow originating outside their borders. Also, Guinea, Mozambique, Cameroon, Gabon, Namibia, South Africa, Tanzania, and Zimbabwe have five or more shared river basins.

The high prevalence of international rivers in SSA presents the Bank with a significant challenge: the promotion of an effective multi-country focus and regional cooperation. Just as countries will need to look towards their co-riparian neighbors, the Bank will need to take a basin-wide approach to development and support the following:

- Support individual countries and groups of countries in conducting water and demand assessment and sectoral planning to forecast future needs for shared waters, paying attention to longer term opportunities for 'win-win' investments, improving water resources for all riparian states in a basin.

- Support capacity building that moves information from water users and monitors at the local level to the policy-makers and negotiators at the national and international level.

- Focus on the Nile Basin in Eastern Africa, explore and promote cooperation among the riparian countries, and support investments for institution building and human resources development in a regional framework.

- Focus on the Southern African basins, particularly the Zambezi, Inkomati, and Pungwe, and explore ways to build Mozambique's capacity to put it on an even playing field with its neighbors; encourage South Africa to become a partner for reasonable and equitable use of shared waters in Southern Africa.

- Support effective river basin organizations (such as the Lesotho Highlands Development Authority and the Organisation pour la Mise en Valeur du Fleuve Senegal) by building the organizational and technical capacity of these RBOs.

- Further support GEF initiatives such as the multilateral efforts on Lake Victoria and Lake Malawi to support the rehabilitation of major watersheds (e.g., the highlands of Eastern and Western Africa), protection of wetlands (e.g., the Okavango Delta), and management of important river basins (e.g., the Congo and Niger Basins).

Focus on Priority Issues. Specifically, the World Bank will offer its priority support to potential crisis areas like the Nile Basin and Zambezi and Inkomati Basins in Southern Africa. Long-term, multisectoral planning should also proceed in the Congo, Niger, and Lake Chad, Senegal, and Volta Basins, as well as in the smaller river and lake basins that impact on development in neighboring countries. A number of straightforward interventions exist for the World Bank.

- Offer assistance to countries which have limited data collection or hydrological monitoring capacity, with the aim of helping nations become secure in their knowledge of their hydrological endowment (e.g., supporting implementation of the WMO/WB African Hydrological Cycle Observing

System; the UNESCO, West Africa and Southern Africa FRIEND Programs).

- Support countries through financial and technical assistance, seeking to make national water policies and strategies in harmony with those of co-basin states.

- Support training and research efforts through operations using the Economic Development Institute (e.g., education and training at the local, national, and regional levels).

Diplomacy. The World Bank will consider using its diplomatic strength to foster basin cooperation, for example in the Nile and Zambezi river basins, providing leadership, if requested by member countries. This would take the form of catalyzing effective communication among riparian countries and actions that would lead to the more efficient allocation of water rights in an equitable and ecologically acceptable manner and to the sustainable management of water resources. The Bank's Operational Directive 7.50 on international waters demands notification and agreement by potentially impacted states if the Bank is to support any national efforts which use transboundary rivers. Mediation may be necessary for such projects to proceed. Moreover, the Bank may consider that in the case of large, multi-country projects that take advantage of economies of scale, senior management may need to play a pro-active role as mediator or conciliator in facilitating joint action by multiple basin states.

Support Regional Institutions. River basin management will also require the Bank to move beyond its traditional support for single-country operations. Special operations will be needed to support multi-national initiatives that involve joint action by co-basin countries. An example already exists with the Global Environment Facility's (GEF) Lake Victoria Environmental Management Project which facilitates scientific and pollution management cooperation between Kenya, Tanzania, and Uganda. In this connection, the Bank will consider supporting effective RBOs (such as the Lesotho Highlands Development Authority and the Organisation pour la Mise en Valeur du Fleuve Senegal) created by basin states.

C. Capacity Building and Human Resource Development

Capacity building will cut across World Bank lending activities throughout the water sector. In the past, the majority of the Bank's, as well as other donors', capacity building efforts often lacked donor coordination, coherence, or results-orientation. Also, these efforts were not in line with country needs, and they often failed to utilize existing capacity effectively and lacked a focus on creating sustainable national institutions. Looking to the future, Bank-supported capacity building and utilization — either as a project component or as the primary aspect of a project itself -- will focus on existing capacity including indigenous institutions, good governance, an enabling environment, good policies, reliable institutions, and human capital. This also implies that the Bank will need to listen more attentively to African needs and facilitate the changes required, particularly in countries which display long-term political commitment to water development strategies.

In SSA countries, the Bank can assist by helping member countries to create an enabling environment, moving towards decentralized management and private sector participation. This effort will encourage countries to (a) address the incentives underlying current policies and institutional arrangements; (b) improve governance so that decision-makers act responsibly and are held accountable; (c) empower the stakeholders at the grassroots level to make decisions and assume responsibility; and (d) allow demand to drive service provision. Capacity is also required for enforcing regulation and providing information on water supply and demand and willingness to pay.

Specifically, the Bank's capacity building and utilization efforts in the water sector will start small, build on existing capacity, and be given the time they need to take hold. They will be rigorously selective on priority management functions and gauged by results on the ground in terms of improved sector performance. The creation of new institutions will occur only when absolutely necessary. Instead, the Bank will emphasize strengthening and using existing institutions and local practices, values, skills, and knowledge. Other vital components include support for on-going human resource development, information management and sharing, promotion of policy dialogue, and helping to link country professionals to each other and to professional and information resources elsewhere (e.g., increasing internet connectivity in SSA).

The Bank can also target those elements of capacity building and utilization that lend themselves to economies of scale—that is, common elements which may be developed at the Africa-wide or regional level, e.g., hardware and software for water management, training materials and programs that can be used without adaptation, and regional monitoring programs. Finally, the Bank may need to support, with limited funding, some capacity building activities 'up front' before sectoral projects begin. Such activities may be necessary for project sustainability and could include human resource development, improvements in physical conditions of institutions, and policy revision or formulation.

D. Policy and Regulatory Reforms

The reality of such reforms in the water sector is that Africans themselves will bear the largest burden. It is vital that reforms take place if water development programs are to succeed, as policy and regulations form part of the enabling environment that either exacerbates or ameliorates the priority challenges of household water security, food production, water pollution, environmental stewardship, and conflict resolution. However, the Bank can make strategic interventions which support this process.

The Bank can assist African countries to adopt policies that move increasingly toward market-oriented solutions and create incentives for the sustainable use of water resources. Markets and prices (the latter reflecting scarcity value of water resources) can, as markets develop in African countries, evolve as important coordinating mechanisms for the efficient allocation and use of water resources. A shift from a centralized command-and-control management of water resources to an economic approach to water utilization will require the Bank to assist African countries in (a) creating an institutional and legal framework to encourage market-oriented incentives; (b) establishing water markets for water trading with tradable water rights; (c) utilizing private sector incentives (through pricing, taxation, subsidies, regulations); and (d) economic pricing of water services. However, it is reasonable to assume that there will be public sector interventions to deal with equity and ecological considerations, safeguarding the interests of the poor as well as those of future generations.

The Bank can also assist African countries to develop implementable 'rules of the game' to manage water resources more efficiently. Regulatory mechanisms are required at all levels to implement and consistently enforce water policies. Mechanisms such as catchment boards and water users associations should encompass both surface water and ground water management. They need to accommodate, and reconcile when necessary, formal laws and traditional laws and practices, which increasingly compete as pressures on water increase. Enforcement should take place at the lowest levels by the people with the greatest stake in the outcome. When local informal mechanisms exist, they should be formalized to the extent possible, or at least recognized by the formal system.

Further, the Bank will need to design projects for national water policy, laws and regulations, and implementation. This will entail the promotion of inter-sectoral coordination at a high level and capacity building. Concomitant with new policies and regulations, countries will require administrative bodies and professionals to monitor and enforce actions at the local and national levels. Capacity building will be necessary for those institutions that monitor environmental standards. The Bank will also promote projects that reinforce coherent national policies, sensibly prioritizing and allocating water—between sectors and between users—through market and pricing mechanisms. Thus, projects will encourage appropriate water pricing and focus on water quality standards.

E. Mainstreaming Environmental And Social Considerations

The Bank will support the mainstreaming of environmental and social considerations in Africa's water sector. If economic and environmental guidelines are not used correctly, social costs could outweigh other benefits. The Bank, through its lending operations, will make these issues integral to African water resources management.

The Bank has a number of tools at its disposal. It will promote national water plans as outcomes of national environmental action plans (or similar environmental strategies). These water plans need to be integrated fully into the overall planning and programming of countries. The Bank can promote the tighter integration of environmental impact assessment and mitigation plans into project design, budgeting, and implementation. Similarly, it will support the widespread application of social impact and beneficiary assessments and promote the role of African national anthropologists and sociologists in project design. Economic methods for determining and incorporating environmental and social costs should be made a standard aspect of projects. Finally, the Bank will not shy away from challenging environmental projects that may not have an immediately high rate of return, such as wetlands restoration or artificial flood release.

The Bank can expand the role of the GEF in Africa's water resources management. Also, through training efforts of the EDI and other institutions (academia and centers of excellence), African professionals will acquire the ability to incorporate environmental impact assessments and economic analysis into their own project designs.

F. Cross-Cutting Themes

Information Systems and New Knowledge

A recurrent element in African water resources management is the need for the collection and dissemination of new data and knowledge that are demand driven. This is necessary at local, national, and regional levels. The World Bank has an important role to play in promoting the establishment of strong water information systems throughout Africa.

The Bank will support both projects that enhance the specific elements needed for hydrological monitoring and assessment as well as those that build broad institutional capacity to accomplish these functions. Projects to support at a country level include those concerned with upgrading of hydrological monitoring networks with new equipment and training of staff and the establishment of internationally accepted standards and guidelines for water data which can be used to determine the economic value of water resources. The Bank will also support regional workshops and training courses. At a broader level, the Bank will stimulate interest in and commitment to monitoring and assessment of water resources among politicians, government agencies, public and private water users, local municipalities and private organizations, and external assistance agencies. The Bank will also support the use of country specific hydrological monitoring systems. The matrices should indicate all the relevant project specifications and the status of priority and implementation. Their public dissemination, in English and French, will make the process transparent and will serve as a catalyst for implementation.

Drought

Drought is an important variable affecting the priority challenges in Africa, thereby impacting water resources management strategies for the World Bank. Drought decreases household water and food security and can lead to increased poverty, water pollution, and environmental degradation. It can also lead to crisis national policy measures that exacerbate a country's fiscal situation. Drought recovery requires budget allocations, and drought mitigation requires foreign exchange earnings to purchase imported food. Drought management is reliant upon a systemic approach to water and land management, market-oriented solutions, incentives, awareness, and regional cooperation. While no single approach to drought management is applicable to the entire continent, the World Bank and its African partners can no longer respond to drought as a random natural disaster. Rather, the contingencies for drought management will be integral to the World Bank's strategic interventions for the Sahel and Eastern and Southern Africa.

Specifically, the Bank will need to make long-term, multisectoral investments in the drought-prone countries of the Sahel and Eastern and Southern Africa. For a broad approach within countries, the Bank will, through investment projects, offer its financial and technical support, and institutional expertise, to countries formulating national drought policies and action plans. Along with policy support, water and agricultural sector programs should emphasize economic reforms that attach appropriate prices to water. Such demand management measures will lead to water conservation, ensuring more water reserves in the event of a drought crisis, together with standby capacity that can be drawn upon. Locally, the Bank will promote the adoption of stress-tolerant production systems. At both a country and regional level, the Bank will offer financial and technical support to climate monitoring efforts. The Bank will consider supporting the Hydrological Cycle Observing System (HYCOS), data collection and processing, and Early Warning Systems (EWS). This will require Bank support for active capacity building and utilization and stakeholder participation within countries. Moreover, the Bank needs to encourage cooperation between countries, both for climate monitoring and for emergency action plans. This necessitates Bank financing targeted at actions in perhaps multiple neighboring countries.

The Bank has already provided loans for projects that focus on these strategic interventions, including emergency recovery and drought area rehabilitation projects in Eritrea, Ethiopia, Zambia, and Zimbabwe. In Kenya, the Arid Lands Resource Management Project has drought management as a core component, aiming to establish an institutional structure for drought preparedness, mitigation, and recovery. This includes (a) creating institutional structures and the capacity to cope with drought at national, district, and community levels; (b) developing districts as the basic unit of drought management (placing EWS responsibility with districts); (c) establishing a clear structure for the coordination of multi-disciplinary recovery activities; and (d) enabling communities to actively participate in drought preparedness, intervention, and recovery (e.g., through consultation to identify potential drought grazing reserves and empowering of communities to be responsible for the management of these reserves).

Involuntary Resettlement

Although the direction of World Bank water sector lending leads away from large projects that will result in involuntary resettlement, a strategy is still needed for the relatively few projects that may remain. When involuntary resettlement is caused by dam projects, valuable land and other land-based resources are lost. There is also a disruption of social systems and networks of the affected populations. Given the disruptive capacity of big dams, it is obvious that involuntary resettlement will increase the magnitude of the challenges facing Africans in the water sector. Finally, the displacement of people can lead to disputes over water in the area to which settlers are relocated.

The World Bank will carry out a policy dialogue with African countries seeking a common framework for projects that will cause involuntary resettlement. The Bank will support policy reform and capacity building within the country before projects can begin. Support is also needed to develop capacity for monitoring project impacts on resettlers. The Bank can also help fund networks among resettlement practitioners and NGOs in order to exchange relevant information. Finally, the reality of large projects is that the project cycle will move slowly. The Bank will withhold project funds until borrowers demonstrate the political will and the ability to implement environmental and social mitigation plans. Moreover, resettlement projects absolutely must have full stakeholder participation from the very first stages of project identification, preparation, and implementation, even if this entails delays or does not conform to budget cycles.

Stakeholder Participation

Stakeholder participation is a guiding principle of development and must be viewed as a strategic intervention in World Bank lending for water resources management in Sub-Saharan Africa. If the main challenges are to be met, the Bank will support a process that incorporates key stakeholders in the project cycle, from the farmer to the industrial water user, and from the local environmental NGO to a national planning agency.

The Bank will need to support basic education and technical training at the lowest levels, particularly for girls and women. Bank projects will specifically recognize indigenous management practices and will facilitate representation and consultation from NGOs and individual users in project design and implementation. This stakeholder representation in projects should be done in a systematic manner. The Bank will also encourage or assist national water authorities in their own efforts to ensure stakeholder participation, particularly in water allocation and catchment management. The Bank can support efforts to link communities with NGOs, and NGOs with government authorities.

A more challenging, but necessary, path for World Bank task managers to follow is one of stakeholder analysis at the initial stages of the project cycle. This involves identification of key stakeholders, defines their respective stakes, and determines their needs and roles in project planning and implementation. Beneficiary assessment is important for achieving this.

G. Change Agenda: A New Dimension

The Bank's mission is to get results on the ground and reduce poverty in Africa by providing timely and effective support to its African partners in order to help them obtain rapid and lasting improvement in living standards for all. Bank interventions in the water sector will support this mission, with emphasis on results in the field and development impact. The Bank will leverage -- through its existing portfolio and lending program concerning water-related operations -- policy changes, capacity building, stakeholder participation, and regional cooperation. The Bank will also promote a new partnership with donor agencies in supporting national programs with long-term commitment.

Existing Portfolio

The Bank will focus on more and better results from ongoing operations in irrigation, water supply and sanitation, urban development, and hydropower. Presently, the Bank has forty-four projects in the sector (US$ 2.3 billion) that can be used to intensify efforts in capacity building, privatization, and involving stakeholders. As appropriate, these operations need to be restructured to move toward integrated sector programs, focusing on successful components. The Bank will also use these operations to promote the development or refinement of water policies, strategies, and action plans. The Bank also will help countries to integrate these projects into the key components of the National Environmental Action Plans dealing with water resources.

Supervision missions will give more attention to assessing results on the ground, using **performance indicators** (such as those used in Table 5.1, plus indicators that deal with water quality, incidence of waterborne or water-related diseases, supply costs, cross-sectoral considerations, etc.). Emphasis will also be given to systematic **client consultation** and **beneficiary assessment** and to involving all stakeholders. The Bank needs to involve donor agencies periodically in joint supervision missions to concentrate on results on the ground and best practices, and to address important implementation issues. Systematically, the Bank will change from a supervision role, which should be the responsibility of the member countries, to a role of implementation review and dialogue.

Broader Sector Approach

To maximize development impact, water-related operations need to be part of a **long-term national programs** based on a broader sector approach that internalizes the country's priorities and builds on existing capacity. The key elements of such a sector investment program approach would be: (a) coherent policies in the sector; (b) sector-wide operations prepared by local stakeholders; (c) inclusion of all donors in the sector; (d) common execution arrangements (implementation, accounts and audits, monitoring and evaluation, management reporting, and procurement); and (e) minimum reliance on long-term technical assistance.

The move to a broader sector approach can be gradual. The Bank can initially support national programs (such as irrigation, water supply and sanitation, hydropower, river basin development, watershed development, and protection of aquatic ecosystems) through integrated sub-sector operations or projects within broader sector-wide programs. In the latter case, it is crucial for the Bank to design simple projects supporting a few objectives and components which are implementable. As countries move toward sector operations, special attention needs to be given to creating an enabling environment through policy reforms, strengthening country capacity, developing human resources, and implementing projects to develop innovative solutions.

In the case of regional programs, the Bank will continue to rely on the GEF as an important vehicle to support regional initiatives that promote the conservation of biological resources, pollution clean up of international waterways, protection of catchment areas affecting international rivers, and capacity building of river basin organizations. The Bank will support initiatives for multi-country efforts in the development of river basins (hydropower, irrigation, water supply for domestic use) involving several riparian states.

Water Resources in Economic and Sector Work

Country Sector Work. Good, cross-sectoral knowledge of water resources in a land use framework is an important element in developing actions (policy reforms, institutional changes, and investment programs) that will lead to the better management of water resources. Sector knowledge needs to be based on physical data on water resources, land use patterns and management, assessment of supply and demand, and lessons learned from past and on-going operations.

The Bank's sector work will be **interdisciplinary** (drawing expertise from the natural and social sciences) and **multisectoral,** incorporating the 'nexus' analytical concept by assessing the linkages among population, environment, poverty, economic activities, and technological variables in a systemic framework. The Bank will avoid undertaking single sector assessment (such as irrigation or water supply and sanitation) unless this assessment is in the context of the entire water resources situation which takes into account the needs and priorities of the entire sector. The Bank's sector work will give special attention to issues relating to demand management factors, including resource pricing and externalities, and transboundary issues. Finally, the Bank will avoid preparing comprehensive sector reports which take an inordinate amount of time and resources to produce. Instead, the Bank needs to develop brief **country strategy papers** of fifteen to twenty pages, including tables, which should be produced in collaboration with the Africans and key donor agencies as input into the country assistance strategies (CAS).

Country Assistance Strategies. More attention needs to be given to addressing issues (e.g., policy choices, investment options, financial sustainability, and cost recovery) relating to the management and utilization of water resources, particularly as they relate to poverty, human health, and environmental degradation. Since multisectoral and transboundary considerations are critical in water resources management in SSA, more clarity needs to be given to the strategic context (development priorities and policy framework). This includes a rationale for individual operations for sustainable management of water resources in a long-term context, fostering regional cooperation. Completion of country strategy papers with inputs from Africans based on rigorous analytical work should provide valuable input into the CASs to shape strategies, policy dialogues, and lending programs.

H. External Agencies: Need for Strong Partnership

As the owners and managers of the region's water resources, African peoples and governments will be primarily responsible for the success of the proposed strategy. However, better coordination among donors and other international organizations involved in the water sector is crucial and can greatly help to accelerate the achievement of water management objectives. Many donors are already providing assistance (finance and technical assistance) to the water sector, either directly to countries or within the framework of regional initiatives. Without coordination, donors will continue supporting narrow objectives in fragmented ways, undermining African national governments, duplicating each other's efforts, or implementing inefficient projects due to limited institutional capacity in the region.

The Bank strategy advocates a systemic approach to water management, focusing on five priority challenges and emphasizing the principle of demand management. As such, many of the proposed actions for Africa differ markedly from the development status quo of the past thirty years. This strategy calls for cooperation and programs that may transcend political boundaries, focus on stakeholders and the private sector, require long time-horizons, or rely upon community-based systems. Such programs are susceptible to failure when donor activity is uncoordinated. For instance, a program promoting participatory watershed management could be undermined if a bilateral agency supports a large dam upstream. Again, a donor placing its own consultants in long-term technical assistance positions could disrupt Bank capacity building initiatives.

Thus, the World Bank and other donors will need to work together in the framework of integrated sector programs in helping African countries to develop appropriate water polices, strategies, and investment programs, and to deal with conflicts in water use at the local, national, and regional levels (the latter including riparian countries). Such national programs will require consultation between the Bank, the African Development Bank, the GEF, UN Agencies, and bilateral agencies. The Bank also will continue its positive dialogue and collaboration with OAU and UN agencies such as UNDP, UNEP, WHO, WMO, UNICEF, FAO, UNHCR, and UNECA, while forming better relationships with ILO, UNCTAD, UNESCO, and UNIDO. Cooperative regional initiatives deserve further support with respect to water resources, such as the Bank/UNDP-sponsored African Capacity Building Foundation, the UNDP/World Bank Water and Sanitation Program, UNICEF country programs, and the UN Secretary-General's Special Initiative on Africa, which among other things, focuses on development of water resources in SSA.

Another potential avenue for a coordinated response to African water resources management issues is the Global Water Partnership (GWP). Still in its infancy, the GWP would consolidate existing UNDP-World Bank programs, not just from the water supply and sanitation sector, but from irrigation, the environment, and other sectors. The partnership will provide knowledge and assistance, support capacity building and regional initiatives, promote innovative approaches, and assist countries in bringing about often difficult reforms.

In the case of SSA, this collaboration will focus on:

- Ensuring governance of regional programs by an appropriate forum of African specialists, building on the experiences gained in developing this strategy.
- Increasing awareness among African leaders and policy makers on the importance of water management issues and challenges.
- Promoting harmonization of procedures relating to project financing and implementation (e.g., disbursement, procurement, financial arrangement, auditing, monitoring and evaluation, etc.).
- Promoting exchange of information and experiences based on lessons learned.
- Ensuring dissemination of information on ongoing and planned operations in SSA, best practices, and cost-effective technologies.

- Identifying areas facing critical threats in regard to water availability, water contamination; and degradation of aquatic ecosystems.

- Supporting national research efforts in integrating soil and water conservation measures, the efficient use of water in irrigated agriculture, and development of low-cost technologies regarding water supply and sanitation.

- Mobilizing resources to assist African countries in capacity building and implementation of investments linked to long-term national programs.

- Facilitating international dialogue on transboundary basins to achieve the equitable development of water resources, promoting regional economic integration.

- Extending support to water utilities, initiated in the Bank-supported UADE Utility Partnership.

- Supporting the work of the UNDP/Bank Water and Sanitation Program for the rural and urban poor.

The Bank will develop these initiatives within a programmatic framework, ensuring optimal coordination and performance.

Annex A

Innovations in the Water Sector in Recent Bank-Sponsored Activities

An integrated approach to water resources management -- focusing on the challenges of household water security, water quality, food security, environmental protection, and regional cooperation -- is already present in the following innovative Bank operations.

- **The Lake Victoria Environmental Management Program**, a GEF-sponsored project in cooperation with the Governments of Kenya, Tanzania, and Uganda, demonstrates how regional cooperation can be used to solve pollution problems in a shared lake basin. The fisheries of Lake Victoria produce exports estimated at US$320 million/year, and support, to some extent, over 100,000 families. The lake also supports unique biological resources of great value to the global community. The project, at a total cost of US$66.8 million, is a comprehensive program aimed at rehabilitation of the lake ecosystem. The project has innovative objectives reflecting the ecosystem approach, including generation of food, employment, and income; an increase in fish exports; supply of safe water; and biodiversity conservation. To this end, project activities include (a) fisheries management; (b) management of lake pollution and water quality; (c) wetlands management; (d) water hyacinth control; and (e) watershed management and soil conservation. The project also has innovations reflecting the international character of the effort, including (a) the signing of tripartite agreements establishing the Lake Victoria Fisheries Organization and calling for joint preparation and implementation and (b) investments by the three governments into a joint trust fund to finance research and extension services.

- **The Utility Partnership (the Capacity Building Program for Water and Sanitation)**, an African regional initiative receiving a special three-year grant from the World Bank for US$1.5 million (representing 20 percent of total program costs), is an innovative step toward enabling African countries to provide water and sanitation services to rapidly growing urban populations. The partnership consists of UADE (Union Africaine des Distributeurs d'Eau, based in Abidjan, Côte d'Ivoire), CREPA (Centre pour l'Eau et l'Assainissement à Faibles Coûts, based in Ouagadougou, Burkina Faso), and TNC (Training Network Center, based in Kumasi, Ghana) and has two main objectives: improving the performance of water utilities through institutional reform and developing the collaboration between utilities and community-based initiatives to improve water and sanitation services. Planned activities include training, documentation of recommended approaches, networking, exchanges of expertise, country seminars, and development of performance indicators.

- **The Tanzania River Basin Management and Smallholder Irrigation Improvement Project** is an important effort in helping Tanzania take a systemic approach to water resources management. The river basin management component is aimed at the Rufiji and Pangani Basins, with the objectives of streamlining the legislative framework, improving resource monitoring and information collection, and researching of basin management issues. Activities include assistance to Water Offices, rehabilitation of hydro-meteorological networks, and studies of the Utengule Swamp and other wetlands. Under the smallholder irrigation component, no new schemes will be established. Rather, the objectives are to adjust the government's role to one of monitoring and guiding irrigation development and to improve the main infrastructure of traditional irrigation schemes. The project plans to rehabilitate schemes at a cost of US$1,500-2,000 per hectare through participatory scheme selection and management, small canal and drain construction, and support for a national extension program.

- **The Zambia Urban Restructuring and Water Supply Project** has been designed with extensive stakeholder consultation and emphasizes the development of capacity within existing ministerial, council, and community structures. This five-year project plans to provide immediate solutions to the most severe water and sewerage infrastructure deficiencies in nine key urban areas, support community-generated and managed water and sanitation demonstration projects, and initiate institutional and financial reforms. Project activities focus on a participatory demand-based approach and include construction, support for community-level projects, and technical assistance and training for local government employees.

- **The Senegal Water Sector Project** combines the lessons of the past in a dramatic effort to integrate planning and management of water supply and sanitation, agriculture, and industry. This project seeks to address sustainability by improving management, pricing, and cost recovery; poverty alleviation and health; and private sector participation. The project will support the Ministry of Hydraulics and the Water Planning Unit in the preparation of a national water strategy, support the national water company in cost accounting, and support the creation of an urban sanitation strategy. The project will also rehabilitate Dakar's water supply and sanitation infrastructure. This effort is innovative in its emphases on treating water as an economic good, demand management, and conservation.

- **The Côte d'Ivoire Second Water Supply Project** is a recently completed effort that successfully increased urban and rural water supply and enhanced water sector institutional capacity. The project optimized existing water production facilities by providing marginal additions for Abidjan and fifty-two other urban systems, promoted the greater use of existing urban systems by providing additional consumer connections, and assisted in the rational development of the village well subsector. It also assisted water sector institutions in the operation, finance, and management of facilities. Among the project activities were the construction of 10,000 service connections and 100 standpipes to develop services to the urban poor, the drilling of 300 wells equipped with handpumps in rural areas, training and technical assistance, and improvement of the land registry system in Abidjan (leading to the improved collection of property and drainage taxes). The success of the rural components of this project is attributed to the reliance on community management. Overall, government agencies in Côte d'Ivoire had a strong sense of ownership and worked as partners with the World Bank.

- **The Kenya Arid Lands Resource Management Project** includes a US$10.9 million Drought Management Component that deals with drought issues through institutional structures and capacity building at the local and national levels. The project seeks to manage all phases of drought, including preparedness, mitigation, and recovery through (a) the establishment of a national level Secretariat to enact polices and carry out operational responsibilities; (b) establishment of district structures for drought monitoring and contingency planning; (c) establishment of a Drought Contingency Fund and Emergency Cereal Reserve at the national level; and (d) drought mitigation interventions, such as the funding of civil works, setting aside of drought grazing reserves, and provision of equipment. The project moves beyond the crisis management of drought response. Rather, it deals with drought before it occurs. Moreover, it should enable government organizations and local people to work together in response to adverse environmental conditions.

- **The Volta River Basin Initiative** is an effort to foster cooperation between the six riparian states of Benin, Burkina Faso, Côte d'Ivoire, Ghana, Mali, and Togo in order to achieve sustainable water resources management at a river basin level. Inadequate water legislation, policy, and institutional structures, particularly in Ghana, severely constrain the effective management and further development of the basin. Water use in Burkina Faso, upstream, impairs the Akosombo Dam in Ghana, downstream, while the dam itself has been responsible for increases in onchoceriasis, malaria, and guinea worm. Thus, in Ghana, the World Bank, in partnership with UNDP, CIDA UK/ODA, and DANIDA, has launched the preparation of a national water management strategy, is discussing a similar effort with Burkina Faso, and is providing opportunities for policy dialogue within projects in Togo, Mali, and Benin. In the next two to three years, the World Bank intends to promote dialogue and data sharing between these riparians and intends to study the possibilities of joint investments and economic integration.

- **The Ghana Water Resources Management Policy Project** is designed to allow Ghanaian leadership from start to finish in the process of designing that country's first genuinely integrated water policy. The World Bank provides resources and technical advice when requested; otherwise, Ghanaian capacity is utilized and built to a maximum degree. The project is being built upon a water resources study of six topics or building blocks: information, regulation, economics and financing, institutions and participation, international rivers, and the socioeconomic and political context. These studies are being conducted by Ghanaian teams based on a Ghanaian time-frame. The World Bank recognizes that a demand-driven policy formulation process cannot be mandated in terms of time. Rather, as building blocks are completed -- not necessarily simultaneously -- the strategic recommendations will be considered by a Ghanaian forum and made into policy.

- **The International Program for Technology Research in Irrigation and Drainage (IPTRID)** is a World Bank-sponsored cooperative effort by multiple international donor agencies which serves as a support program for research and innovation in irrigation. Based on a 1992 workshop on the problems facing irrigated agriculture in West Africa, IPTRID and its West African partners developed research projects organized around seven themes: (a) assessment and management of shallow aquifers in support of small-scale irrigation; (b) optimization of components for small-scale irrigation; (c) low land development with partial water control; (d) improvement of communal irrigation; (e) restructuring large and medium water management schemes; (f) salinity control and reclamation of saline soils; and (g) information exchange.

As of 1995, various research projects had been planned or implemented according to these themes. For example, regarding the optimization of components for small-scale irrigation, the World Bank-sponsored Pilot Private Irrigation Promotion Project in Niger aims to improve manual irrigation technologies through improved hand-dug wells, more efficient manual water lifting methods, and the training of local artisans to produce manual irrigation equipment. In relation to salinity control, IPTRID is working with CORAF (an African NGO) to diagnose the causes and extent of salinity problems, experiment with improved management techniques, test the suitability of drainage and maintenance practices, and train personnel in the Senegal River Valley.

Annex B

Summary Report of Workshops on Water Resources Management in Sub-Saharan Africa

In February 1996, the World Bank sponsored two Workshops in Africa with the theme *Water Resources Management.* The first was held in Nairobi, Kenya, on February 12-15, with 119 participants from 21 countries of eastern and southern Africa and from UN agencies, bilateral donors, and non-governmental organizations (NGOs). The second workshop was held in Dakar, Sénégal, on February 19-22, with 115 participants from 20 countries of west and central Africa and from external support agencies. The participants included several water sector Ministers and senior government officials from African countries, as well as representatives of bilateral and multilateral agencies, non-governmental organizations (NGOs), and the private sector.

Full proceedings of the two workshops are available from the World Bank. This Summary Report combines the conclusions and recommendations of the two workshops to present an African perspective on Integrated Water Resources Management.

Workshop Theme and Focus

The high attendance and the evident commitment of all participants to the same objectives make it clear that the Workshop topic is a highly relevant one for all African countries. In preparing its Strategy Paper, the World Bank undertook an extensive consultation exercise, spanning 18 months. It included the active involvement of an African Advisory Group and the preparation of some twenty background papers. The aim was to include all the different domains of water resources to obtain as wide a perspective as possible. The Theme and Focus for the Workshop (see box) was selected when it became apparent that the issues of sustainability, equity, efficiency and integrated management were emerging as critical throughout the continent. It also reflected the prevalent view that the social aims of governments and other sector stakeholders merit as much attention as economic and environmental ones.

> **WORKSHOP THEME AND FOCUS**
>
> **Theme:**
>
> *African Water Resources: Challenges and Opportunities for Sustainable Development*
>
> **Focus:**
>
> *Partnership and a broad coalition for promoting more efficient and equitable use of water resources in Sub-Saharan Africa*

The Workshops brought together a range of stakeholders (governments, sector agencies, NGOs, UN agencies, and bilateral donors). The aim was to convert the analyses and action-oriented recommendations in the Strategy Paper into results which will improve the livelihood of all Africans. The process needs to continue by extending the discussion to include more stakeholders (the private sector, community groups, academia, and research institutes).

The World Bank is seeking to set its own agenda, by integrating the African perspective into its analysis, including the many achievements highlighted during the Workshops. The Workshops' conclusions will influence World Bank thinking on assistance to Africa. In particular, the messages will be taken into account as the Bank begins to implement the African Water Resources Management Strategy.

At both venues, the discussions demonstrated convincingly that a New Agenda is needed. The old supply-driven, sectoral approach has been effectively laid to rest. African countries are committed to new imperatives, which will focus on their needs, identified and converted into action programs by them, and implemented, making maximum use of a wealth of indigenous talent and resources.

Countries have much to share, and the opportunity to get together to compare and contrast experiences was immensely valuable. It was valuable to the donors and the World Bank too, giving fresh insights into the major issues analyzed in the Strategy Paper and helping to define a new responsive role for development support agencies. Clearly, the countries are going to be the driving forces in implementing the New Agenda, and it is their determination and commitment which will be the cornerstones of its success. Opportunities to share information like that provided through regional and specialist groups are a key part of the process, and the participants in Nairobi and Dakar indicated a strong desire to continue the sharing process through all means available.

The Emerging Imperative

The enthusiasm of the Workshop participants to learn the lessons of the past, but base their future programs on strengths and achievements, is captured in a three-part Emerging Imperative (see box).

Repeatedly, in both plenary and Working Groups, participants insisted on the positive view, focusing on ways of redirecting available resources and mobilizing previously untapped ones. Threatening scarcity and environmental degradation add weight to the acknowledged need to make sustainability a primary objective. The dilemma of limited resources to meet even the high-priority needs of all sectors at the same time makes equity a key issue too. Most importantly, though, the imperative is to ensure that African development policy is put together by Africans for Africans and that its implementation builds on (and continues to build) Africa's indigenous capabilities.

THE EMERGING IMPERATIVE

- Enthusiasm by African countries to accelerate transition to sustainable and equitable use of water
- Development to be country-driven making, optimum use of African capabilities, resources, and experiences
- Cooperation among sectors and among riparian countries, including multisector and multicountry programs

With very few exceptions, Sub-Saharan countries share the waters of international rivers with at least one of their neighbors. There is a strong desire to achieve rational and equitable sharing of the waters and to manage the river basins in an integrated way. That poses challenges both for the riparian countries and for the donor agencies seeking to support them. New approaches are needed, which will enable donors to provide support on a multisector and multicountry basis, so as to foster effective joint management of international resources.

Developing from these emerging imperatives, the Workshops have reaffirmed some important goals that countries should set themselves to create the enabling environment for the 'New Agenda.' These are the important milestones on The Road Ahead (see box).

The Road Ahead

Political Will and Commitment

Government commitment to the changing agenda is crucial to achieving progress.

THE ROAD AHEAD

- Political will and commitment
- Stakeholder participation at all levels
- Demand management and water conservation
- Equitable sharing of international resources
- Effective policy and regulatory framework
- Capacity building, utilization, and retention
- New forms of country/donor partnership

Stakeholder Participation at All Levels

Active participation of all the parties involved in the development process is now widely accepted as both a route to successful planning and an effective way of mobilizing previously untapped resources from local agencies, communities, farmers, NGOs, and the private sector. Any process for involving stakeholders needs to recognize the different needs and potential contributions of men and women, through gender-sensitive approaches in the consultative process and throughout program implementation.

Demand Management and Water Conservation

Greater stakeholder participation is a powerful mechanism for raising awareness of the value of water and the need to conserve its quality and quantity. Demand management approaches using economic instruments, conservation measures, etc., are an important part of strategies to extend the life of existing resources and defer investment in costly new water resources development projects. The old supply-driven approach is no longer an acceptable way to plan and implement projects.

Equitable Sharing of International Resources

The Workshops repeatedly returned to the topic of transboundary water problems - an indication of the high importance attached to this issue across the continent. Transboundary water sharing is important for all African countries and fundamental to future economic growth in some downstream riparian countries. Participants heard of recent progress both on bipartite agreements and on regional protocols, but many intractable issues remain (information sharing, joint research, mechanisms for conflict resolution, new treaties and agreements, etc.). The World Bank expects regional cooperation over shared rivers to be part of its policy dialogue with partner countries through the next decade.

Effective Policy and Regulatory Framework

Thoroughly prepared policies matched by effective regulation are fundamental as a means of demonstrating government commitment and creating the enabling environment for integrated water resources management. With community management and private sector involvement as important parts of the way ahead, government's regulatory role will need to be reinforced.

Capacity Building, Utilization, and Retention

The emphasis here is on equipping all stakeholders to play their parts and on starting by using existing capacity to the full. Through their multisectoral plans, countries can determine ways of maximizing use of their own indigenous resources (human, financial, and institutional) and identify effective ways in which donor support can be used to plug capacity gaps. Many countries emphasized at the Workshops that their existing capacities are underutilized.

New Forms of Country/Donor Partnership

The country-driven nature of development programs calls for a responsive approach from donors, working in partnership with government agencies and guided by nationally determined priorities.

THE NEW AGENDA

The elements of the New Agenda (see box) reflect the continual affirmation at each Workshop of some now widely accepted common principles:

THE NEW AGENDA

- Integrated approach to WRM
- Cooperation in WRM of shared rivers
- Partnership, integration, and pluralism
- Water as a social and an economic good
- Health and environmental sustainability
- Public awareness and indigenous knowledge
- Gender sensitivity

Integrated Approach to Water Resources Management

The old water agenda was supply-driven, engineering-based, single-sector, and usually involved only a single stakeholder. It was also materialistic and utilitarian.

Cooperation in WRM of Shared Rivers

Integrated river-basin planning and management are seen as key elements in national WRM strategies. They are equally valuable for international rivers, as a way of allocating water equitably and protecting ecosystems. Riparian states and donors need to seek ways of extending principles of stakeholder involvement, multisectoral planning, and legislative reform into the international arena. The 'win-win' scenario of mutual benefit from water sharing initiatives is one pointer to the way forward.

Partnership, Integration, and Pluralism

A number of countries have shown that commitment to stakeholder-driven policy development, with all partners having a voice and contributing resources, leads to more effective and sustainable programs. Examples include Sénégal, Ethiopia, Malawi, Zimbabwe, and South Africa.

Water as a Social and an Economic Good

Water pricing has always been a sensitive political issue. The Workshops generated interesting discussions on ways of achieving equitable use of available water supplies and ensuring the prime aim of extending services to the urban and rural poor, while at the same time recovering costs for operating existing projects and constructing new ones.

Health and Environmental Sustainability

Improving human health and safeguarding the environment are linked objectives which need to be integrated into water sector strategies.

Public Awareness and Indigenous Knowledge

The benefits of stakeholder participation come when all sections of society are well-informed and empowered to contribute to program planning and can help to put societal interests alongside individual demands.

Gender Sensitivity

The gender issue is not simply one of recognizing women as victims. Both men and women have vital roles to play -- sometimes different roles. The aim has to be to use approaches which take gender issues into consideration as a way of making programs more effective.

DEVELOPMENT PRIORITIES

Countries' commitments to achieving sustainable management and use of their water resources need to be backed by government-formulated programs which recognize and cater for the linkages and trade-offs among sectors. The choices spread across a range of development priorities (see box).

Enhanced Service Coverage with Priority for the Poor

The African Advisory Group steered the Strategy Paper towards a focus on rural and peri-urban problems. Workshop discussions confirmed this emphasis on tackling the urgent needs of the poor.

DEVELOPMENT PRIORITIES

- Enhanced service coverage with priority for the poor
- Food security through irrigation and water harvesting
- Water quality and human health
- Protection of watersheds and wetlands
- Intercountry river-basin cooperation

Food Security through Irrigation and Water Harvesting

The potential for much more small-scale irrigation has been confirmed by several countries (for example, Ethiopia, Madagascar, Sahelian countries, Nigeria, Tanzania, Kenya). World Bank analyses show that doubling the irrigated area used for growing cereal crops would produce enough extra food to meet needs up to the year 2025. Water harvesting is an attractive way of using low-cost technology to boost production from the 200 million hectares of land presently used for rainfed agriculture in Africa.

Water Quality and Human Health

Protecting water resources from pollution is important as a way of safeguarding precious current and future sources. It is also vital to combat the many threats to human health from contaminated water.

Protection of Watersheds and Wetlands

Land degradation has serious implications for water quality and quantity. Appropriate land management and catchment protection programs are an integral part of the river-basin approach.

Intercountry River-Basin Cooperation

Shared water resources feature prominently in national WRM strategies in most African countries. Resources need to be assigned to the development of basin-wide agreements, which may involve sacrifices as well as gains.

KEY STRATEGIC ACTIONS

The most powerful message emerging from the Workshops is that future water resources management strategies in Africa will be country-driven, making optimum use of indigenous resources and with external technical assistance limited to plugging capacity gaps identified by the countries. Summarized in the box, the key strategic actions have a common goal - sustainable and equitable use of water resources - and seven strategic elements:

KEY STRATEGIC ACTIONS

Goal:

- Sustainable and equitable use of water resources

Strategies:

- Utilize and build local capacity and human resources
- Develop knowledge and approaches through applied research
- Strengthen data/information systems
- Involve all stakeholders and build awareness
- Establish mechanisms for regional cooperation and conflict resolution
- Support long-term national investment programs
- Implement country-driven coordination

Utilize and Build Local Capacity and Human Resources

External support for capacity building will be responsive to country demands and will include institutional and human resource development involving all stakeholders, not just government agencies.

Develop Knowledge and Approaches through Applied Research

Applied research is crucial for countries and donor agencies with limited financial resources. Applied research should be demand-driven and be based upon stakeholder input and participation.

Strengthen Data/Information Systems

Needs include the hydrological and other physical data required for planning and monitoring programs, but also social and economic data as a basis for multisectoral strategies and priority setting.

Involve All Stakeholders and Build Awareness

A necessary condition for more efficient and lasting management of water resources is the participation of all stakeholders (public agencies, private sector, NGOs, local communities and special interests) in all aspects of decision-making, planning and implementation. The challenge for African countries at this time is to involve local communities more fully in policy formulation and project design and execution. Public awareness campaigns and education initiatives can be important steps in building awareness among stakeholders.

Establish Mechanisms for Regional Cooperation and Conflict Resolution

This may well be the biggest challenge for the region as a whole. Cooperation is going to involve trade-offs and income transfer for which there are as yet no models available.

Support Long-Term National Investment Programs

African countries recognize the need to depart from a single-project approach which has resulted in fragmentation and inefficiency in water utilization, and to develop long-term national programs for development and management of water resources. These national programs can be an important vehicle for mobilizing support of all stakeholders and for coordinating donor support.

Implement Country-Driven Coordination

These last two elements are closely linked, as program-oriented approaches are a helpful way of coordinating donor activities at the country level and directed by the country.

WORKSHOP RECOMMENDATIONS FOR PRIORITY ACTION

Following analysis of five key issues by Working Groups, the Workshops developed recommendations under the same five thematic headings:

Strategies and Investment Options

Governments and donors are in agreement that water resources management strategies need to be **country-driven**, making maximum use of indigenous resources and local capacity. Donor support should be responsive to the needs and priorities identified by the countries, minimizing the use of technical assistance.

STRATEGIES AND INVESTMENT OPTIONS

- Country-led strategies with responsive donor support
- Community-level management and resource mobilization
- Mobilization of domestic financial resources
- Commercialized approach to service provision
- Equitable and environmentally sustainable development

Community management of water supplies for drinking purposes and small-scale irrigation has been shown to be effective in rural areas. As well as improving the reliability and performance of the water services, **community-level resource mobilization** provides a major source of project financing. It needs to be introduced with a high level of stakeholder participation.

The degree to which privatization could improve institutional performance will vary from country to country. However, a more **commercialized approach** is a vital part of improving the performance of public service providers. Successful approaches have included private sector participation in large urban water supply and sewerage services and small commercialized public utilities at the district level.

Strategies with the twin objectives of **equitable and environmentally sustainable development** enable countries to extend water and sanitation services to the urban and rural poor in an affordable way, to provide water to increase food production, and to conserve water resources for future generations.

Capacity Utilization, Building, and Retention

Exploitation of **indigenous capacity** and plugging of gaps through external support will be accompanied by incentives to retain qualified staff.

CAPACITY UTILIZATION, BUILDING, AND RETENTION

- Increased use of indigenous resources
- Decentralized agencies with a commercial approach
- Equipping all stakeholders for an effective role
- Regional cooperation in capacity building
- Policy, institutional, and legislative reform
- Training and education

Support for the necessary **decentralization** will focus on establishing a commercialized approach in public sector agencies as well as seeking opportunities for privatization where appropriate.

Donors need to find innovative ways of **building capacity not just in public sector agencies** but in communities, NGOs, the private sector, among farmers, and other water sector stakeholders. Capacity building is not a one-way process; the different stakeholders have much to teach governments and donors.

Special thought needs to be given to appropriate frameworks for continuing **cooperation among riparian states**. **Intercountry exchange** of African expertise and experience is both appropriate and cost-effective.

The overall aim is to create the right **enabling environment** for reaching the common goal of efficient and equitable water use through partnership. The right policy framework, backed by effective legislation, is the foundation for this enabling environment. **Training and education** initiatives need to match identified needs.

Regional Cooperation

In helping to resolve transboundary issues, donors need to look for mechanisms which will allow them to assist through **multicountry interventions**.

REGIONAL COOPERATION

- Multiple country focus based on simple common objectives
- Equity for upstream and downstream riparians
  - identify "win-win" solutions
- Enhance support for River Basin Organizations
- Foster cooperation through:
  - training
  - sharing of information
  - institutions and organizations
  - treaties and agreements
  - joint investments
  - applied research

Conflicts can be resolved if **'win-win' solutions** can be found and an even playing field can be created, so that discussions are acknowledged to be among equals. **International river basin organizations** need commitment and support from both governments and donors if they are to achieve the desired objective.

Networking and information-sharing among countries will help to stimulate water-sharing agreements. Informal get-togethers and formalized institutional arrangements both have parts to play in improving transboundary relationships. **Cooperation** can be further increased through joint (intercountry) projects, training, and applied research programs, particularly those related to the management of shared water resources.

Information and Knowledge Base

Information and data generation needs to be demand-driven and cost-effective. Restoration and improvement of hydrological networks and routine collection and updating of other physical data have to be accompanied with programs to assemble and analyze socioeconomic data.

INFORMATION AND KNOWLEDGE BASE

- Strengthen water information services
  - physical
  - socioeconomic
- Set economic objectives for information systems
- Support demand-driven information systems
- Build on and integrate recent initiatives
- Raise stakeholder awareness of the economic and social value of water
- Support pan-African sharing of information and knowledge

Combination of **physical and socioeconomic information** can help to determine how social systems interact with natural ones, providing important planning information on issues such as the effects of changed land use on watershed degradation and the resulting impact on available water resources over different time horizons.

The strengthening of water information services and analytical methods will lead to **multiple benefits**, including: improved planning, programming, and monitoring; identification of opportunities for applied research; effective management of multipurpose projects; improved mitigation of droughts and floods; and more cost-effective and environmentally sound projects.

Raising awareness among all stakeholders is a vital part of building partnerships within countries, while regional and pan-African information sharing, both formal and informal, fosters enhanced intercountry cooperation.

Donor Collaboration

Donors need to view their links with African countries not as a provider-recipient relationship but as part of a **partnership of mutual respect**, in which solutions to problems come from both sides.

DONOR COLLABORATION

- Strengthen African partnership
- Support country-driven national programs
- Respond to multisectoral and multicountry challenges
- Rely on African capacity and human resources
- Enhance client consultation – listening
- Focus on results on the ground
- Harmonize procedures and approaches
- Replicate successful examples of international cooperation

Countries can help to build the partnership by sharing information on national strategies and programs. Donors are committed to respecting **national priorities** and do not gain from being paternalistic.

The widely accepted multisectoral approach is a challenge for both countries and donors, which can be helped significantly by **regular dialogue** and by networking among countries, among donors, and in workshops and conferences.

By listening to the experiences and ideas emerging from stakeholders, donors can help to ensure that support is better tailored to national needs, taking account of **indigenous capacity**.

The **development impact** of programs should be the focus of donor project assessment. Recognizing that donors are responsible to their governments and taxpayers and the Bank to its stockholders, there is scope for **harmonization of approaches** at the country level to match national goals and priorities.

Where Do We Go from Here?

The Strategy Document is intended to shape the way that the World Bank does business in the water sector in Africa. The Workshop messages will influence country-assistance strategies and help the Bank to develop partnerships with countries and other donors.

AN AFRICAN PARTNERSHIP

- Establish an informal pan-African framework
- Foster intercountry dialogue
- Build partnerships
- Develop consensus on key issues and actions
- Share knowledge, experience, and best practices (country and subregional)
- Review progress on agreed action plans

The impact of the Workshops is also expected to spread through the participants to a wider audience, fostering the stakeholder participation in strategy development that is seen as so important.

The partnership process needs to continue under **African leadership**, and future meetings will wish to review what has happened as a result of the Workshop recommendations. The concept of a **Pan-African Partnership** (see box) was widely debated at both Workshops, with the consensus in favor of an informal framework. The World Bank's African Advisory Group, which helped to steer development of the Strategy Paper, is to be asked to pursue ideas for such a partnership.

Bibliography

Alaerts, G., T.L. Blair, and F.J.A. Hartvelt. 1991. *A Strategy for Water Sector Capacity Building.* Proceedings of the UNDP Symposium, Delft, 3-5 June, 1991. Delft, The Netherlands: International Institute for Hydraulic and Environmental Engineering.

Andrews, Anthony. Undated. "The Friend Network." UK: Institute of Hydrology.

Aw, Djibril and Chantal Dejou. 1996. "Recent Developments in the Office du Niger, Mali." Draft paper. Washington D.C.: World Bank.

Barker, Randolph. 1996. "Priorities for Research in Irrigation and Water Management in West Africa." Paper prepared for World Bank Water Resources Management Technical Workshop. Dakar, Senegal, 19-22 February, 1996.

Benson, Charlotte and Edward Clay. 1994. "The Impact of Drought on Sub-Saharan African Economies: A Preliminary Examination." Draft. London: Overseas Development Institute.

Caponera, Dante. 1992. *Principles of Water Law and Administration.* Rotterdam: A.A. Balkama.

Carter, T.R., et al. 1992. "Preliminary Guidelines for Assessing Impacts of Climate Change." IPCC Working Group II. Environmental Change Unit and Center for Global Environmental Research. United Kingdom.

———. Undated. "Groundwater Development for Small Scale Irrigation in SSA." United Kingdom.

Climate Prediction Center. 1991. In World Bank, *Toward Environmentally Sustainable Development in Sub-Saharan Africa: A World Bank Agenda.* Draft. Washington D.C.: World Bank.

Elder, John and L. Cooley. 1995. *Sustainable Settlement and Development of the Onchocerciasis Control Programme Area.* Proceedings of a Ministerial Meeting. Technical Paper No. 310. Washington D.C.: World Bank.

Falkenmark, Malin and Gunnar Lindh. 1993. "Water and Economic Development." In P. Gleick (ed.), *Water in Crisis: A Guide to the World's Fresh Water Resources.* New York: Oxford University Press.

FAO. 1986 *Atlas of African Agriculture.* Rome.

———. ARC/90/4. *The Conservation and Rehabilitation of African Lands: An International Scheme.* Rome.

Garn, M. 1985. *Water Supply Investments in Developing Countries: Some Technical, Economic, and Financial Implications of Experience.* Proceedings of Drinking Water Supply and Sanitation Workshop - Water Supply Investments. Washington D.C.: World Bank.

Gleick, Peter. 1993. *Water in Crisis: A Guide to the World's Fresh Water Resources.* New York: Oxford University Press.

Grove, A.T. 1989. *The Changing Geography of Africa.* Oxford: Oxford University Press.

Husain, Ishrat. 1993. *Overview on Population, Environment, and Development.* Technical Working Paper No. 10. Africa Technical Department. Washington D.C.: World Bank.

ILM (International Legal Materials). 1988) "Agreement on the Action Plan for the Environmentally Sound Management of the Common Zambezi River System," *ILM* 27(5):1109-1143.

ILRI. 1993. "Review of Water Resources Issues in Sub-Saharan Africa." Paper prepared for World Bank by the International Institute for Land Reclamation and Improvement. Wageningen, The Netherlands.

International Conference on Water and the Environment - Development Issues for the 21st Century. January 26-31, 1992. Dublin, Ireland

Kirmani, Syed and Robert Rangeley. 1994. *International Inland Waters: Concepts for a More Active World Bank Role.* Technical Paper No. 239. Washington D.C.: World Bank.

LeMarquand, David. 1990. "International Development of the Senegal River," *Water International* 15(4):223-231.

Le Nay, Jean and Jean Mathis. 1989. "The Impact of Drought on the National Accounts for Livestock in Sahelian Countries." *Review of Income and Wealth* 35 (2).

Listorti, J.A. 1996. "Bridging Environmental Health Gaps," Volumes 1-2. Draft. Washington DC: World Bank.

Munasinghe, M. 1993. *Environmental Economics and Natural Resource Management in Developing Countries.* Washington DC: World Bank.

Purcell, Randall. 1996. "Memorandum on Status of IPTRID Projects for West Africa." Washington D.C.: World Bank.

Obeng, L. A. and Locussol A. R. 1992. "Sanitation Planning: A Challenge for the 90s." Presentation to the Union of African Water Suppliers Congress, Cotonou, Benin, 3-6 February, 1992. Regional Water And Sanitation Group - West Africa UNDP/World Bank Water and Sanitation Program. Washington D.C.: World Bank.

Parra, Antonio. 1987 "The Role of the World Bank in the Settlement of International Investment Disputes." Draft. Washington DC: World Bank.

Rangeley, Robert, e. al. 1994. *International River Basin Organizations in Sub-Saharan Africa.* Technical Paper No. 250. Washington DC: World Bank.

Rogers, Peter. 1993. "The Value of Cooperation in Resolving International River Basin Disputes," *Natural Resources Forum*, May 1993, pp. 117-131.

Southern African Development Community (SADC). 1993. "SADC Environment and Land Management Sector: An Outline." Public document available from Ministry of Agriculture, Co-operatives and Marketing, Lesotho.

———. "Protocol on Shared Water Course Systems in the Southern African Development Community Region."

Scudder, Thayer. 1994. "Recent Experiences with River Basin Development in the Tropics and Subtropics." *Natural Resources Forum* 18(2) 101-113.

Sub-Saharan Africa Hydrological Assessment: 1992. West African Countries. African Development Bank, French Ministry of Cooperation, UNDP, and World Bank.

Trolldalen, J.M. 1992. *International Environmental Conflict Resolution: The Role of the United Nations.* Washington, DC: World Foundation for Environment and Development.

UNEP. 1992. *World Atlas of Desertification.* London: Edward Arnold.

UNICEF. 1994. *The State of the World's Children 1994.* New York.

Vernard, J. L. 1994. "Perspectives de la Banque Mondiale pour un developpement durable en Afrique subsaharienne: Planification urbaine et environnnement en Afrique au Sud du Sahara." Document de reflection. Paris: Caisse Francaise de Developpement.

Wisner, Benjamin. 1976. *An Overview of Drought in Kenya.* Natural Hazard Research Working Paper 30. Boulder, Colorado: University of Colorado.

World Bank. 1987. "Ethiopia - Small-scale Irrigation and Conservation Project." Staff Appraisal Report 6393. Washington D.C.

———. 1988. "FY88 Annual Sector Review Water Supply and Sanitation." Infrastructure and Urban Development Department Report INU 32. Washington D.C.

———. 1990a. Central African Republic Natural Resource Management Project. Report P-5225-CA. Washington D.C.

———. 1990b. Uganda Second Water Supply Project. Report P5214. Washington D.C.

———. 1990c. "FY90 Sector Review Water Supply and Sanitation." Sector Policy and Research - Infrastructure and Urban Development Department. Report INU - OR6. Washington D.C.

———. 1991. *Water Supply and Sanitation in Africa: Laying the Foundation for the 1990s.* Proceedings of the All-Africa Rural Water Supply and Sanitation Sector Conference, Volumes 1 and 2. Abidjan, Côte d'Ivoire, May 1990. Washington D.C.

———. 1992. *World Development Report 1992.* New York: Oxford University Press.

———. 1993a. *Water Resources Management.* Policy Paper. Washington, D.C.

———. 1993b. Burundi, Rwanda, Zaire - Regional Power Projects. Performance Audit Report 12157. Washington D.C.

———. 1994a. Malawi - SADC Lake Malawi/Nyasa Biodiversity Conservation Project. Report 13044. Washington D.C.

———. 1994b. Uganda - Small Towns Water and Sanitation Project. Report 12296. Washington D.C.

———. 1995a. Madagascar - Irrigation Rehabilitation Project. Report 14671. Washington D.C.

———. 1995b. Nigeria Impact Evaluation Report. Report 14767-UNI. Washington D.C.

———. 1995c. *OED Report on Water Supply and Sanitation Projects: The Bank Experience 1967-1989.* Washington D.C.

———. 1995d. "Water Management in Road Works Design in the Sahel Region." Draft Report 14408 AFR. Washington D.C.

———. 1995e. *World Development Report 1995.* New York: Oxford University Press.

———. 1995f. *World Populations Projections 1994 - 95: Estimates and Projections with Related Demographic Statistics.* Baltimore: The Johns Hopkins University Press.

WHO/UNICEF. 1993. "Water Supply and Sanitation Sector Monitoring Report." In *WHO/UNICEF Joint Monitoring Programme Annual Report.* Geneva and New York.

WMO. 1995. African Conference on Water Resources: Policy and Assessment, Addis Ababa, Ethiopia, 20-25 March 1995. Report of the Conference.

World Resources Institute. 1994. *World Resources 1994 - 95: A Guide to the Global Environment.* Oxford: Oxford University Press.

Water Resources Management Strategy for SSA: Draft Background Papers

Appelgren, B.G., Burchi, S. 1995. "Water Resources Policy Reform - Issues and Effects in the Agriculture Sector." Rome: FAO.

Brown, D., Grimble, R., Morton, J. 1995. "Small Scale Irrigation in Sub-Saharan Africa: Prospects for Development." UK: The Natural Resources Institute.

Busia, A. 1995. "A Strategy for Integrated Water Resources Management in Sub-Saharan Africa: A Water-Based Land Management Approach." Technical Department, Africa Region. Washington DC: World Bank.

Clones, J. 1995. "Gender and Water Resources Management in Sub-Saharan Africa." Washington, DC: World Bank.

Damhaug, T. 1995. "An Analysis of the Urban Water Supply and Sanitation Sector." Technical Department, Africa Region. Washington, DC: World Bank.

Damhaug, T. and Matthews, G. 1995. "Water Information Services." Technical Department, Africa Region. Washington DC: World Bank.

Fisiy, C., "Africa Region: Involuntary Resettlement in Water Projects." Technical Department, Africa Region. Washington, DC: World Bank.

Garn, M. and Rouleau, M. 1995. "The Role of Economic Instruments in a Water Resources Management Strategy for SSA - A Summary Presentation." Technical Department, Africa Region. Washington, DC: World Bank.

Gilgan-Hunt, E., with A. Bichara, R. Tillman, E. Aikins-Afful, A. Elahi, I. Valencia. 1995. "An Overview of Past, Current, and Future Bank Lending." Technical Department, Africa Region. Washington, DC: World Bank.

Grey, D. 1995. "Management of Rural Water Supply and Sanitation Services." Technical Department, Africa Region. Washington, DC: World Bank.

Grey, D. "An Overview of the Intersectoral Issues affecting Water Resources Management." Technical Department, Africa Region. Washington, DC: World Bank.

Hirji, R. 1995. "River Basin Management in Sub-Saharan Africa: Challenges and Opportunities." Washington, DC: World Bank.

Jordan, V. 1995. "Sub-Saharan Africa Water Resources Management: An Assessment of the Health Situation in Sub-Saharan Africa." Washington, DC: World Bank.

Keck, A., Dinar, A. 1995 "Water Supply Variability and Drought in Sub-Saharan Africa: Physical and Economic Perspectives for a Comprehensive Water Strategy." Washington DC: World Bank.

Muntemba, S. 1995. "Towards Sustainable Water Resources Management in Sub-Saharan Africa: Stakes and Stakeholders." Technical Department, Africa Region. Washington, DC: World Bank.

Okaru, V. 1995. "Legal and Institutional Framework for Preventing/Resolving Disputes in the Use, Management, and Ownership of Africa's Shared River Basins." Technical Department, Africa Region. Washington, DC: World Bank.

Patorni, F.-M. 1995. "Water Resources Management Strategy for Sub-Saharan Africa: Capacity Building in Water Resources Management." Technical Department, Africa Region. Washington, DC: World Bank.

Rothberg, D. 1995. "International River Basins in Sub-Saharan Africa: A Strategy for Fostering Co-Riparian Cooperation." Durham: Duke University.

Stone, P., J. Boesen, and S.O. Fye. 1995. "Improving Water Resources Management in SSA Through Capacity Building." Washington, DC: World Bank.

Vandeweerd, V. 1995. "Key Monitoring and Assessment Considerations for Sound Watershed Management in Sub-Saharan Africa." Nairobi: UNEP.

COUNTRY PAPER SUBMISSIONS: WATER RESOURCES TECHNICAL WORKSHOPS

Nairobi, Kenya. February 12 - 15, 1996.

Angola, Botswana, Burundi, Eritrea, Ethiopia, Kenya, Lesotho, Madagascar, Malawi, Mozambique, Namibia, Rwanda, Somalia, South Africa, Sudan, Swaziland, Tanzania, Uganda, Zaire, Zambia, Zimbabwe

Dakar, Senegal. February 19 - 22, 1996.

Benin, Burkina Faso, Cameroon, Cape Verde, Central African Republic, Chad, Congo, Côte d'Ivoire, Gabon, The Gambia, Ghana, Guinea, Guinea-Bissau, Mali, Mauritania, Niger, Nigeria, Senegal.

Distributors of World Bank Publications

Prices and credit terms vary from country to country. Consult your local distributor before placing an order.

ALBANIA
Adrion Ltd.
Perlat Rexhepi Str.
Pall. 9, Shk. 1, Ap. 4
Tirana
Tel: (42) 274 19; 221 72
Fax: (42) 274 19

ARGENTINA
Oficina del Libro Internacional
Av. Cordoba 1877
1120 Buenos Aires
Tel: (1) 815-8156
Fax: (1) 815-8354

AUSTRALIA, FIJI, PAPUA NEW GUINEA, SOLOMON ISLANDS, VANUATU, AND WESTERN SAMOA
D.A. Information Services
648 Whitehorse Road
Mitcham 3132
Victoria
Tel: (61) 3 9210 7777
Fax: (61) 3 9210 7788
URL: http://www.dadirect.com.au

AUSTRIA
Gerold and Co.
Graben 31
A-1011 Wien
Tel: (1) 533-50-14-0
Fax: (1) 512-47-31-29

BANGLADESH
Micro Industries Development Assistance Society (MIDAS)
House 5, Road 16
Dhanmondi R/Area
Dhaka 1209
Tel: (2) 326427
Fax: (2) 811188

BELGIUM
Jean De Lannoy
Av. du Roi 202
1060 Brussels
Tel: (2) 538-5169
Fax: (2) 538-0841

BRAZIL
Publicacões Tecnicas Internacionais Ltda.
Rua Peixoto Gomide, 209
01409 Sao Paulo, SP.
Tel: (11) 259-6644
Fax: (11) 258-6990

CANADA
Renouf Publishing Co. Ltd.
1294 Algoma Road
Ottawa, Ontario K1B 3W8
Tel: 613-741-4333
Fax: 613-741-5439

CHINA
China Financial & Economic Publishing House
8, Da Fo Si Dong Jie
Beijing
Tel: (1) 333-8257
Fax: (1) 401-7365

COLOMBIA
Infoenlace Ltda.
Apartado Aereo 34270
Bogotá D.E.
Tel: (1) 285-2798
Fax: (1) 285-2798

COTE D'IVOIRE
Centre d'Edition et de Diffusion Africaines (CEDA)
04 B.P. 541
Abidjan 04 Plateau
Tel: 225-24-6510
Fax: 225-25-0567

CYPRUS
Center of Applied Research
Cyprus College
6, Diogenes Street, Engomi
P.O. Box 2006
Nicosia
Tel: 244-1730
Fax: 246-2051

CZECH REPUBLIC
National Information Center
prodejna, Konviktska 5
CS – 113 57 Prague 1
Tel: (2) 2422-9433
Fax: (2) 2422-1484
URL: http://www.nis.cz/

DENMARK
SamfundsLitteratur
Rosenoerns Allé 11
DK-1970 Frederiksberg C
Tel: (31)-351942
Fax: (31)-357822

EGYPT, ARAB REPUBLIC OF
Al Ahram
Al Galaa Street
Cairo
Tel: (2) 578-6083
Fax: (2) 578-6833

The Middle East Observer
41, Sherif Street
Cairo
Tel: (2) 393-9732
Fax: (2) 393-9732

FINLAND
Akateeminen Kirjakauppa
P.O. Box 23
FIN-00371 Helsinki
Tel: (0) 12141
Fax: (0) 121-4441
URL: http://booknet.cultnet.fi/aka/

FRANCE
World Bank Publications
66, avenue d'Iéna
75116 Paris
Tel: (1) 40-69-30-56/57
Fax: (1) 40-69-30-68

GERMANY
UNO-Verlag
Poppelsdorfer Allee 55
53115 Bonn
Tel: (228) 212940
Fax: (228) 217492

GREECE
Papasotiriou S.A.
35, Stournara Str
106 82 Athens
Tel: (1) 364-1826
Fax: (1) 364-8254

HONG KONG, MACAO
Asia 2000 Ltd.
Sales & Circulation Department
Seabird House, unit 1101-02
22-28 Wyndham Street, Central
Hong Kong
Tel: 852 2530-1409
Fax: 852 2526-1107
URL: http://www.sales@asia2000.com.hk

HUNGARY
Foundation for Market Economy
Dombovari Ut 17-19
H-1117 Budapest
Tel: 36 1 204 2951 or 36 1 204 2948
Fax: 36 1 204 2953

INDIA
Allied Publishers Ltd.
751 Mount Road
Madras - 600 002
Tel: (44) 852-3938
Fax: (44) 852-0649

INDONESIA
Pt. Indira Limited
Jalan Borobudur 20
P.O. Box 181
Jakarta 10320
Tel: (21) 390-4290
Fax: (21) 421-4289

IRAN
Kowkab Publishers
P.O. Box 19575-511
Tehran
Tel: (21) 258-3723
Fax: 98 (21) 258-3723

Ketab Sara Co. Publishers
Khaled Eslamboli Ave.,
6th Street
Kusheh Delafrooz No. 8
Tehran
Tel: 8717819 or 8716104
Fax: 8862479
E-mail: ketab-sara@neda.net.ir

IRELAND
Government Supplies Agency
Oifig an tSoláthair
4-5 Harcourt Road
Dublin 2
Tel: (1) 461-3111
Fax: (1) 475-2670

ISRAEL
Yozmot Literature Ltd.
P.O. Box 56055
Tel Aviv 61560
Tel: (3) 5285-397
Fax: (3) 5285-397

R.O.Y. International
PO Box 13056
Tel Aviv 61130
Tel: (3) 5461423
Fax: (3) 5461442

Palestinian Authority/Middle East
Index Information Services
P.O.B. 19502 Jerusalem

ITALY
Licosa Commissionaria Sansoni SPA
Via Duca Di Calabria, 1/1
Casella Postale 552
50125 Firenze
Tel: (55) 645-415
Fax: (55) 641-257

JAMAICA
Ian Randle Publishers Ltd.
206 Old Hope Road
Kingston 6
Tel: 809-927-2085
Fax: 809-977-0243

JAPAN
Eastern Book Service
Hongo 3-Chome,
Bunkyo-ku 113
Tokyo
Tel: (03) 3818-0861
Fax: (03) 3818-0864
URL: http://www.bekkoame.or.jp/~svt-ebs

KENYA
Africa Book Service (E.A.) Ltd.
Quaran House, Mfangano Street
P.O. Box 45245
Nairobi
Tel: (2) 23641
Fax: (2) 330272

KOREA, REPUBLIC OF
Daejon Trading Co. Ltd.
P.O. Box 34
Yeoeida
Seoul
Tel: (2) 785-1631/4
Fax: (2) 784-0315

MALAYSIA
University of Malaya Cooperative Bookshop, Limited
P.O. Box 1127
Jalan Pantai Baru
59700 Kuala Lumpur
Tel: (3) 756-5000
Fax: (3) 755-4424

MEXICO
INFOTEC
Apartado Postal 22-860
14060 Tlalpan,
Mexico D.F.
Tel: (5) 606-0011
Fax: (5) 624-2822

NETHERLANDS
De Lindeboom/InOr-Publikaties
P.O. Box 202
7480 AE Haaksbergen
Tel: (53) 574-0004
Fax: (53) 572-9296

NEW ZEALAND
EBSCO NZ Ltd.
Private Mail Bag 99914
New Market
Auckland
Tel: (9) 524-8119
Fax: (9) 524-8067

NIGERIA
University Press Limited
Three Crowns Building Jericho
Private Mail Bag 5095
Ibadan
Tel: (22) 41-1356
Fax: (22) 41-2056

NORWAY
Narvesen Information Center
Book Department
P.O. Box 6125 Etterstad
N-0602 Oslo 6
Tel: (22) 57-3300
Fax: (22) 68-1901

PAKISTAN
Mirza Book Agency
65, Shahrah-e-Quaid-e-Azam
P.O. Box No. 729
Lahore 54000
Tel: (42) 7353601
Fax: (42) 7585283

Oxford University Press
5 Bangalore Town
Sharae Faisal
PO Box 13033
Karachi-75350
Tel: (21) 446307
Fax: (21) 454-7640
E-mail: oup@oup.khi.erum.com.pk

PERU
Editorial Desarrollo SA
Apartado 3824
Lima 1
Tel: (14) 285380
Fax: (14) 286628

PHILIPPINES
International Booksource Center Inc.
Suite 720, Cityland 10
Condominium Tower 2
H.V dela Costa, corner
Valero St.
Makati, Metro Manila
Tel: (2) 817-9676
Fax: (2) 817-1741

POLAND
International Publishing Service
Ul. Piekna 31/37
00-577 Warzawa
Tel: (2) 628-6089
Fax: (2) 621-7255

PORTUGAL
Livraria Portugal
Rua Do Carmo 70-74
1200 Lisbon
Tel: (1) 347-4982
Fax: (1) 347-0264

ROMANIA
Compani De Librarii Bucuresti S.A.
Str. Lipscani no. 26, sector 3
Bucharest
Tel: (1) 613 9645
Fax: (1) 312 4000

RUSSIAN FEDERATION
Isdatelstvo <Ves Mir>
9a, Kolpachniy Pereulok
Moscow 101831
Tel: (95) 917 87 49
Fax: (95) 917 92 59

SAUDI ARABIA, QATAR
Jarir Book Store
P.O. Box 3196
Riyadh 11471
Tel: (1) 477-3140
Fax: (1) 477-2940

SINGAPORE, TAIWAN, MYANMAR, BRUNEI
Ashgate Publishing Asia Pacific Pte. Ltd.
41 Kallang Pudding Road #04-03
Golden Wheel Building
Singapore 349316
Tel: (65) 741-5166
Fax: (65) 742-9356
e-mail: ashgate@asianconnect.com

SLOVAK REPUBLIC
Slovart G.T.G. Ltd.
Krupinska 4
PO Box 152
852 99 Bratislava 5
Tel: (7) 839472
Fax: (7) 839485

SOUTH AFRICA, BOTSWANA
For single titles:
Oxford University Press Southern Africa
P.O. Box 1141
Cape Town 8000
Tel: (21) 45-7266
Fax: (21) 45-7265

For subscription orders:
International Subscription Service
P.O. Box 41095
Craighall
Johannesburg 2024
Tel: (11) 880-1448
Fax: (11) 880-6248

SPAIN
Mundi-Prensa Libros, S.A.
Castello 37
28001 Madrid
Tel: (1) 431-3399
Fax: (1) 575-3998
http://www.tsai.es/mprensa

Mundi-Prensa Barcelona
Consell de Cent, 391
08009 Barcelona
Tel: (3) 488-3009
Fax: (3) 487-7659

SRI LANKA, THE MALDIVES
Lake House Bookshop
P.O. Box 244
100, Sir Chittampalam A. Gardiner Mawatha
Colombo 2
Tel: (1) 32105
Fax: (1) 432104

SWEDEN
Fritzes Customer Service
Regeringsgaton 12
S-106 47 Stockholm
Tel: (8) 690 90 90
Fax: (8) 21 47 77

Wennergren-Williams AB
P. O. Box 1305
S-171 25 Solna
Tel: (8) 705-97-50
Fax: (8) 27-00-71

SWITZERLAND
Librairie Payot
Service Institutionnel
Côtes-de-Montbenon 30
1002 Lausanne
Tel: (021)-341-3229
Fax: (021)-341-3235

Van Diermen Editions Techniq
Ch. de Lacuez 41
CH1807 Blonay
Tel: (021) 943 2673
Fax: (021) 943 3605

TANZANIA
Oxford University Press
Maktaba Street
PO Box 5299
Dar es Salaam
Tel: (51) 29209
Fax (51) 46822

THAILAND
Central Books Distribution
306 Silom Road
Bangkok
Tel: (2) 235-5400
Fax: (2) 237-8321

TRINIDAD & TOBAGO, JAM.
Systematics Studies Unit
#9 Watts Street
Curepe
Trinidad, West Indies
Tel: 809-662-5654
Fax: 809-662-5654

UGANDA
Gustro Ltd.
Madhvani Building
PO Box 9997
Plot 16/4 Jinja Rd.
Kampala
Tel/Fax: (41) 254763

UNITED KINGDOM
Microinfo Ltd.
P.O. Box 3
Alton, Hampshire GU34 2PG
England
Tel: (1420) 86848
Fax: (1420) 89889

ZAMBIA
University Bookshop
Great East Road Campus
P.O. Box 32379
Lusaka
Tel: (1) 213221 Ext. 482

ZIMBABWE
Longman Zimbabwe (Pte.)Ltd
Tourle Road, Ardbennie
P.O. Box ST125
Southerton
Harare
Tel: (4) 6216617
Fax: (4) 621670

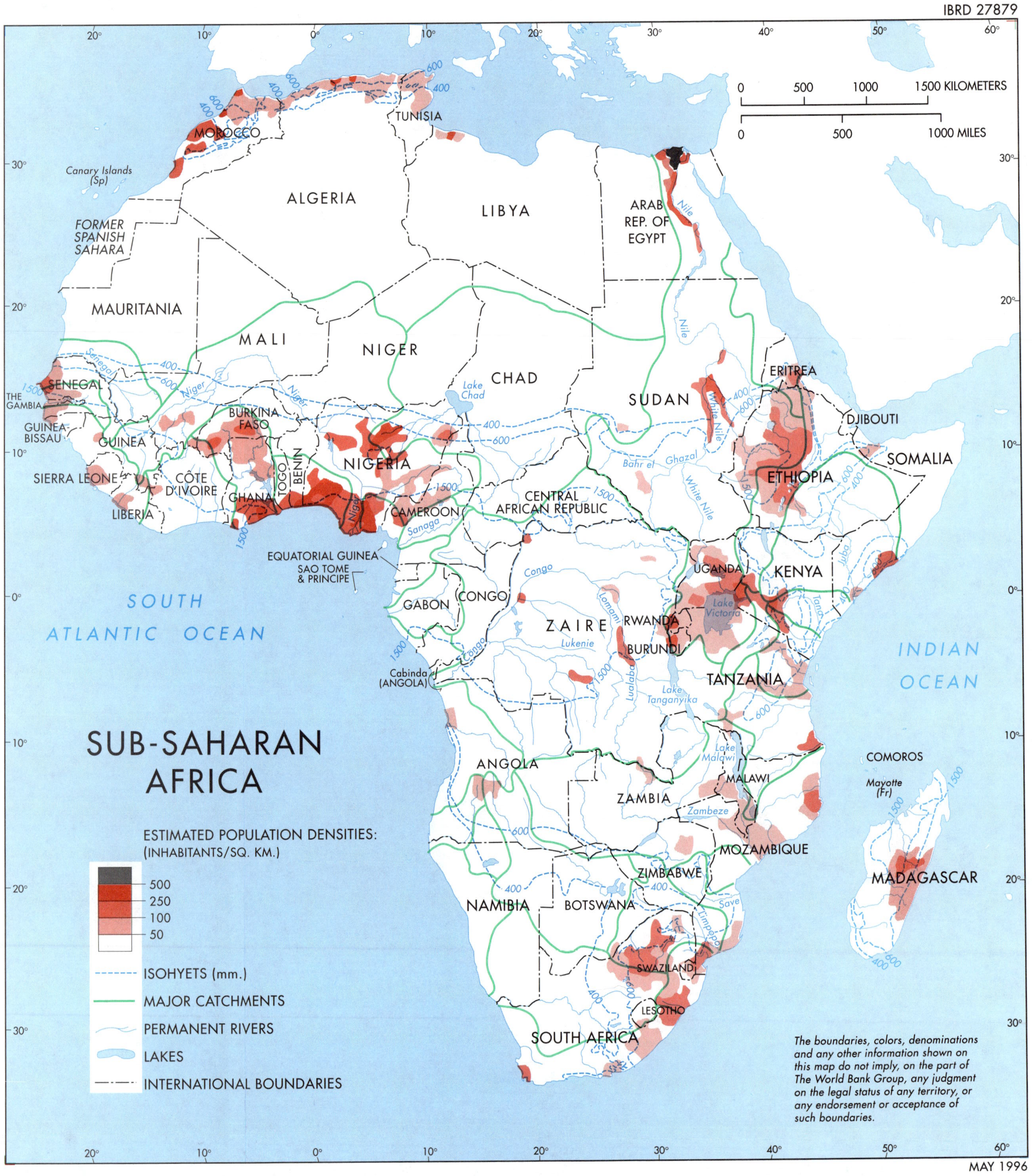
IBRD 27879
SUB-SAHARAN AFRICA
ESTIMATED POPULATION DENSITIES: (INHABITANTS/SQ. KM.)
500
250
100
50
ISOHYETS (mm.)
MAJOR CATCHMENTS
PERMANENT RIVERS
LAKES
INTERNATIONAL BOUNDARIES
0 500 1000 1500 KILOMETERS
0 500 1000 MILES
SOUTH ATLANTIC OCEAN
INDIAN OCEAN
MOROCCO
TUNISIA
ALGERIA
LIBYA
ARAB REP. OF EGYPT
Canary Islands (Sp)
FORMER SPANISH SAHARA
MAURITANIA
MALI
NIGER
CHAD
SUDAN
ERITREA
DJIBOUTI
SOMALIA
ETHIOPIA
SENEGAL
THE GAMBIA
GUINEA-BISSAU
GUINEA
SIERRA LEONE
LIBERIA
CÔTE D'IVOIRE
BURKINA FASO
GHANA
TOGO
BENIN
NIGERIA
CAMEROON
CENTRAL AFRICAN REPUBLIC
EQUATORIAL GUINEA
SAO TOME & PRINCIPE
GABON
CONGO
ZAIRE
Cabinda (ANGOLA)
UGANDA
KENYA
RWANDA
BURUNDI
TANZANIA
ANGOLA
ZAMBIA
MALAWI
MOZAMBIQUE
COMOROS
Mayotte (Fr)
MADAGASCAR
ZIMBABWE
NAMIBIA
BOTSWANA
SWAZILAND
LESOTHO
SOUTH AFRICA
Lake Chad
Lake Victoria
Lake Tanganyika
Lake Malawi
Nile
White Nile
Bahr el Ghazal
Niger
Senegal
Congo
Sanaga
Lukenie
Lomami
Lualaba
Zambeze
Limpopo
Save
Tana
Juba
The boundaries, colors, denominations and any other information shown on this map do not imply, on the part of The World Bank Group, any judgment on the legal status of any territory, or any endorsement or acceptance of such boundaries.
MAY 1996